The Uncertain Center

The Uncertain Center

Essays of Arthur C. McGill

ARTHUR C. McGILL

Edited by Kent Dunnington
Foreword by David Cain
Afterword by Stanley Hauerwas

CASCADE *Books* • Eugene, Oregon

THE UNCERTAIN CENTER
Essays of Arthur C. McGill

Copyright © 2015 Wipf and Stock Publishers. All rights reserved. Except for brief quotations in critical publications or reviews, no part of this book may be reproduced in any manner without prior written permission from the publisher. Write: Permissions, Wipf and Stock Publishers, 199 W. 8th Ave., Suite 3, Eugene, OR 97401.

Cascade Books
An Imprint of Wipf and Stock Publishers
199 W. 8th Ave., Suite 3
Eugene, OR 97401

www.wipfandstock.com

ISBN 13: 978-1-62564-215-8

Cataloging-in-Publication data:

McGill, Arthur C.

The Uncertain Center : essays of Arthur C. McGill / Arthur C. McGill.

xxviii + 190 p. ; 23 cm. —

Includes bibliographical references and indexes.

ISBN 13: 978-1-62564-215-8

1. Death—Religious aspects—Christianity. 2. Suffering—Religious aspects—Christianity. 3. Theology. I. Title.

BT732.7 M282 2015

Manufactured in the U.S.A.

COPYRIGHT NOTICES

Every effort has been made to trace copyrights on the materials included here. If any copyrighted material has nevertheless been included without permission and due acknowledgement, proper credit will be inserted in future printings once notice has been received.

"The Twilight World of Popular Songs" by Arthur C. McGill from: *Religious Education* 49.6 (1954) 382–88. Reprinted by permission of Taylor & Francis LLC (http://www.tandfonline.com).

"Reason in a Violent World" by Arthur C. McGill, originally published by Wesleyan University Press, 1959. Reprinted by permission of Lucille McGill.

"The End of Intimacy" by Arthur C. McGill, originally published by the Christian Faith and Higher Education Institute, 1965. Reprinted by permission of Lucille McGill.

"The Education of the Specialists" by Arthur C. McGill from: *The Christian Scholar* continued as *Soundings*, vol. 49.1 (1966) 24–32. Copyright © 1966 by The Pennsylvania State University Press. Reprinted by permission of The Pennsylvania State University Press.

"The Death of God and All That" by Arthur C. McGill from: C. W. Christian and Glenn R. Wittig, eds., *Radical Theology: Phase Two*, copyright © 1967. Reprinted by permission of C.W. Christian.

"Critique II" by Arthur C. McGill from: *Theology Today* 25.3 (1968) 317–19. Reprinted by permission of SAGE Publications Ltd.

"Is Private Charity Coming to an End?" by Arthur C. McGill from: *Vanguard: A Bulletin for Church Officers* 6.2 (1969) 3–6, 16. Copyright © 1969 Board of Christian Education of The United Presbyterian Church in the United States of America. Used with permission.

"The Ambiguous Position of Christian Theology" by Arthur C. McGill from: Paul Ramsey and John F. Wilson, eds., *The Study of Religion in Colleges and Universities*. Copyright © 1970, 1998 Princeton University Press. Reprinted by permission of Princeton University Press.

"Suffered Under Pontius Pilot—Theological Brief" by Arthur C. McGill from: Robert A. Evans and Thomas D. Parker, eds., *Christian Theology: A Case Method Approach*, copyright ©1976. Reprinted by permission of Wipf and Stock Publishers.

"The Religious Aspects of Medicine" by Arthur C. McGill from: Donald W. Shriver, Jr., ed., *Medicine and Religion: Strategies of Care*, copyright © 1980. Reprinted by permission of the University of Pittsburgh Press.

"Human Suffering and the Passion of Christ" by Arthur McGill from: Flavian Dougherty, C. P., ed., *The Meaning of Human Suffering*, copyright © 1982. Reprinted by permission of Lucille McGill.

However far Christians may want to advance beyond the "old" dispensation of the Jews, and however rhetorically they want to stress the fullness of the revelation given in Jesus Christ, they still cannot break out of the condition of recurrent uncertainty and tension and change in which all religious truth stands. A hiddenness remains ... In Christianity what is uncertain is the very center, the viability of Christ as Lord and Savior.

—ARTHUR C. MCGILL,
"THE AMBIGUOUS POSITION OF CHRISTIAN THEOLOGY"

Contents

Foreword by David Cain xi
Acknowledgments xv
Introduction by Kent Dunnington xvii
Chronology of McGill's Life xxiv
The Work of Arthur C. McGill xxvi

1. The Twilight World of Popular Songs (1954) 1
2. Reason in a Violent World (1959) 13
3. The End of Intimacy (1965) 30
4. The Education of the Specialists (1966) 47
5. The Death of God and All That (1967) 58
6. The Radicals Are Not Immanent Enough (1968) 71
7. Is Private Charity Coming to an End? (1969) 75
8. The Ambiguous Position of Christian Theology (1970) 81
9. The Crisis of Faith (1974) 109
10. Structures of Inhumanity (1975) 115
11. Suffered Under Pontius Pilot (1976) 133
12. The Religious Aspects of Medicine (1980) 139
13. Human Suffering and the Passion of Christ (1982) 155

Afterword by Stanley Hauerwas 181
Bibliography 185
Index of Names 187
Scripture Index 189

Foreword

"That One Expend Oneself in Gratitude"

Read at your own risk.

Arthur McGill is dangerous. He overturns assumptions. He upsets expectations. He uproots opinions. McGill mischievously delights in leading his listeners-readers down a path to nowhere, a path to which he provides a decisive dead end.

McGill liked to cause trouble—writing reflective provocations with snarl and bite. "None of us believes any more in our health. We believe in sickness." "We who live today [1959] see ourselves surrounded by a dreadful world." "What happens to the university when the demons rule?" "Reason . . . must declare what it finds when it too lives in the shadow of death, and this is the work of theology." "The prevailing personalistic notion of Christian love must be challenged." "God's victory and grace do not cease when a man enters the city." "Unfortunately the church is not, it seems for most people, a place where anything happens . . . It is . . . therefore a place where the only god one can let in is a god who is too impotent to bother you." "God—this transcendent, vacuous something—is killing Christianity!" "At the religious level *the truth-question is never closed*." "Every act of theological reflection begins with a *question*." "The person who finds it hard to believe in Jesus is exactly the person who is beginning to know Jesus." "Only those who are free to be needy are free to be grateful." "Our hope, I think, therefore must be that the crisis of faith in our churches will grow worse." "For Jesus throws upon our existence a strange and difficult light and overturns our basic assumptions." "Death belongs part and parcel to the overcoming of evil and the perfecting of love." "I mean I'm now convinced after my operation that it's only the healthy that can survive the hospital." Etcetera. But then: "Victory, therefore, is the decisive and final fact of human existence." Thank goodness. Thank God.

McGill is not often reassuring but often unnerving and disconcerting. What he writes of the "Death of God" theologians (among whom he counts Paul van Buren, William Hamilton, Thomas Altizer, and Harvey Cox) could be applied to McGill himself: "Their whole vocabulary has been on the negative, with the positive only very elusive, very latent." Also: "They are not demolishers, they are gadflies." McGill was a gadfly. He was not a demolisher but ultimately a builder, constructive in demanding, arduous ways. Still, in reading McGill, it is easier to see what he is denigrating than what he is commending.

Right next to "gratitude," "glory," and "expenditure" in McGill's theological (and existential) vocabulary is "power." Religions are all about power, but many different perceptions and impressions of power persist, as McGill knew well and evidenced well. "The word 'God' in terms of religion is any life- or death-giving power, any power that a person feels is capable of enhancing or crushing his life. Sex, war, penicillin may therefore be gods in this very special sense." What comes through forcefully is McGill's emphasis on *service*, warranted by his reading of the New Testament. Can the Good Samaritan be far away? And right next to "service" are, again, the words "expend," "expenditure," and "self-expenditure," which true service demands and entails. Yet sustenance, satisfaction, and fulfillment come dialectically creeping in.

Kent Dunnington declares, "McGill's theology does not make it easier for us to believe . . . Rather McGill's theology makes it harder for us to believe." I am reminded of Johannes Climacus' cigar-smoking resolution: since his "limited capabilities" do not permit him to join the acclaimed "celebrities . . . who know how to benefit humankind by making life easier and easier," he will "with the same humanitarian enthusiasm as the others have, take it upon [himself] to make something more difficult."[1] "Rather," Dunnington continues, "McGill's theology makes it harder for us to believe [but potentially this "harder" belief *becomes more meaningful*] by exposing the strange power of the God we would believe in and by suggesting the strange power may be vindicated in our lives only as we learn to die." "Strange power" is exactly right. And learning to die: there is death and then there is death. McGill is concerned with "the *kind of dying* which occurred in Jesus" (italics added). Yes, there are kinds of dying; and the "kind

---

1. Kierkegaard, *Concluding Unscientific Postscript*, 186.

Foreword

of dying which occurred in Jesus" is the center of the "uncertain center" of McGill's Christian theology.

Kent Dunnington has chosen to arrange the essays he selected for this volume chronologically, not thematically. Themes of course recur, but meanwhile one never knows what is coming next. Some unlikely comings come along. We have the fun and adventure of surprise.

I am so glad that a colleague in the appreciation, commendation, celebration, and fascination of Art McGill (I never called him "Art"; he was "Professor McGill" to me but was Art to his friends), Kent Dunnington, has come forward with this volume to which he has provided a sensitive and perceptive introduction. Dunnington writes of "the sense of urgency, the implacable push for the extremes of human experience, the 'strong stomach' by which McGill stares unflinchingly at the realities of suffering, breakdown, disease, disintegration, and death—these distinctive marks of his theological approach reveal a theologian writing from the depths." From where else should a theologian write?

The last paragraphs of "Structures of Inhumanity" give us McGill's essential theological—which is to say, christological—conviction and depiction (uncertainty still abounds): not the way of exorcism but the way of the cross.

McGill's Christian faith was relentless, tough, and painful. If true life somehow cost God death, then we of God's image can face no less. But there *is* true life. That is what death—true death—and the Christian theology of Arthur McGill are all about.

Read at your own risk.

—David Cain

Acknowledgments

I am grateful to Lucy McGill, for delightful conversation about "Art" and for her blessing of this project; to David Cain, student of McGill and caretaker of the papers of McGill, for his wonderful editions of previously unpublished McGill writings, for agreeing to write a foreword to this volume, and for much helpful correspondence about McGill; to my teacher and friend Stanley Hauerwas, for introducing me to McGill in a footnote and for agreeing to write an afterword to this volume; to the late Allen Verhey, my teacher whose own thought was so shaped by McGill that I learned from McGill before I ever knew it; to the cheerful librarians at Greenville College—Georgann Kurtz-Shaw, Jane Hopkins, and Diana Hoffman—for their help with the detective work of tracking down the various contents and copyrights for this volume; to Kirsten Norsworthy, for help transcribing McGill's lecture on "The Crisis of Faith"; and to Ben Wayman, whose faithful friendship is a source of energy and encouragement, for joining in my enthusiasm about McGill and lending a helping hand or critical eye at a moment's notice.

Introduction

Bringing together the essays of Arthur C. McGill began with a crisis and a footnote. In the midst of my first year of teaching I was reaching my limit, trying to cope with undiagnosed illness and struggling to go on. As academic types are prone to do, I read. I read everything I could find on suffering, casting about for some new perspective. Much of what I could find on suffering was beside the point. My problem was not that of theodicy—how a good God could allow suffering. Rather, my problem was how to live with suffering in a way that did not destroy my humanity and agency. How can we go on when the future requires energy, vitality, and confidence, which are threatened by suffering?

In an essay by Stanley Hauerwas titled "Suffering the Retarded: Should We Prevent Retardation?" I read:

> We believe that our identity derives from our independence, our self-possession. As Arthur McGill suggests, we think "a person is real so far as he can draw a line around certain items—his body, his thoughts, his house—and claim them as his own." Thus death becomes our ultimate enemy—the intimation involved in every form of suffering—because it is the ultimate threat to our identity.[1]

I did not know who Arthur McGill was, but the suggestion that we are unable to endure suffering because it threatens our cherished identities seemed right to me. The footnote led me14011 to Arthur McGill's book, *Suffering: A Test of Theological Method* (1968), and I have been reading McGill since.

It is fitting I would encounter McGill from a position of existential desperation, not only because he saw neediness as the human situation, but

---

1. Hauerwas, *Suffering Presence*, 169.

also because he did theology as though our lives depend on it. Although he spent his intellectual life in Ivy League schools, McGill was not a typical academic theologian. He wrote comparatively little, publishing only two short books and a handful of essays. Nearly everything he wrote was in response to invitations, often to meet with laypersons or practitioners who were gathered around a pressing need. He avoided the scholarly style of footnotes, appendices, and bibliographies. He cited *Time* magazine more often than Karl Barth despite having written his dissertation on Barth. In other words, he was after something other than academic reputation or legacy. He believed the theological task was always provisional, always piecemeal, and always urgent. The theologian constantly strives "to penetrate through a particular religious confusion and to attain a clarifying insight regarding Christ's lordship over life and death in some specific area of existence."[2]

There is no escape when reading McGill. He relentlessly exposes the distance between Jesus and us. As he expresses it in "The Crisis of Faith," every attempt to make Jesus relevant to *our* lives is a lie. Rather we must see that *we* are irrelevant to *him*, that our lives cannot survive him, that following him would be the death of a recognizable self. Reading McGill as I now do from a position of relative health is an uncomfortable experience, for McGill denies that health is a "blessing" since health lulls us once again into the lie of a secure and independent self. Who can hear this? Who can say such a thing without endless qualifications that restore us to our shibboleths? As McGill puts it, "One has really to have a fairly strong stomach to be able to be a theologian responsibly."[3]

On the other hand, McGill's relentless assault on our common hopes and dreams suggests he has something to say to those whose hopes and dreams have been shattered. I suspect such unflinching honesty is why McGill is one of few writers I know who can provide nourishment in the face of serious affliction (Weil, Bernanos, and the Psalmist are others for me).

McGill's essential insight is a distinction between what he calls the way of having and the way of giving. The way of having is at the heart of our common hopes and dreams: hopes for health, security, wholeness, dignity, power, and acclaim. Central to the way of having is the seemingly unassailable assumption that our lives are sustained by what we can lay claim to. Thus we may give our excess money to those in need but we must keep

2. See below, 89.
3. See below, 70.

what is necessary to sustain our own livelihood; we may give surplus time to those who need us but at some point we must learn how to say no if we are not to be abused. McGill argues that such a perspective cannot make sense of Jesus whose death was freely willed as the revelation of the triune life of God. The death of Jesus reveals another way of being a person—God's way—a way in which our personhood is constituted by receiving *everything* with gratitude, staking claim to *nothing*, and freely giving away *everything*.

McGill's position should not be confused with a soul-making theodicy. Suffering is not good on McGill's account, nor is suffering instrumentally valuable as a mechanism for further projects of self-development. Such a theodicy tries to recover suffering as something within the ambit of human aspiration. But McGill knows that suffering cannot be harnessed by a program of virtue; indeed, we must admit that extreme affliction more often destroys people, dominating not only their bodies but also their souls: their personality, their virtues, even their faith. Thus it is reasonable to resist suffering with all our might. For in suffering we encounter the demonic, a powerfulness that exceeds all human resourcefulness. Suffering destroys the illusion of humanism according to which the world is ultimately disposed to our hopes and dreams.

But what about the resurrection? Doesn't the resurrection show that, despite all evidence to the contrary, our hopes and dreams may end up being fulfilled? Not for McGill. Resurrection does not mean that Jesus received back health, security, wholeness, dignity, power, and acclaim on the other side of death. Rather, resurrection is a way of describing a life of eternal neediness, receptivity, and generosity. If death is the process of the continual relinquishment of the self then death is not antithetical to eternal life, since the Trinity is constituted by relations of self-donation. It is in this sense that McGill claims, "Death, I believe, will not be removed in heaven."[4] Resurrection describes an altogether different human horizon, an altogether different way of being a self, one that boggles the limits of our imagination and could only be good news to those who live in the continual awareness that their life is an ongoing death.

McGill lived most of his life with such an awareness of his fragility and ongoing death. Born in Canada in 1926, he was a diabetic from childhood and his life was entangled with the world of medicine from an early age. His family moved from Wolfville, Nova Scotia to Brookline, Massachusetts the same year he was born, and he was to spend the majority of his life on the

---

4. McGill, *Death and Life*, 80.

Introduction

East Coast, attending college at Harvard and graduate school at Yale, teaching at Amherst, Wesleyan, Princeton, and finally Harvard. He died in 1980 at the age of fifty-four after an ultimately unsuccessful kidney transplant in 1978. Almost everything he wrote connects to this experiential matrix, the three most recurrent themes being the meaning of human suffering, the religious significance of medicine, and the methods and ends of education. McGill does not write autobiographically, indeed he rarely refers to personal experience in his essays. Nevertheless the sense of urgency, the implacable push for the extremes of human experience, the "strong stomach" by which McGill stares unflinchingly at the realities of suffering, breakdown, disease, disintegration, and death—these distinctive marks of his theological approach reveal a theologian writing from the depths.

McGill wrote in the 1960s and '70s when the promise of Protestant liberalism had wilted into the pronouncements of the death of God. It was an exciting time for theology in one sense, with the buzz surrounding Bonhoeffer's "religionless Christianity" and Harvey Cox's "secular city." But theology was also capitulating to what John Milbank would later describe as "false humility,"[5] a failure of nerve with respect to the categories of Christian discourse and the duty to edify the church. McGill was one of the few theologians who during this time preserved the work of theology as a discipline of the church without lapsing into a reactionary conservatism. His essay in this volume, "The Death of God and All That," brilliantly illustrates his willingness to learn from the "radical theologians" without conceding Christian grammar. The radical theologians rightly expose an incommensurability between the encrusted "transcendent God" of liberal theism and the phenomenological experience of "modern man," but McGill argues this should come as no surprise to those who read the New Testament. "I just think the New Testament is nonsense as the revelation of a transcendent God who creates the whole universe, who fills people's stomachs and gets rid of evil," McGill writes. "I don't know what you do with Jesus! He's just a disaster with his crucifixion in that kind of gospel!"[6] In other words, the god rejected by the radical theologians is not the God revealed in Jesus.

McGill played an important role in maintaining the centrality of God and Christian grammar in the practice of theology, and my generation benefited tremendously. We have moved beyond the false humility of modern theology. Nowadays we have the high metaphysics of radical orthodoxy

---

5. Milbank, *Theology and Social Theory*, 1.
6. See below, 68.

Introduction

(for instance, John Milbank) and the political and ethical reclamations of the ecclesial theologians (for instance, Stanley Hauerwas). Contemporary theology seeks to "position" or "out-narrate" so-called secular discourse; it seeks to recover a bygone Christian confidence. Yet I am convinced McGill remains resonant exactly because he was disturbed by the concerns of the radical theologians even if he did not follow their response. It may be, after all, that no amount of metaphysical or politico-ethical *ressourcement* can retrieve Christian confidence in such a time as this. It may be that we are stuck in a position of uncertainty and uneasiness.

"The Ambiguous Position of Christian Theology" is the heart of this collection, both the best and the most fundamental of the essays herein. In that essay, McGill describes what I take to be our position still, nearly fifty years after it was written.

> The gods who seemed so clearly to have control over a people's life and death yesterday now become impotent and irrelevant. No reality has so clearly, so universally, and so unavoidably manifested its lordship over all life and death that every new experience at the level of actual existence immediately confirms that lordship. To be sure, people may use the term "God" to refer to something so abstract, so devoid of any manifestation in contemporary existence that it is unaffected by the shifts and surprises of concrete experience. But by the same token all that then remains to them is a god void of all religious significance, who stands in no relation to the concrete actualities of life and death.[7]

If this description is still a description of those of us who call ourselves Christian, as I believe it is, then we still need McGill. McGill does not write from a position of confidence or advocacy. He writes as a Christian living in a time when the beliefs and rituals that once sustained us have become empty or inadequate. He writes, not with false humility, but with the humility of what Kierkegaard calls "contemporaneity with Christ" (*Practice in Christianity*). That is, McGill believes we always must discover again who Jesus is and whether we can believe in him. McGill is less assured than the postliberals and the radically orthodox, but no less vital or urgent. On the contrary, as McGill argues, if the work of theology is not ultimately academic, if it does not simply require more precision or conceptual creativity, then "theologians do not themselves have the means of disposing of the confusions which they face."[8] McGill's theology does not make it easier for

7. See below, 85–86.
8. See below, 90.

us to believe by assuring us once again of the conceptual firepower of a "Christian worldview." Rather, McGill's theology makes it harder for us to believe by exposing the strange power of the God we would believe in and by suggesting this strange power may be vindicated in our lives only as we learn to die.

When I discovered McGill in 2007, only three short books and scattered essays were available. (Since then, I am delighted that David Cain, McGill's student and now caretaker of the papers of McGill, has brought out two volumes of previously unpublished writings of McGill in a series called Theological Fascinations: first, *Sermons of Arthur C. McGill* in 2007, and then *Dying Unto Life: Arthur C. McGill on New God, New Death, New Life* in 2013, both published by Cascade). As I began to locate the published McGill essays, I discovered they were not readily accessible. Only one of the journals in which McGill's essays were published is still in print, and none of the books is. Several essays were available only at one or two libraries, evidently because they were part of very small print runs. I began then to gather all of the essays with a mind to edit and republish them. They are all here, with three caveats. First, I did not include the introduction to *The Many-Faced Argument*, a collection of essays co-edited with John Hick on Anselm's ontological argument. I did not include it because it is long, co-written, currently available in a reprint, and less clearly germane to McGill's defining thematic concerns. Second, one of McGill's published essays, "Technology and Love—A Human Problem," is nearly a replica of an earlier published essay, "The End of Intimacy." I chose the "The End of Intimacy" for this volume because it is the original and there were no substantive changes in the later essay. Finally, one of the essays that appears here, "The Crisis of Faith," was not a published essay, but rather a recorded lecture McGill gave that I have transcribed. It is the only recorded lecture of McGill's.

I have made minimal adjustment to the texts of the various essays. I have removed obvious spelling or punctuation errors and tried to make punctuation patterns consistent across the essays. I have also added several citations for material McGill quotes, following his citation method from other essays. And I have arranged the essays in chronological order and contextualized each one with a short introductory paragraph. I have also included a chronology of the life of Arthur McGill, a bibliography adapted and updated from David Cain, and an index of names and Scripture cited by McGill in these essays.

Introduction

When I was considering bringing these essays together, a colleague asked if there is anything in the essays we do not already get in *Suffering*, McGill's essential book. The answer is yes. I will mention four important contributions among several.

First, "The Ambiguous Position of Christian Theology" is both a remarkable summary of McGill's theological method and also a trenchant analysis of the state of "religious studies" that is still highly relevant. That essay alone is worth the price of the book.

Second, McGill's direct engagement with radical theology is on display here as nowhere else.

Third, in both "The End of Intimacy" and "The Education of the Specialists," McGill enters the debate between technical and humanistic modes of education, between the research university and the liberal arts college.

Fourth and finally, we see in the chronological progression here what I would argue is the most significant shift in McGill's thinking. In "The End of Intimacy" and "The Education of the Specialists" McGill takes aim at personalistic forms of religiosity such as that advocated by Martin Buber. Buber's privileging of I-Thou intimacy and face-to-face relationship are subjected to critique. McGill argues that in the New Testament we are simply commanded to meet the needs of others, not to get to know them as "whole persons." But in his later writings, especially his last two essays, "The Religious Aspects of Medicine" and "Human Suffering and the Passion of Christ," McGill begins to advocate personal presence and companionship as the heart of New Testament service. Indeed, at one point he critiques those who give pride of place to the Matthew 25 command to remove the suffering of the needy, arguing that "the New Testament writings seem to give equal emphasis to the work of simply *accompanying* the sufferers in their suffering."[9] These developments seem to be in tension if not outright contradiction with his earlier antipathy to personalism although in both cases he consistently rejects the language of "wholeness" as antithetical to the God who lives by receiving and expending.

But consistency was not a virtue McGill held central to the theological task. The theologian knows that the truth-question will always become unsettled and therefore system-building is a distraction at best, idolatrous at worse. Honesty, openness, gratitude, and courageous endurance—these are the virtues McGill extolled, and the virtues he exemplified.

---

9. See below, 163.

Chronology of McGill's Life

1926	Born Aug. 7, Wolfville, Nova Scotia; family moved to Brookline, MA same year
43–47	BA in physics, Harvard
47–48	Taxi driver in San Francisco
48–51	BD Yale Divinity School
50–51	Summer pastor of Congregational Church in Pettibone, ND; met Lucille ("Lucy")
51	In June married Lucy, with whom he had three children, two daughters and a son
51–61	PhD at Yale Divinity School
52	Ordained in Hamden, CT, in the Congregational Christian Church (now UCC)
52–54	Instructor, Amherst College
53	Elected Kent Fellow in the National Council on Religion in Higher Education
55	Fill-in pastor of the Congregational Church, Hatfield, MA
55–59	Assistant Professor of Theology, Wesleyan University
57–58	Academic year Fulbright Fellow at University of Louvain, Belgium

Chronology of McGill's Life

59	Awarded Vedder Prize for distinguished undergraduate teaching in a private American college
60–68	Taught at Princeton University, Full Professor by 1964
65	Founding member, Academic Council Ecumenical Institute for Advanced Theological Research, Jerusalem
67–68	Senior Fellow in Humanities, Princeton
68–69	Sabbatical year in London; Edward Cadbury Lecturer at the University of Birmingham, England
69–80	Professor, Harvard Divinity School; elected Bussey Professor of Theology in 1971
1980	Died Sept. 10, Boston, MA

The Work of Arthur C. McGill

(arranged chronologically with contents of this volume in bold)

"**The Twilight World of Popular Songs.**" *Religious Education* 49.6 (1954) 382–88.

"**Reason in a Violent World.**" In *The Distrust of Reason: Alumni-Faculty Seminar, June 1959*, 34–50. Middletown, CT: Wesleyan University Press, 1959.

"The Place of Dogmatic Theology in the University." PhD diss., Yale University, 1961.

"The Power of God and the Problem of Suffering." Princeton University. 1963. Series of six lectures.

The Celebration of Flesh: Poetry in Christian Life. 1964. Eugene, OR: Wipf and Stock, 2008.

"**The End of Intimacy.**" National Campus Ministry Association Study Conference. June 1965, Michigan State University. East Lansing, MI: Christian Faith and Higher Education Institute, 1965.

"**The Education of the Specialists.**" *The Christian Scholar* 49.1 (1966) 24–32.

The Many Faced Argument: Studies on the Ontological Argument for the Existence of God. With John Hick. 1967. Eugene, OR: Wipf and Stock, 2009.

"**The Death of God and All That.**" In *Radical Theology: Phase Two*, edited by C. W. Christian and Glenn Wittig, 45–58. Philadelphia: Lippincott, 1967.

"Technology and Love—A Human Problem." *Fifth Combined Plan Conference.* November, 1967, Columbia University. Harriman, NY: Arden House, 1967.

Suffering: A Test of Theological Method. 1968. Eugene, OR: Wipf and Stock, 2007.

"Critique II." *Theology Today* 25.3 (1968) 317-19. Published here as "The Radicals Are Not Immanent Enough."

"Is Private Charity Coming to an End?" *Vanguard: A Bulletin for Church Officers* 6.2 (1969) 3-6, 16.

"The Ambiguous Position of Christian Theology." In *The Study of Religion in Colleges and Universities*, edited by Paul Ramsey and John F. Wilson, 105-38. Princeton, NJ: Princeton University Press, 1970.

"The Crisis of Faith." Pittsburgh: Thesis Theological Cassettes, 1974. Audiocassette.

"Structures of Inhumanity." In *Disguises of the Demonic: Contemporary Perspectives on the Power of Evil*, edited by Alan M. Olson, 116-33. New York: Association Press, 1975.

"Suffered Under Pontius Pilate—Theological Brief." In *Christian Theology: A Case Method Approach*, edited by Robert A. Evans and Thomas D. Parker, 148-53. 1976. Eugene, OR: Wipf and Stock, 2001.

"The Religious Aspects of Medicine." In *Medicine and Religion: Strategies of Care*, edited by Donald W. Shriver, Jr., 77-93. Pittsburgh: University of Pittsburgh Press, 1980.

"Human Suffering and the Passion of Christ." In *The Meaning of Human Suffering*, edited by Flavian Dougherty, C. P., 159-93. New York: Human Sciences Press, 1982.

Death and Life: An American Theology. Edited by Charles A. Wilson and Per M. Anderson. 1987. Eugene, OR: Wipf and Stock, 2003.

Sermons of Arthur C. McGill. Edited by David Cain. Eugene, OR: Cascade, 2007.

Dying Unto Life: Arthur C. McGill on New God, New Death, New Life. Edited by David Cain. Eugene, OR: Cascade, 2013.

The Twilight World of Popular Songs

Written in his late twenties while he was an instructor at Amherst College, McGill's first publication appeared in the journal Religious Education *in 1954. Here McGill examines the titles and lyrics of popular music to expose an abiding "emotional apathy" underlying everyday experience in 1950s America, and an emotional skepticism he contends has crept into church music and Christian life. This is where McGill begins in his publishing, but not where he goes. The essay is dated but nevertheless hints at some patterns of thought that would become characteristic: his gift for phenomenological description, his conviction that human experience is mediated through images rather than propositions, and his penchant for discovering traces of the holy or the demonic in the banalities of middle class American life.*

|

Man does not live by bread alone, but in this country also by entertainment. Clichés to the contrary, this entertainment is no casual diversion, but provides a treasured source of vital life. It draws from the people considerable portions of their time and money, and, more important, absorbs their whole imaginative energies. It seems to offer them what was previously associated with religion—not just escape, but a kind of re-creation.

The most pervasive form of entertainment, that which accompanies us through the whole course of our lives—our reading and eating, our resting and travelling, our loving and loneliness—is popular music. For the average person, perhaps, popular represents only a very limited part of life, found in special places, and enjoyed by a special, highly excitable age group. What is not apparent is the astonishing extent to which hit songs drench the American scene, and the vast industry which provides them.

First, of course, there are the phonograph records, available no longer just at music shops, but also in every dime, drug, and department store. Without considering the smaller companies which number in the hundreds, the major record firms in 1952 sold one hundred million dollars worth of popular records alone, and along with this, of course, an avalanche of affiliated paraphernalia. Next there is radio, where popular music provides perhaps three-quarters of all the material which is broadcast, and receives the exclusive attention of one or more stations in every city. On the newsstands, we meet song magazines, established to throttle the illegal bootlegging of lyrics, and selling one and a half to two million copies a month. In the cinema, a few songs may form the basis of an entire picture, or some background music may be a popular hit in disguise.

Finally there are the jukeboxes. Having replaced their neon glitter with dignified respectability, these find a corner in almost every eating place in the United States, and probably devour from four to five billion nickels annually. They are equipped with a devilish electronic volume control which automatically keeps the volume of the music at a preset margin above the varying din of the room. Any attempt, therefore, to drown out the music for the sake, say, of conversation, will only make it roar louder. At the same time there are remote control devices that allow a customer to play the machine in the secrecy of his booth, and thus protected from disapproving frowns, he escapes taking any public responsibility for what he inflicts on his neighbor. Wherever or whenever America stops to eat, the jukeboxes provide the atmosphere for digestion.

Such a complex distributing process as this is maintained by a vast production line of writers, publishers, pluggers, performers, and recorders, each one of whom is surrounded in turn by his own entourage of personnel—contact men and advisers, managers and secretaries, agents and accountants.

That the enormous size of the music business is not generally recognized is no accident, for it prefers to keep many of its statistics secret. The industry, like its product, is most effective when in the background. Here the technique is the reverse of Hollywood's. There is no frontal assault upon the public awareness with staggering figures, world premieres, full-page newspaper advertisements. Instead, just as the music industry remains inconspicuous and self-effacing, so its songs insinuate themselves quietly at strategic points in our lives, as a kind of background atmosphere—the theme song of a motion picture, the disc jockey that precedes the news program, the jukebox during a sandwich.

Night and day, year in and year out, this whole elaborate apparatus turns out about as bad a music as has ever been sung in Western society. It lacks the variety or ingenuity to arouse musical interest; it has no spontaneous sincerity to give it human interest. Therefore, the people, it is widely believed—and especially such a well-schooled people as in the United States—could not possibly of themselves desire such an inferior product. The apparent popularity of this music must therefore be traced to an extraneous factor. Some hold up adolescence and its emotional disorders as the villain, for it is the young people who patronize popular music most conspicuously. Nevertheless, behind this excitable front, there lies a vast covert audience of more stolid adults. The success of disc jockeys who direct their programs to housewives, the popular music shows on television with their genteel rococo style, the continuing profitable sale of Bing Crosby records, the enormous success of hits revived from the days when the present middle-aged population was courting, and the adult craze for such crooners as Johnny Raye, who packed the Copacabana for weeks without a bobby soxer in sight—all indicate that the popularity of this music cannot be explained away as adolescent.

Even more common is the view that barbaric businessmen have fabricated the whole enterprise of popular music, and that invincible press agents have foisted it upon the helpless public. Actually, however, there is no business more frantically responsive to public whims than the music industry, and no sooner does a midwestern disc jockey receive twenty requests a week for a new song than recordings of it swarm off the presses of a number of companies. Moreover, the one financial goldmine in the music business is the song which first meets a new public fancy, and such a fancy cannot be anticipated or provoked even by the most skillful promotion. Mercury Records, for instance, vigorously plugged "Boogie Woogie Santa Claus" as its Christmas hit, but while this flopped, the six-year-old tune used to fill the reverse side of the record was "The Tennessee Waltz" which sold four million copies. Occasionally a song like "Oh, Happy Day" (1953) may become popular without any promotion and in the face of widespread scorn from the disc jockeys.

Folk music has, of course, been commercialized since the beginning of capitalism, and has provided as attractive an opportunity for the entrepreneur as any other field of venture. The charming Elizabethan madrigals made their way by means of the same plugging that propelled "Beat Me, Daddy, Eight to the Bar." They were promoted by slogans, like "delicate dainties to sweeten lovers' lips withal," and so crudely hawked at every church festival, May dance, and country fair that the "ballad monger" became a familiar type of rogue in seventeenth-century drama. Modern song hits have a synthetic quality that distinguishes them from the usual folk music, but neither this characteristic nor their popularity can be blamed on the music industry. Somehow they actually appeal to the people, and an analysis of them may disclose the reason.

II

In spite of the surprising variety of songs offered to the public each year, among those that become popular hits there is an appalling uniformity. In fact, when one reviews the tunes that have been popular in the last decade, it is impossible to tell from their lyrics or their music which ones are revivals from the 1890s ("When You Were Sweet Sixteen") or the 1920s ("Together"), and which ones are current compositions. Such uniformity threatens to become unbearable, and outright monotony is avoided only by maintaining a continual succession of new performers, new styles, and new fads, only by keeping the surface of the situation in a constant ferment of change.

The craving for such persistent uniformity is something that should not surprise us. Life for most people in the United States is full of change and motion. For their work, for their neighborhood activities, for their social life, for their vacations, and for their religious worship they must in each case go to a different place and associate themselves with a different group. Their feeling for the places and objects around them, therefore, is weak and unsure; their relation with any one person is confined to one situation and one kind of activity. They cannot stay still long enough to live deeply into one place or one friendship. Now and then, this instability is further disrupted when they move to a different community.

The Twilight World of Popular Songs

In the midst of such shifting sands, people try to stabilize their one possession which is not caught in this sea of change—their inner imaginings. If their dreams and musings can retain a fundamental sameness, then at least one part of their intimate life can have a kind of permanence. For such an imaginative world of stable, patterned happenings and compelling emotions, they depend on the mass media. If these do not change, if the movie plots all tell the same story, if the comic strip situations and soap opera crises faithfully repeat themselves, if popular songs preserve the same mood—then the ordinary flitting life can find at least one source of coherence and continuity. As the directors of the mass media know, the people crave the same old thing, offered with only such variety of surface details as to prevent monotony. Any threat of fundamental change in these popular arts—like the intrusion of jazz on the musical scene—is resisted with deep anxiety.

For some understanding of the imaginative life of our culture, we might now turn to a close examination of the basic characteristics of popular music. And the one that comes immediately to mind is the theme of romantic love. This has been described, analyzed, and explained countless times, so that it might be well for me to focus on a single characteristic of the love lyrics.

The feature any love must have to be worthy even of the name is an absorbing involvement in another person. Because a sensitive awareness of the other is present in every case, we use the same word for such various things as the child's love for his parents, the husband's love for his wife, the disciple's love for his teacher. But in what is surely a remarkable achievement, song lyrics adopt an uncompromising vagueness toward the object of their romantic passion. With deliberate care, it seems, nothing is said by which he or she might become an identifiable human being. In the course of romantic love as endlessly portrayed in our songs, after an initial period of vague unfulfilled longing, suddenly and quite fortuitously "I Meet My Dream." The body suffers physiological changes ("My heart is down in my shoe"), the world grows strange, and all conventional aspirations are set aside ("I Don't Want to Set the World on Fire").

Now who is it that effects such a wondrous transformation? "You and only you." But who exactly is this "you" which fills the consciousness and transfixes the mind? We are never told. Any vivid communication of her physical charms, of something as concrete as her laughter or mode of speaking is deleted. "I Dream of You," not of "Jeannie With the Light Brown Hair;" "I See Your Face Before Me," although it is not worth describing.

This extraordinary vagueness in the lyrics becomes more marked as the romance collapses, for the rival who brings about this disaster remains an even more shadowy figure than the loved one herself. Not only is his description restricted to the words "another," "somebody else," or, at most, "an old friend I happened to see," but his very conquest of the girl proceeds invisibly. The lover sees nothing of it, and in the end discovers it indirectly, not, to be sure, from anyone in particular. "They" tell him—the nameless ones.

On close inspection, what emerges as vividly real from this world of popular songs is neither love nor despair in any proper sense, but a group of personal feelings that rise and fall by themselves without contact with actual people. When we hear how "my heart cries for you, sighs for you, dies for you," it is my crying and sighing and dying—not "you"—that attracts our attention. The "you" is vague because for all practical purposes it is unreal, an abstract excuse for "Falling in Love with Love," for an orgy of feeling. The thrill of being intensely committed—this, and not the loving awareness of another person, is what the songs express. Likewise, the defection of the girl brings no disillusion, no unexpected intrusion of an actual world which shames and depresses the lover. It rather provides him with the enjoyment of a new feeling. It is as if he had become bored with the thrill of self-importance, and now sought the anguish of self-pity.

But we must go further than this, and say that the world presented in popular music is not only devoid of any awareness of persons, but is carefully detached from the whole expanse of daily life. The songs themselves openly characterize their realm as a dream world, "a sweet, improbable, unreal world," where either "My Dreams Are Getting Better All the Time" or "My Dreams Are Old and Lonely." They actually take pains to emphasize the disjunction between romantic experience on the one hand and the actual world on the other.

If the romantic experience is consciously divorced from actual life, surely this would affect the quality of its emotions, and would somewhat inhibit "The Greatest Feeling in the World." This is exactly what we do find when we consider the music itself. As in the case of the lyrics, there has been a single dominating element which has pervaded the vast majority of popular tunes since the early nineteenth century. This element is melancholy, and immediately we are reminded of sobbing nostalgia ("Old Folks at Home," "The Old Oaken Bucket," "Ol' Man River") or of the endless laments to separated and broken love ("Red Sails in the Sunset," "Sweet Genevieve," "The Tennessee Waltz"). What is perhaps not so obvious is the way in which our songs provide a melancholic mood for every imaginable situation. Whether one wakes up to the glories of nature ("Mockin' Bird Hill") or proclaims a creed of freedom ("Don't Fence Me In") or rejoices in college companionship ("The Wiffenpoof Song") or invokes his love at bedtime ("Goodnight, Sweetheart") or praises heroic fidelity ("Lili Marlene")—the music creates a melancholic atmosphere.

In ordinary life, melancholy occurs when, in the midst of joys, we realize their limitations, when we remember experiences both deep and irretrievable—"so sad, so strange the days that are no more"—or when we suddenly sense the mortality of a present happiness. Because melancholy involves this peculiar fusion of joy and sorrow, it has found repeated expression in literature. What is so unusual about our popular music is that here, in a media designed primarily to arouse feelings, melancholy tinges the entire range of emotional experience. This indicates that our culture must feel some profound limitation, not in the pleasure of any particular situation, but in the pleasure of feeling as such. And the song lyrics have indicated what that limitation is: deep feelings do not belong to the actual world, for nothing there apparently is capable of arousing or sustaining them. They can be found, if at all, only in a dream world like that of popular music. When a people believes that its ordinary emotional life is condemned to starvation, every imagined experience of deep feeling will be touched by melancholy

III

If we turn from the songs themselves and ask about the conditions of life which they reflect, two things especially deserve to be noticed. One observes first the apparent belief that the actual relations between men and women have become bankrupt of really significant joys. The song romances lack all sense of the vibrant presence of another person; the beloved is simply the occasion for a feeling which she does not inspire. Apparently the general urban lack of confidence in interpersonal life has now extended to this last important refuge of mutual affection.

Yet the fact that the people should enjoy the mass entertainment media at all is itself a symptom of this distrust. For the most extraordinary thing about this entertainment is not its commercial character, but the isolation which it imposes on any who enjoy it. Magazine literature is to be read alone in silence, not out loud to others. Once the party turns its attention to the television screen, latecomers are hardly noticed. To sit in a movie theater, where, swathed in darkness, you may draw up your knees, is like a return to the passivity and shelter of the womb. And when the popular music is played and "the piano builds a roof of notes above the world," whether the listener lies alone late at night or sways wordlessly in the arms of a girl, he is lost in the privacy of his own dreams. Genuine works of art, of course, impose a temporary isolation because of the concentration they demand. But that isolation should be a condition of *entertainment* is indeed unusual, and betrays, like the songs themselves, a profound distrust of interpersonal life.

A second feature of the American scene is disclosed especially by the excessive emotionalism of the songs; this is the emotional apathy of its daily existence. Many aspects of our culture are affected by the effort to escape this apathy, and newspaper headlines, for instance, speak to a condition where the emotions seek to be aroused by sensation, not quieted with wisdom. In the case of the popular songs, the effort involves no attempt to dress up actual life in deep emotions; actual life is simply ignored in the song world of feelings. In other words, people no longer expect to be deceived about the dullness of life. Boredom is inevitable, and it would therefore be foolish to trick out their imagined emotions in the pretense of concrete situations. Songs should simply display lavish feelings *in vacuo*. No more can be expected. This attitude amounts to a convinced skepticism about the emotional richness of ordinary existence. No one is deceived about life by the exaggerating headlines or the emotionalism of the songs. In fact, it is usually the unskeptical—those for whom the actual world has some possibility of excitement and ultimate importance—who are revulsed by the blatant unreality of popular entertainment.

We have only to take note of the kind of real life goals and hopes in which our culture is submerged to see the reason for this emotional skepticism. Taught that a kind of natural necessity undergirds objects, events, and personal experiences, compelled to find the meaning of work in terms of income or competitive prestige, and inspired by the overarching aim to control life through various impersonal techniques like personality display or greeting cards or petting, most people completely resign actual life over to monotonous ennui.

The Twilight World of Popular Songs

It would appear that the function of our popular songs is to provide us with a consciously unreal world of simulated feelings, and to engage the higher degrees of our emotional intensity, which daily life cannot absorb. It is therefore in the midst of life, during the very moments when they are enduring the apathy of daily routine, that the people crave their music. The worker in the factory, the housewife at the sink, the salesman on the road, the shopper in the supermarket, the vacationers in the restaurant, the school girl at her homework—all try to supplement, but make no attempt to replace, their awareness of actual life with song emotions.

Because the people have made their songs instruments of emotional compensation, these songs have lost their integrity. They do not express what is actual, but seek to arouse what is artificial. Hence they are tense, uneasy, struggling to impose themselves upon us and to engage our imagination. Like instruments, whose only meaning is to be kept by usage in continual activity, they have none of the repose of other folk music. They have a synthetic quality, not because they have been machine made, but because they are themselves machines. There is a pitiful irony here, for in the people's effort to compensate for the bleak impersonal world of synthetic techniques they turned their music itself into such a technique. For this reason, in spite of all its simulated passion, the whole realm of popular songs fades into a masquerade of emotion.

IV

Because the whole state of mind behind our popular music relates to attitudes of basic importance to the religious community, we must consider whether it has had an effect upon the people's fellowship of worship. Have relations between people, for instance, become as devoid of a personal quality as the songs indicate? When we examine the meaning of love of neighbor, such in fact seems to be the case. Throughout the American scene, both in the popular religion encountered in the mass media and to a large extent in the official religion of the churches, love of neighbor is advocated as a technique to affect the world out there—to combat communism, to bring political peace, to make the constant attrition of people in city life a little more tolerable. The goal of the ethical life is not love of neighbor as such, freed from its perversions, perfected and fulfilled; not the incomparable joy of inter*personal* life; and certainly not the honor of another's inviolable dependence on God. Love is only a means of achieving something else.

We hear little penetrating criticism of the motives that may be operating under the guise of love, and no large segment of the American population believes that it might be difficult, if not impossible, for any of us to apply this technique properly. All we have to do with love, as with any tool, is simply settle down and use it. In fact, we usually hear it recommended on the basis of its efficiency for doing things, not because of its moral or personal dimensions. "Hire the handicapped," reads the official postmark on United States mail. "It's good business"—a lesson Sunday school children have been taught for years. Separated from the difficulties of inner moral decisions and from the personal richness of human intercourse, love of neighbor has been divested of all humaneness, and been transformed into an impersonal technique.

But this is only one in the jungle of such techniques that submerge the religious institution. Consider some of the tendencies in religious education. A Bible story is useful because, like a scientific experiment, it provides us with data. From it a neat moral lesson can be drawn, which may be applied elsewhere to life by a student with engineering aptitude. The catechism resembles the laws of physics which we learned in school. It is a set of general principles, by which the expert figures life out, but which are too vast for the ordinary person to do anything with but memorize. While this kind of education at least gives the student manageable bits of information which he can pull out efficiently whenever needed, it hardly confronts him with the awesome, mysterious, absolutely unmanageable God that spoke on Mt. Moriah and on Calvary.

It is quite false, however, to single out religious education. How else do many people think of their offering of money, their praying, and even their churchgoing itself, except as techniques for getting something else done? Don't forget, "Bring a friend to church. You both may benefit."

This atmosphere of inhuman instrumentalism severely colors American religious communities, and one therefore wonders whether it has provoked the same emotional skepticism there that we find elsewhere in our culture. In view of the popular (though not always clerically approved) church music, this would seem to be the case. First, little attention is given to the words of the hymns and anthems, since apparently few expect anything vital to be expressed by them. No discrimination is made in these words between faithful and contradictory expressions of belief, so that singing for the people is usually not part of their response to believed realities, but an important habit.

Secondly, we find recurring in the music the same melancholic mood that inspires our popular songs. Consider the enormous popularity in the Roman Catholic Church of certain sorrowful Lenten pieces, where, according to the music, the sense of sin is not felt bitterly or hopefully or sorrowfully, but with a sweet sadness. Even more obvious are some of the familiar Protestant hymns. When many churches, for instance, gather at the Lord's table, there is no "remembrance of me," no awareness of the real Person, nor of the Event with its horror and dazzling hope. All is dissolved away by the lugubrious "Break Thou, the Bread of Life," and any feeling that "my spirit pants for thee" or any expectation that "then shall all bondage cease" is relegated by the music to the unreal dream world of sweet regret. Perhaps more striking yet is the fact that when all American Christians unite to celebrate the miracle of Christmas, their most popular carol is not a tune vibrant with joy, but the slow and melancholy "Silent Night."

It should be understood clearly that the pall of skepticism which operates here is not due to intellectual conviction, for people do not, at least in our time, make *conscious* discriminations between attitudes by referring to overarching ideas. In order to judge how to believe an assertion, they refer to their emotional response. If a statement rings a modest set of practical, unpretentious emotional buzzers, then it belongs to the actual world of daily life. But if it begins to prompt an intense and total response, like adoration or joyous hope, then it belongs to the regretted world of consoling dreams. Emotions in the religious life have something of the character of the romantic experience in the popular songs. They seem unreal, like a masquerade for which people are grateful, but which they do not confuse with actual life.

Whatever may be required to meet this situation, it seems to me that greater emotional clarity on the part of religious leaders and teachers is indispensable. By this I do not mean a display of emotionalism. Exaggerated feelings have a quality of self-indulgence and artificial excitement, which makes us doubtful about the emotional adequacy of whatever inspired them. But I do mean a conscious emotional appropriation of things religious, a strong and controlled awareness in every corner of the religious life of joy or fear, of confidence or disgust. Because attention is focused and defined only to the extent that its object is real, skepticism breeds on vagueness, and this is as true in the emotional life as in the intellectual.

The Uncertain Center

The dead weight of skepticism which is now flourishing in and around the American religious communities will not be burned away by intellectual argument or factual precision. It can be met only by emotional clarity. This, like the development of any other kind of awareness, requires concentration and discipline, but for those who have the necessary gifts and patience, it offers an avenue of genuine service to our religious life.

2

Reason in a Violent World

This essay was written for an alumni-faculty seminar in June 1959 at Wesleyan University. McGill was finishing his tenure at Wesleyan and on his way to Princeton. McGill had spent the 1957–58 academic year as a Fulbright Scholar in Belgium, and surely he drew on that experience to sketch his contrast here between European and American modes of education. In this essay we find McGill developing the analysis of violence that would frame his masterpiece, Suffering: A Test of Theological Method *(1968). "The Age of Reason is over," McGill declares, since we no longer believe in the powerfulness of reason in the face of the terrors we confront. McGill is hypothesizing the shift from humanism to demonism that would mark most of his later output. The closing paragraphs of this essay are particularly striking given the course McGill's life would take. "Even the intellectual man can be an example of creative suffering," McGill concludes.*

Power-mad killers . . . notorious, untamed women clashing in a sun-scorched sin spot.
   —Motion Picture Advertisement

|

I should like to ask what is behind modern man's distrust of reason. But I find that the term means rather different things to different people. For instance, it often appears in connection with those modern intellectual movements, like psychoanalysis and existentialism, which belittle the power of reason. These views make human existence a matter of subconscious impulses or willful decisions. Our poor minds are left in the lurch.

It seems to me, however, that this use of the phrase "distrust of reason" is wholly misleading. The real concern of all these modern movements is not to attack reason, but only to attack the kind of reason which uses abstract and general ideas, which insists on making everything clear and logical. Contemporary thought wants to stop reducing reality to a system of concepts. It wants reason to forget about absolute moral principles and neat scientific laws. It wants the mind to get out of its ivory tower of abstractions and to recover contact with all those parts of the world that are not logical. The Marxists emphasize the dynamic thrust of human history; the psychoanalysts expose the power of unconscious instinctual drives. Critics of literature talk about action and gesture rather than themes. And the existentialists call men to get rid of moral principles and to face each moment of their lives as a unique situation that demands a total decision all its own. Thus, in every area, contemporary thought extends the concern of reason to those areas of reality that are not rational, that cannot be mastered by a formula or reduced to an idea, that can only be respected and experienced and followed. It tries to prevent men from hiding behind their reason, from putting their minds *between* themselves and the world. It wants them to have the courage to open themselves fully to whatever is there.

American thought also shares this concern, though in its own special way. It insists on always going beyond the abstractions of theory and solving the *practical* problems of life. Pragmatism, as this viewpoint is called, is not just a philosophic movement; it informs the whole intellectual life of America, from theoretical physics to first-grade education. Whenever we are presented with an idea, we always ask: How can we "use" it? What is it "good" for?

Now does this contemporary thought distrust reason? Yes, from the viewpoint of those who identify reason purely with logical procedures or with the abstract ideas of science. For them, the Marxists and the psychoanalysts, the existentialists and the American pragmatists all seem dangerously preoccupied with the irrational. Yet in truth all these movements deserve no such condemnation. They reject the tyranny of ideas, not to hurt reason but to revive it and enrich it, to put it in touch with the forces and decisions and turgid confusions of real life. If they have "distrust of reason," it is only for that particular kind of reason which has flourished in science and philosophy for the past three hundred years. They represent a bold and adventurous effort to bring reason back to reality, so that, if it cannot conquer the world, it can at least put men in touch with the world.

Here, then, is one common use of the phrase "distrust of reason," but it is not the only one. In recent years, the term has become associated with the educational system in the United States. One often hears that, in America, high school is primarily a matter of football games and dating rituals; college consists largely in extracurricular activities and fraternity life; and people endure what schooling they must simply for the practical purpose of getting a job or improving their social status. If one compares this with the much more intellectual emphasis of European education, which minimizes everything social and stresses the importance of philosophy and the classics, then one may well decide that the American school system is anti-intellectual.

But before deciding this question, we should consider for a moment the meaning of education. Why do human societies train their young? The purpose of education is *to enable people to belong to their communities,* so that, when they become adults with freedom and initiative, they will use their powers in a way that does not disrupt the community life but helps and enriches it. Every human individual is full of creative passion and ambition and persuasion. He is capable of directing his talents to advance the general welfare; he is also capable of using them to overthrow and destroy it, to assert his own self-interest at the expense of the group. No society can ever afford to let the individual go his own way. No society can be so sure of itself that it can ignore him. Every group has had its Hitlers and its Al Capones, men with sufficient drive and mastery to arouse unholy passions in others and to subvert the whole community life to their own purposes.

The crucial work of education, therefore, is to help every individual to learn how to belong. That is, it teaches him to share in the community life, to learn its hopes and fears, to discover the kind of conduct which is helpful and the kind which is destructive and alienating. By concrete experiences of praise and punishment, it teaches him to make the community's goals his own, and to modify whatever *he* wants to do privately in the interests of the common life. Whether education fully develops the peculiar talents of an individual or not is therefore a completely secondary concern. In fact, without the primary training in how to belong and serve, the more effectively an individual learns how to use his personal talents, the more dangerous he becomes. On the other hand, even if a person never realizes all his potentialities, as long as he knows how to fit his own drives into the common life, his work will be fruitful to the community and to himself.

If we look at Europe, the content of community life is expressed primarily in terms of a tradition, and in terms of a tradition that is both social and intellectual. For instance, in the Latin countries, the legal codes are derivatives of Roman law, the political groupings reflect the boundaries of long-extinct medieval dukedoms, Roman Catholic rituals and symbols mold the moral and religious life, and everything is pervaded by a certain intellectual atmosphere.

The process of educating a person in Europe and integrating him into the community life naturally consists in teaching him this tradition. He must learn to participate in its fundamental concepts and in its long historical development. Education, then, must involve rigorous study. From the age of six onward, every child goes to school from eight in the morning until six at night. Except for such refreshment as is necessary, his time is spent wholly in learning, and at night he lugs a briefcase home for further work. The purpose here is not to develop whatever intellectual capacities the individual may have—that is the work of the university. The purpose of the school is to infuse into the mind of every person a sense of the intellectual tradition which constitutes the common life. Then, whatever he may do as an adult, he at least can be trusted to fit in and serve that life.

When we turn to education in the United States, we must remember that the community life here has no such intellectual or traditional content. On the contrary, American life consists precisely in the confrontation and compromise of *different* traditions. The United States exists because minority groups, each with its own viewpoint and self-consciousness, each with its own history and customs and traditions, have agreed to live together, have agreed not to impose their own particular viewpoints on each other, and, where common action is necessary, have agreed to compromise.

The most dramatic example of this that I know is Statuary Hall in the national Capitol. Last year Professor Schattschneider of Wesleyan escorted a group of visiting Germans through the hall, and it took them only a minute to discover Louisiana's statue to Huey Long. "Doesn't this embarrass you," one of the Germans asked, "to have the statue of such a man in your national Capitol?" Professor Schattschneider explained that he and his state—his minority group, so to speak—had no respect for Huey Long. But the law allowed each state to commemorate any two of her citizens that she wished. Whatever the views of the rest of the country about Huey Long, everyone acknowledged to Louisiana her right to honor him. Driving his point home, Professor Schattschneider pointed to the statues of other embarrassing persons—a Cherokee Indian from Oklahoma; a polygamist, Brigham Young, from Utah—men who might have seemed disreputable by our standards, that is, by the standards of our particular racial or religious minority group. At the end, he showed them there, in the shrine of our national Capitol, statues to the Confederate leaders and generals who dedicated their lives to destroying this nation. Needless to say, the German visitors were dumbfounded.

The United States is not guided by a particular moral viewpoint or a specific political theory or a philosophic conviction or a historical tradition. Nor is it a melting pot where all viewpoints and theories and traditions are dissolved away. The content of community life in America is an unqualified *respect* for our mutual differences, the freedom for everyone to live by the convictions of his *own* group as long as this does not threaten the freedom and security of others. The United States is a place where minority groups live side by side, where there is always tension, but where the tension is always kept in check by a willingness to compromise. We live in a pluralistic, many-sided, ever-changing society, where one generation can never tell in what direction the compromises of the next generation will go, where no particular thing is certain except the variety and competition and compromise of many particulars.

The primary education of young people in the United States, therefore, must *not* be intellectual. Everything that belongs to the common life in Europe—religion, legal codes, moral conventions—is treated in America as part of a man's personal life. What is communal here is the *social experience* of confronting each other's differences and achieving common action by mutual compromise. This, therefore, is also the content of our education. The development of intellectual self-consciousness is quite unnecessary. Our young people do not need to gain a clear understanding of their own private moral principles or political loyalties or religious beliefs. Before everything else, the individual must learn—through games and cheerleading and committee work and extracurricular activities and dating—to submit his own personal traditions to the group action, in the continual give and take of democracy. We know only too well what happens when individuals refuse to compromise the traditions of their minority group, and if last year

The Uncertain Center

we had juvenile gangs and Orval Faubus, next year we will be threatened by someone else.

Is the American educational system anti-intellectual? Of course, by the very nature of American life. Individuals belong to our community, not by intellectual participation in a tradition, but by social discipline, and we leave the tradition to humanities courses in college. But if the intellect has a peripheral place in our education, this does not mean that we distrust reason. We distrust only its use at this point. In fact, at other points and especially in the practical world, we have pursued reason far more intensely than the Europeans. We have made it dominate the whole realm of active affairs. That is why, in spite of our educational needs, we have always had a profound confidence in reason, but a confidence typified by the inventor rather than the philosopher.

I have discussed here two examples of distrust of reason—modern intellectual movements on the one hand, American education on the other. And I have done so in order to show that neither involves a real distrust of reason. There is, however, a third use of the phrase, which I should like to consider in detail. It is associated with the headlines of our newspapers: juvenile delinquency and racial tension, concentration camps and hydrogen bombs, art works that idealize chaos and motion pictures that idealize brutal sensuality. Here the term "distrust of reason" does not refer to any specific movement. It denotes, rather, a quality of violence that seems to touch all of modern life. Here we do not have to do with a preference for one kind or one use of reason over others. These phenomena are expressions of an undercurrent of fear and anxiety that undermines all rationality whatsoever. This attitude cannot be dismissed as a matter of immaturity or emotional instability. It is shared by too many different kinds of people and affects too many human situations.

There may be something misleading about the titles of alumni seminars. "Distrust of reason" not only calls our attention to certain features of life today, but also suggests what is wrong. It seems to say that men act irrationally *because* they distrust their reason, *because* they do not take a mature and sensible approach to things. My own view is that our distrust of reason does not grow out of our attitude toward reason itself. It is only the symptom of an entirely different problem, concerning the world where our reasoning takes place. Therefore I should like to ask, not about the distrust of reason, not whether we believe in it and live by it, but rather about that world. In what kind of world do we think we live?

Reason in a Violent World

II

For this purpose, observe the stories that make up the front pages of our newspapers. Here, for instance, are the headlines in the Hartford *Courant* at the end of a typical week: "Ike Warns Russia to Ease War Scare"; "Nile Boat Sinks, 200 Feared Lost"; "Murderer Hanged as London Mob Storms Prison." Two days later, as a new week begins, we read: "Ex-Boxer Held in Slaying of Wife"; "Hoover Urges Sterner Treatment for Delinquents"; "Tornadoes Spin Death and Destruction." Here are typical daily records, not perhaps of the world as it really is, but of those incidents which we consider newsworthy, those events which we want etched on our memories with headlines and pictures.

The first thing that strikes us is that all these stories have something to do with disaster, with the way a storm or a murderer or a threat of war breaks suddenly into the lives of people with anguish or death. Disaster always has news value. But another curious thing is the way these focus, not on what people do, but on what they suffer, on what is done to them. A man is murdered, a woman is raped, a house is blown over, an airplane is forced down, a city is disturbed by riot, a country is under crisis. In all such newspaper reports, the vividly human element is found in the suffering. In contrast, the source of disastrous action is always something nonhuman, even when people are involved. Notice how, according to these stories, we are not troubled by particular boys, but by juvenile delinquency. Notice how the police are not battling specific men with individual problems, but a crime wave. We do not know the murderer or the rapist. The airplane was forced down by a faceless government, the city threatened by a faceless mob, the house destroyed by an invisible wind. And in the national crisis, even the most powerful leader is to some degree the victim of circumstances.

The newspapers most forcefully highlight this nonhuman, or superhuman, quality of events by painting every disaster as if it were wholly unexpected, wholly miraculous. Whatever acts here does not belong to the region of ordinary human purposes; it does not even show traces of its coming beforehand. Look at this typical example from *Time* magazine for May 11, 1959:

> In Manhattan, Nancy Alverson left her 2-year-old daughter in their Greenwich Village apartment while she went shopping. Back in "a few minutes," she found the child dead of suffocation, with her head swathed in the adhering layers of a plastic garment bag.

Notice what pains are taken to set the disaster in the normal routine of life, as if it meant to conceal itself there. Mrs. Alverson just went shopping for a few casual minutes, and nothing was involved but an ordinary garment bag. So we are told how the murder victim was attacked while "on his usual walk," how the plane that was forced down was "regularly scheduled," how the now rioting city "seemed perfectly calm."

We should not imagine that this style of reporting is an inseparable part of all journalism. In fact, one of the marks of our newspapers seventy-five years ago was their deliberate effort to avoid the unexpected. If there was a murder, we were given a clear description of the locale, a brief history of the town, and some perfectly intelligible reasons for the deed. Similarly, if tension erupted in the Middle East, we read three columns of detailed history of the area before the crisis itself was described, and by then it seemed to be no crisis at all, but the normal outworking of everything that went before. Apparently in those days people wanted the newspapers to *remove* the surprise from disaster, to extinguish the idea of accident, and make each tragedy seem the obvious effect of previous events. Today the opposite is true. Something is newsworthy only to the extent that it is unexpected. Even the international crisis is made to look like an accident, and the disorganized layout of the front page, the way unrelated items are bunched together, reinforces this impression that events are without order and without background.

Thus a picture begins to emerge from the newspapers, the picture of men in the midst of life suddenly smashed by an outbreak of violence from beyond their normal world. Call it crime, call it weather, call it war, the picture is consistently the same.

Now the extraordinary thing is that, if we turn from the newspapers to our own daily lives we find everywhere this same grim picture. Consider, for example, the matter of health. None of us believes any more in our health. We believe in sickness. Even if we feel fine, glowing with juvenile vigor, we know that it cannot last, that it is only momentary and may even deceive us. Every day, therefore, we take our vitamins. Every month we pay our health insurance. Every year we submit to the examination and wait for the X-ray to discover the spot on our lungs or for the smear to reveal the presence of cancer. We have no confidence in health because we know that what threatens us is not just certain bacteria or faulty organs or inadequate diet. What threatens us is something mysterious and aggressive, which appears in all these things but can be conquered in none of them. We do not think of sickness as the absence of bodily strength, but rather as the presence of disease. It is a power outside of us, a vital and cancerlike force that attacks us and cripples us and destroys us. It is a reality that since childhood we have been taught to picture in terms of germs or viruses, weird undetectable terrors. And we know that finally for each of us this something will be more powerful than all health or all science.

Naturally we fight these dreadful powers. We construct immense black machines studded with glittering eyes. We use invisible rays that penetrate everything. We invent uncanny drugs, with side effects no one can predict and names no one can pronounce, to be administered by long, sharp needles. We marshal in our defense weapons that are comparable to the enemy's. And the hospital—the place where the battle is joined and where the monstrosities of medicine meet the monstrosities of disease—is a holy place of awe and stillness, where the only people who can walk with safety are the white-robed initiates, the doctors and nurses. Yet even these defenses do not reassure us. What if we conquer one disease? Remember that for Mrs. Alverson's baby death came in an innocent garment bag. Suppose we keep away from dirt? Remember that even the air around us may be filled with deadly pollution. When Dr. Salk announced the success of his vaccine, did any of us feel closer to victory? Did any of us reduce his hospital insurance? For us, health is not a permanent state. It is only that momentary condition when the powers of disease are held back and bide their time. Each day we wait for their attack, much as Arthur Godfrey recently waited to see if the tumor on his lung was cancerous. "I never felt better in my life," he said. "Then boom. This horrible, skulking 'thing,' visible only as a ghostly shadow on an X-ray negative. This 'thing' that no longer gives me pain, probably because I can't feel it through the cold, clutching fear that's gnawing at my vitals" (*Time,* May 11, 1959).

Turning from our bodies, consider how the place in which we live promotes our anxieties. It is a place of machines, and all life is touched by their quiet hum. I wake up in the morning to the hum of the oil burner. I eat breakfast to the hum of the refrigerator. I go to my office by the hum of my car. I talk to people through the hum of the telephone, and correspond by the hum of the Dictaphone and even think to the hum of the electric typewriter. I drink to the hum of the water cooler. I buy my food to the hum of the cash register. And in the evening I sit at home and dream to the hum of the television set. Everywhere I am enclosed by strange supersensible forces, which these machines channel and which betray their terrific power only in this hardly audible noise. Beyond my own home and office hums the city, a place of endless motion, which has no purpose and no rest, which pulsates twenty-four hours a day, seven days a week, fifty-two weeks a year. The city itself is a gigantic machine, throbbing with power and engulfing everyone in its own pointless haste. Even the suburbs, which were designed originally for escape from the city, have now become encircled by the eight-lane superhighway and never escape the city's glare or the airplanes' roar in the night sky.

In this world of humming power, everyone keeps on the watch for it suddenly to break forth. My oil burner is working fine, though the one down the street exploded last year and killed three people. The electric system is safe, provided the fuses are in order and my children do not play at the outlets. We like our gas stove, though before we go to sleep we make a point of seeing that the burners are turned off. If we leave home for the city, we know that, for all our caution, we may happen to be in the way when the car lurches out of control, or when fire guts the theater, or when the holdup occurs or the juvenile gang attacks. We defend ourselves as best we can—with safety fuses and safety valves, with air brakes and power brakes, with constant checkups by the repairman and comprehensive year-round insurance. Against the crime wave and other human explosions we maintain our police forces, with their squad cars and machine guns. Here, as in medicine, the defense must be comparable to the enemy. But when the plane is overdue, when the boy is out late with the car, when it is not certain whether we turned off the gas, we know that these defenses are useless.

Consider our attitude toward romantic love. According to the popular songs, the final truth about love is that it will leave us. However real it may be now, the day will come when we will "wonder who's kissing her now," and we will "sit all alone at a table for two," "laughing on the outside, crying on the inside," and slobbering our soup all over our broken heart.

This silly despair in our songs becomes dreadfully real in the divorce courts. For some reason, love in our lives is a great agony, not something to be played with, but a power and an endless struggle to be endured. We are continually forced either to submit to it with violence or to suppress it into empty habit. We are like Dr. Courrèges in Mauriac's novel, *The Desert of Love*. We have a sterile home life and a disturbed dream life. We have to keep choosing between the lie of decency, where we stifle the vigor and excitement of love, and the lie of gratification, where we degrade ourselves in unmanageable lust. Love for us is not a lush garden of the Orient, filled with gentle breezes and the quiet intoxication of fulfillment. Love, as Mauriac says, makes life into a burning desert. Every morning the newspaper tells us of another person in whom love became frustration, became divorce, became murder. If we have vital love, we know that we hold a terribly destructive force. Our only hope is to keep it calm, keep it weak, keep it habitual. With Jean Anouilh and our popular songs, we know that vital love "is not the business of honest people" (*The Lark,* Act I).

If we turn to more public issues, we find even there this same sense of disaster. We may remember the good old days of economic optimism in America. Every man had his life in his own hands; his future was a golden road of opportunity; and millionaire success awaited anyone with get-up-and-go. But today we cannot believe in our economy. Remembering 1929, we know that a terrible momentum of disaster lurks within it, ready to break forth at any moment. We have our graphs and charts to peer into the future. We tinker with the interest rate here and withdraw money from circulation there. We take a job with some big company which, we hope, will shelter us through all storms. But however steady the market, however promising the statistics, few of us believes in prosperity. The anxious worrying about the economy goes on and on and on, at the dining table, at the university, at the White House, like an endless conference of baffled doctors around a sickbed. Prosperity is no longer for us a real condition, but only that fragile moment between the two monsters—inflation on the one hand, depression on the other.

There is, finally, our concern for peace. Over us hangs the threat of *total war,* not war in the old sense where victory and defeat were both possible, but war in the modern sense where there can be only defeat. We have no illusions about getting rid of this threat. Our hope is simply to keep it at a distance, by having huge defenses and incredible weapons at our disposal. We must discourage our enemies with the threat of "massive retaliation." In other words, the only kind of peace we know or can expect consists in keeping ready for war. Like health and prosperity, peace too is a matter of continually fighting a *cold war* against the threat of destruction.

I have made this survey of our lives intentionally one-sided. I realize that we have all enjoyed the rigor of healthy bodies. We have all cherished and respected the affection of our children. We know the security of a steady income and the peace of our quiet towns. But I did want to highlight the thread of pessimism which seems to characterize our life, the constant feeling that disaster may be lurking somewhere in the background, a sense of enormous evil that comes perhaps from seeing the gas chambers at Dachau and the atomic bomb at Hiroshima.

This anxiety is perhaps the distinctive mark of us modern men. It gives us a certain grim wisdom. We can understand Camus when in his novel *The Plague* he criticizes the townspeople of Oran for not taking seriously the terrible epidemic which has struck them:

> Our townsfolk were like everybody else, wrapped up in themselves; in other words they were humanists: they disbelieved in pestilences. A pestilence isn't a thing made to man's measure; therefore we tell ourselves that pestilence is a mere bogy of the mind, a bad dream that will pass away. But it doesn't always pass away and, from one bad dream to another, it is men who pass away. Our townsfolk were not more to blame than others; they forgot to be modest, that was all, and thought that everything still was possible for them; which presupposed that pestilences were impossible. They went on doing business, arranged for journeys, and formed views. How should they have given a thought to anything like plague, which rules out any future, cancels journeys, silences the exchange of views. They fancied themselves free, and no one will ever be free so long as there are pestilences (37).

We who live today are not humanists. We do not fancy ourselves free. We know that there are pestilences. As the newspapers teach us day after day, life is in the hands of unseen forces which are ever ready to attack us, to shatter the security of our bodies or the security of our loves or the security of our homes or the security of our land. And, worst of all, we know that disaster may strike just when the situation seems most secure—just when, like Arthur Godfrey, we never felt better in our lives, just at the height of prosperity, as in 1929, or just after the perfect agreement has been reached at Munich.

This may be why the loss of the *Titanic* has a peculiar fascination for us today. If you saw the motion picture *A Night to Remember*, you know the theme: the sinking of the unsinkable, the defeat of triumphant humanism, the collapse of man's science and self-confidence. When the boat sets sail, all humanity is assured, the rich in first class, the officers on deck, the immigrants in steerage. Then the iceberg and disaster. As the ship settles, we see different reactions—the intoxication of the bottle, hysterical violence and grief, the worried busyness of trying to cope with little problems, the aimless running about for some escape. It is a perfect picture of us in our everyday living, awaiting our iceberg or plastic garment bag or atomic bomb. As one of the officers said at the end of the movie, "We were all so sure—the unsinkable *Titanic*. Now I can never be sure again."

III

It is in terms of this feeling of terror that I would understand the distrust of reason in our time. This distrust is not simply a protest against neat logical thinking, like the modem intellectual movements. It is not an effort to withdraw reason from the community life and limit it to practical affairs, like American education. Indeed, it is not primarily an attitude toward reason at all. We who live today see ourselves surrounded by a dreadful world. Regardless of our wishes, therefore, we cannot help but feel that in such a world reason is no more reliable than man himself. In fact, our only sane attitude is to distrust it.

This attitude may seem disturbing and unnatural, but it has actually been prevalent in most ages of human history. By its technical name it is called demonism. Demons, of course, are not little creatures with horns and pitchforks, but powers that break into life and bring destruction. They have no form that can be named, because their very essence is to disrupt and annihilate forms. They have a darkness which defies the mind. What is dreadful in cancer, for instance, is not the virus itself but its strange vitality to kill healthy cells. The awful thing about economic depressions and wars is the terrific energy of destruction which they let loose in the world, an energy that not only overthrows institutions and demolishes cities but that even invades the human spirit and carries it to inconceivable heights of brutality.

Most human societies are quite frank in acknowledging these demonic powers. Take, for example, the Christian church, with its confession that God is "the Creator of heaven and earth." "Earth" in the Christian confession means everything contained within our human capacities, everything we can objectify and conceptualize, everything we can arrange and understand. The sun and the galaxies and all nature belong to what is here called "earth," since they can be understood by us in terms of our experience. Similarly the world of ideas, the domain of spiritual values, and all the ideals which men have pursued since the beginning of time are part of this "earth."

In addition to this earthly realm, however, there also exists the heavenly realm. Heaven, here, is not the stratosphere or the starry ether; it is the reality inconceivable to man and superior in power to everything earthly (See Karl Barth, *Dogmatics in Outline*, ch. 9). The Christian confession asserts quite unambiguously that there are impenetrable mysteries of glory and evil within creation itself, real inconceivable terrors that we cannot describe, but only suggest with grotesque symbols. When we have reached what to us is inconceivable, we have not reached God, but only heaven. Creation has within it depths of being and immensities of power that stagger our consciousness. The children and the poets and the newspapers that speak of these mysteries are not wrong.

Yet, for the Christian church, though the demonisms of life are quite real, their power is only relative and limited. That is the good news which the church proclaims when it confesses that *God* created heaven and earth. For all their seeming power and finality, the demons of heaven are in the hands of a Lord, the same Lord who has chosen man for eternal life. Neither cancer nor accident nor war nor death, but only the Lord God is God; only he holds the lives of men in his hands. That is why the first and second commandments hold good. Because nowhere in heaven or on earth is there a divine power which men ever have to love or ever have to fear, therefore "ye shall not fear other gods, nor bow yourselves to them, nor serve them, nor sacrifice to them" (2 Kgs 17:35).

Extraordinarily enough, the church's confession finds it necessary to speak of supersensible evils in another place, this time in relation to Jesus Christ, who "suffered under Pontius Pilate, was crucified, died and was buried, descended into hell, and on the third day rose from the dead." Notice how Jesus' whole life is summed up under the one word "suffered," and how it ends in the agony of crucifixion. He receives all the earthly evils men must endure, and in him, as in us, these evils bear their fruit. He was dead and buried, covered over, wiped off the face of the earth and from the mind of man. Yet, after submitting to these conceivable evils, "he descended into hell," into the region of inconceivable evil, of dreadful demonic powers that exist only to corrupt and destroy. Thus, for a second time, the confession brings the demonic into the foreground.

Yet here, too, what the church announces is not simply the existence of these horrors, but their limitation and defeat. For "on the third day he rose again from the dead." He who is *the* man, who is the reality of all men, triumphed over both the earthly and the heavenly evils. Victory, therefore, is the decisive and final fact of human existence. That is why in every disaster Jesus' command holds good: "Be not anxious" (Matt 6:25). Neither cancer nor accident nor war, neither death nor life, neither angels nor principalities nor powers nor anything else can take from us the victory that is ours in Jesus Christ. For Christianity, then, the demons are there, but they are not to be feared. Their dreadful power over men is ruled by him who created the heavens and is broken by him who rose from the dead.

I mention Christianity here as an example of how familiar, even to us civilized Westerners, is the sense of the dreadful. Today, of course, our anguish is not Christian. We do not experience the power of destruction as something the Lord created or the Savior suffered. As a newsman reported Easter morning, "In spite of the resurrection hope, there is great anxiety about tension in the Middle East" (CBS, April 5, 1959). For us, the power of war is infinitely more real than any Christian fairy tale.

The background for our modern experience is not Christianity but the Age of Reason, the belief in universal rationality. According to this view, we do not need to fear the demons because they simply do not exist. Reality is rational through and through, and ordered like a clock or a slowly growing flower. To the human mind it is a completely open book. There are no heavens in the old Christian sense; there is only starry space dominated by the same laws of gravity and motion that govern the earth. There are certainly no demons or witches or hell. These are the figments of a fear-ridden imagination. Nature is beautifully ordered and moves flawlessly toward its own perfection. The battle cry of the Age of Reason, therefore, was: Dare to think! Dare to behold the world with your reason! For then you will know that everything dreadful exists only in your mind, that you have nothing to fear but fear itself. Then you will become free—free from the terrors that enslave you to tyrants, free from brutal superstitions and inhuman magic, free to see the world in its rational order. This freedom is the glory of enlightenment.

Today, as I see it, the Age of Reason is over. Men have discovered demonic ferocities in themselves and in their world, and have learned with terror that these ferocities cannot be explained away. People do not make their own rational minds the measure of reality. They no longer believe that education will make them wise, that science will make them healthy, that law will make them peaceful, that freedom will make them happy, or that love will make them good. Even in the midst of pestilences, of course, there are a few humanists, still insisting that everything is possible. Here and there a commencement speaker will exhort the young to rely on themselves, will prescribe initiative and self-confidence as a solution to their troubles. But these voices make no impact. For the people of today have had enough of the dreams of reason and order. They have seen the Enlightenment proved a lie. They have seen the democratic experiment breed dictators abroad and juvenile delinquents at home. They have watched the League of Nations unwittingly contribute to the rape of Nanking. They do not wonder about "the distrust of reason." The distrust of reason is no longer even a question: it is a fact they all accept. Their fundamental attitude is rather a distrust of life; and before this the glory of reason is swept away, along with moral conventions and self-discipline and civilized diplomacy.

To be sure, people in such a state of mind suffer an almost intolerable hunger for security. They pile up insurance policies, and flock to uplifting meetings to hear about a Never-Never Land where love is king, where nothing is insoluble, and where no one is ever damned. But they know that they can never trust such security. They have no real knowledge of, say, a Savior's descent into hell to limit their fears. For them there is only one rule of life: Be ye anxious, for tomorrow—or even today—ye die. Indeed, what really worries them is the fact that they may not fear *enough*. They are afraid that the defense budget or the Securities and Exchange Commission will lull them into confidence. That may be why, each morning and each evening, they demand a newspaper to feed their fear, to remind them that evil is not static but volcanic, not anticipated but sudden and unpredictable. At the same time, even in the midst of this terror, they have found a new and peculiar excitement. There is an intensity to a life that awaits disaster, a nihilistic exuberance which the ordered world of polite decency can never know. Why be reasonably cautious when at eighty miles per hour you can drive some glory road to nowhere with a thrill in every instant? Why fritter away forty billion dollars for meaningless luxuries when you can risk them in a cold war?

Yet we must ask: what does reason do in this violent world? What happens to the university when the demons rule? And the answer is clear: today, as always, reason must simply share the human condition. It must not fly to a world of neat abstractions. It must, like all the rest of man's consciousness, turn its vision to the darkness. That means, first, that it must search for powers of life and marshal them to resist the demons. This becomes the work of natural science. Secondly, it must fashion new words, new ideas, and new forms of expression to enable men to speak their anguish to one another. This is the work of art and philosophy. Above all, it must declare what it finds when it too lives in the shadow of death, and this is the work of theology.

Yet something quite different may happen. Perhaps in the future reason will cease to be important. Perhaps for guidance in time of trouble, people will turn not to human thought, but to the human capacity for suffering. Not the universities with their thinkers, but the places and people in distress, the inmates of asylums and concentration camps, the helpless decision makers in bureaucracy and the helpless soldiers in foxholes—these will be the ones to lighten man's way, to refashion his knowledge of disaster into something creative. We may be entering a new age. Our heroes may not be intellectual giants like Isaac Newton or Albert Einstein, but victims like Anne Frank, who will show us a greater miracle than thought. They will teach us how to endure—how to create good in the midst of evil and how to nurture love in the presence of death. Should this happen, however, the university will still have its place. Even the intellectual man can be an example of creative suffering.

3

The End of Intimacy

This essay was delivered at the study conference of the National Campus Ministry Association at Michigan State University in June 1965. The theme of the study conference was technology and its revolutionary impact on society and higher education. McGill, then professor of religion at Princeton, was the only theologian to speak at the conference. His assignment was "to demonstrate the way in which a theologian would think through the change in one significant theological concept as an illustration to churchmen of the process of rethinking theology in the age of technological mass man." McGill chose to focus on the concept of Christian love. He argues that the personalism advocated and popularized by Martin Buber in I and Thou (1923) finds no correlate in the New Testament accounts of love. McGill's critique of personalism is recurrent in much of his writing during the 1960s, but it is muted if not overturned in his writing on suffering near the end of his life.

Christians today are addressing themselves to the specific problems created by technology, the problems of automation, of nuclear war, of overpopulation. There is, however, a question of much deeper proportions: why should the Christian give his consent and support to technology at all? What basis is there within the Christian life for accepting and encouraging technology?

Of course, there is no problem when technology causes suffering. Then Christian duty is clear-cut and unqualified: suffering should be relieved. But the question, "What should the Christian do to help the victims of technology?" is *not* the question, "Why should the Christian give his support to technology itself?" In fact, if on balance technology seems to be more harmful than helpful to the human side of man's life then the Christian is bound to oppose it with all his power.

This is what actually happens today more often than is generally realized. Christians feel a profound pessimism about technology itself. They do not often say this in so many words, of course. They eagerly inform themselves about the latest advances in computers and the latest techniques in genetic surgery. They have no illusions about the enormous importance of technology for day-to-day life. But in their hearts they just cannot gather this highly rationalistic and impersonal world into the driving center of the Christian faith. In short, they cannot relate the doing of technology to the *Christian life of neighborly love.*

If this is the case, then it is really pointless for Christians to ask seriously about automation or cybernetics from the viewpoint of their Christianity. If the technological world cannot be a living and vital action of Christian loving, if it must always stand as something alien, that should be said clearly and forcefully. Christians should not mask their condemnation behind an "interest" that really amounts to a kind of intellectual voyeurism.

The first task, therefore, is to seek out the roots and the meaning of this Christian pessimism over technology.

|

It is necessary to secure a picture of what this technological world is, not simply or primarily in the rarefied atmosphere of original research, but in the day-to-day living of the people who work within it. Perhaps the simplest way of doing this is to consider the impact of the machine on human life, since the heart and soul of technology is the machine.

The first thing which a machine requires is someone with the necessary technical knowledge to operate it. The machine establishes such knowledge as an indispensable part of work. Today no one can be a secretary without being familiar with the different control buttons on her machine, and without mastering the correct technical specifications for the necessary ribbons (quality, color, spool number) and paper (weight, texture, erasability).

Secondly, the machine requires that people work together. This may involve the cooperation of several men in running a single machine. But it certainly involves the integration of different stages of work into a smooth show. There is the idea-man who first conceives of some product. There is the financier who provides the money, the planner who works out production techniques and specifications, and the workers who carry out the production. There then are the distributors who must transport the product and the salesmen who must find purchasers for it. Each of these roles is a very complex and specialized task. If the machine is to be used fruitfully, each of them has to be carefully and smoothly and continually integrated with the others. Everywhere and always the machine creates the need for the *organization of human labor.*

Out of these two developments there results a third, which is the most important for our purposes: the individual person in his unique individuality begins to disappear from the realm of work. For instance, the work of the machine does not represent something done by one individual for another on the basis of a personal interrelationship which exists between them. The machine makes work an organizational matter. It is performed *by* a collective—by a corporation or institution; it is performed *for* a collective—for the public or the "consumers" or the "patients." Because of the complexity of the machines, only a huge collective can build them and use them and own them. Because of the huge volume of work which they do—which they must do if they are to be economical—only a huge collective can make use of their service.

Similarly, when an individual speaks in the world of machine-work, he cannot use a language which arises out of his own personal life. He must use the technical and impersonal language which the organization itself has established for its collective action. This is true whether he plans the machine, or runs the machine, or sells or buys the products of the machine. When he speaks in this role, he never uses his own language but the language of the collective.

This sketch of the impact of the machine indicates its human meaning. The individual has been eliminated as a conspicuous presence. He is still there, to be sure, but he does not—indeed, he cannot—make his own particular individuality felt. And this aspect of technology has penetrated into every corner of public life today.

At one extreme, consider the scholar who works at the intellectual frontiers of our culture. He does not work as a private individual out of his own personal identity. The years of study for the PhD degree have seen to that. This educational process has completely saturated his mind with technical knowledge. It has drenched him with such a thorough acquaintance with what other experts have done before him that he no longer even knows what it means for him to work "on his own." In our culture, before any thinker is allowed anywhere to use the expensive libraries and laboratories available at the universities, he must have his PhD degree, which means that he must be thoroughly indoctrinated into the *collective* activity of his particular field, so that when he does work and publish, it is not in the name of his own private personhood, but in the name of the corporate scholarly effort that has authorized him with a degree and employed him with a salary. Technology has made even the university a place of impersonal collective work. And woe be unto the young student who goes to college with the idea of nurturing his own unique individuality.

The research scholar represents one extreme. The housewife shopping at the supermarket represents the other. Before anything else, shopping today requires first of all a technical mastery of trade names, prices, and specialized uses, and secondly it requires an assessment of competing chain stores and competing product companies. Consider the relatively minor task of purchasing breakfast cereal. The housewife cannot casually reach up for just any box on the counter. She must have enough technical knowledge to choose among the paralyzing variety of products in front of her. She must know the difference between puffed rice full of air and Rice Krispies full of sound, between packages which offer coupons for toys on the outside and those which contain actual toys on the inside, between the small-sized boxes that are soon devoured and the large-sized boxes that will not fit between her cupboard shelves. Above all, she must be alert to any new, new, new product that is impressing her children on television. And all the time she recognizes that all this technical knowledge is simply her way of entering into and benefiting from the productive work of vast and hopelessly complex organizations.

The modern child does not require many trips to the store to discover this situation. When he accompanies his mother shopping, he quickly learns that the process of buying and selling has nothing whatever to do with his own person, talking to and purchasing from some other person. He stands with his mother in the crowd of nameless shoppers, an evanescent presence trying to compete for the attention of a nameless clerk. He soon recognizes that here the only names which count for anything are not the names of people, but the names of the *product,* specified with complete technical accuracy—four General Electric seventy-five-watt bulbs, or one quart of Sherwin-Williams sand-dune brown A-100 latex outside paint. A child quickly learns the kind of names which are important in this world—DuPont, Kellogg, 15 Denier—and the kind of names which are not important—Bill Smith and Terry Johnson.

Today the collective, technical, highly organized and impersonal activity which is required by the machine and its technology has now penetrated every corner of public life. This world which it has created is what today we call the life of the city. When we speak of technology, therefore, we should not think simply of research and industry, but of the whole urban environment which they have produced.

II

With these relevant features of technology in mind, we must now turn to the question of its relation to the Christian life—or rather, to the question of why Christians feel that it is at enmity with their Christian life.

When we speak of the interhuman aspect of Christian life, we are speaking about the Christian love of neighbor. For the Christian knows that, as a Christian, he can have *no other* way but the way of love. As John writes, "Beloved, let us love one another, for love is of God. He who does not love does not know God" (1 John 4:8). But the Christian also knows that, as a Christian, he can have *no higher* way than the way of love. It is the consummation of his social existence with others; it is his fulfillment of the entire divine law (Rom 13:8); it is the crown of his salvation.

What, then, is the prevailing nature of Christian love, in terms of which Christian believers must assess the world of technology? The answer is obvious enough. Today Christian love is usually identified with the relationships of *personal intimacy* between two individuals. It involves their being considerate and sensitive to each other, and, for better or worse, of always affirming each other's value as individual persons.

One of the finest descriptions of what is involved here on the human side has been given by the Jewish theologian, Martin Buber, in his little volume *I and Thou.* There Buber sets up a contrast between what he calls the I-It world and the I-Thou world. The I-It world, he says, is essentially one of alienation. It is where the ego, withdrawn inside itself, looks out upon a realm that stands over against it. This world involves a basic separation, a basic over-againstness between the self and all other beings. That is why Buber calls it the realm of "experience," since experience occurs when we are aware of something as standing over against us in some independent realm. In this world the mind merely passes over the surface of things. It never penetrates them, never apprehends them from within, but only looks at them from the outside, as if from a distance. In this I-It world, no object has any kind of absolute status or claim. Each thing is seen as bounded by other things, as one item in a world of items. This is the world of objectivity, and therefore of intellectual analysis and rational explanation.

According to Buber, however, there exists another world with altogether different laws and structures. This he calls the I-Thou world. Here there are no objects, no things standing in external space. Here the person has his whole existence in a relationship with another. He is encountering a *Thou*, who for him fills all the heaven and from whom everything else in the universe derives its meaning. In that world, the Thou is never known as an object which stands separated from us and which exists by itself somewhere out there in the world. We know the Thou as within our own depths, as the soul of our soul and the life of our life. In other words, says Buber, our relationship with a Thou is absolutely direct. There are no obstacles, no distances to be crossed. There is meeting—genuine, direct, and total meeting. That is why only in the I-Thou relation is the present a full and rich present and not just that empty moment where the past has ended and the future not yet begun. According to Buber, this I-Thou relation is the realm of love. Genuine love, he contends, can never appear in the I-It world, can never be the act or attitude of an isolated ego which throws itself outward toward alien objects. Genuine love is relationship, is a unity of two, where each is present and genuinely open to the other. True love does not belong to either; it lies between the I and the Thou, embracing them both. It is the substance of the I-Thou relation.

Such is Buber's account of man's two worlds. And we can see how easily this view can be transcribed into a Christian perspective. It can be maintained that the Thou world of intimacy and love is precisely the world of reconciliation which Jesus brought. His message is that God works upon men to cleanse them of their hostility and pride and indifference to one another. By his grace he enables them to step out of their self-enclosed separateness from each other, and to enter into genuine relationship. Through the example and encouragement of Jesus, men are taken out of the I-It world and placed in an I-Thou world. They are called to love each other with precisely that directness and intimacy which Buber describes. The good news of Christ is that men may trust each other as persons, as Thous and not as Its, as ends and not as means. When we stand before another person, the grace of Christ permits us to recognize him for what he is, a child of God, a person who claims our love, a center around which the whole universe should turn, and *not* just as one objective item in the external world of items.

Bishop John Robinson gives a strong statement of this version of the Christian gospel in his book *Honest to God*. He contends that statements about God are really statements about the ultimacy of personal I-Thou relationships. It is *only* in this experience of intimate love that we come to know anything of God. "Our sense of the sacredness of love," he writes, "derives from the fact that in this relationship as nowhere else there is disclosed and laid bare the divine Ground of all our being . . . To assert that 'God is love' is to believe that in love one comes into touch with the most fundamental reality in the universe" (53). "God, since he is Love, is encountered in his fullness only '*between* man and man' . . . God, the unconditional, is to be found only in, with and *under* the conditioned relationships of this life: for he is their depth and ultimate significance" (60). According to Bishop Robinson, then, we have man's entire saving relationship to God seen as the depths within his I-Thou relationship with his neighbor. In this regard I expect that Robinson expresses the version of the gospel which is most prevalent today in our American churches.

III

We are now in a position to understand the subterranean pessimism toward technology which seems to pervade the Christian scene. For if this I-Thou relation represents the indispensable arena for Christian love, what can possibly be said about the impersonal, highly collective and functionalized public life that technology has brought? What can be said, not just about automation and cybernetics, but about the office and the supermarket and the university?

There is only one thing that can be said, and Buber has said it: the modern city represents a world of dreadful alienation. It is an exclusively I-It world from which all love is necessarily excluded. It is a universe of things, where people are merely things too. In the congestion and hurry and impersonality of urban life, there can be no private intimacy. It is

The End of Intimacy

physically and psychologically impossible. Love—genuine I-Thou love—is out of the question. Wallace Stevens describes the ever-present pressure of people which besieges the mind of anyone in the city.

> If only fifty private houses were built in New York this year, it would be a phenomenon. We no longer live in homes, but in housing projects, and that is so whether the project is literally a project, or a club, a dormitory, a camp, or an apartment in River House. It is no longer that there are more of us and that we are actually close together. We are closer together in every way. We lie in bed and listen to a broadcast from Cairo, and so on. There is no distance. We are intimate with people we have never seen and, unhappily, they are intimate with us (*The Necessary Angel*, 18).

Where men have no sheltered space for private intimacy, where strangers are constantly obtruding into their lives, they have all that they can do just to protect themselves from abuse. Buber is quite correct in saying that the world of urban congestion and technology has deprived people of their power to enter into intimate relations. It teaches them how to deal with what is external, to manipulate objects and to use things, but it has prevented them from discovering the possibility of personal love. From the viewpoint of personal love, Buber's thesis is unarguable.

In fact, it has often been contended that the conditions of the modern city have the effect of splitting people into two loveless worlds. On the outside, in their surrounding environment, they are submerged in the congestion and haste of urban life. Their actions *must* be tightly regulated so that they will not collide with other figures on the scene. The volume of people requires that everything there be meticulously organized. Individuals may plan their day, but it is the institutions which plan for them. People naturally feel that their personal private world is being crushed by this vast network of collective control—by timetables, office routines, stoplights, and government regulations. Within themselves, therefore, they create an altogether different world, a world of daydreams and unexpressed feelings, an incommunicably secret world that can find no roots in the surrounding environment. As Buber rightly points out, neither world contains a Thou for the individual to love and cherish. Outside there are regulated collectives, with "members" and "workers" and "officials," but no persons. Inside there are only dreams and feelings, but again, no persons. The outside world is dominated by a collective will to power and a collective will to profit. The inside world is dominated by private, impotent, and irresponsible wishful thinking. Since there are no meetings here, no moments when one individual opens himself to another and stands directly before him as a Thou, there can be no love. This is how Kenneth Fearing pictures the situation, in his poem "American Rhapsody (4)" (*Collected Poems*, 131).

> First you bite your fingernails. And then you comb your hair again. And then you wait. And wait . . .
> Then the doorbell rings. Then Peg drops in. And Bill. And Jane. And Doc.
> And first you talk, and smoke, and hear the news and have a drink. Then you walk down the stairs.
> And you dine, then, and go to a show after that, perhaps, and after that a night spot, and after that come home again, and climb the stairs again, and again go to bed . . .
> But first the stairs.
> And do you now, baby, as you climb the stairs, do you still feel as you felt back there?
> Do you feel again as you felt this morning? And the night before? And then the night before that? . . .
> Or do you feel: What is one more night in a lifetime of nights?
> What is one more death, or friendship, or divorce out of two, or three? Or four? Or five?
> One more face among so many, many faces, one more life among so many million lives?
> But first, baby, as you climb and count the stairs (and they total the same), did you, sometime or somewhere, have a different idea?
> Is this, baby, what you were born to feel, and do, and be?

The world where technology reigns is a world where people have no power and no possibility for genuine personal relationships. They *function* together, but they *live* alone.

From the point of view of the gospel of intimate personal love, then, this world of collective technology can only be a threat. The Christian cannot embrace it with the passion of his religious faith. He cannot affirm it as the work and instrument of Christian love. There is nothing personal or intimate about a traffic jam, or an office conference, or a laboratory experiment, or a hurried visit to the crowded supermarket. In such situations a person may be friendly and polite, but he is completely caught up in the vast movement of impersonal structures. However hard he may try, the technical aspects of his work will demand his attention and will leave him

The End of Intimacy

little opportunity to grasp the concrete personal individuality of the people around him. However conscientious he may be, he will still feel the alien, thing-like impact of voices over the telephone or faces at the committee meeting. With a few exceptions, the customers and clients and students will remain faceless names. Too many technical problems must be handled and too many collective activities must be pursued to allow room for intimacy.

Whatever Christians may pretend to themselves, so far as they believe in the gospel of personal love, in their heart of hearts they must condemn the machine and the frantic urban world it has produced. However realistically they may view the actual power of technology over modern life, they must see Christianity as a *redemption from* this dreary loveless world. They must see it as serving the cause of intimacy, as providing people with a mode (kindness) and a discipline (service) and a reason (Jesus Christ) and a community (the church) for personal love. They certainly should not claim that their Christianity will help the industrialist, for example, with his problem of automation. This is a complex problem in the technology of mass production. In order to solve it at that level and in those terms, the Christian preoccupation with personal love is a useless and perhaps harmful distraction. Personalistic Christianity may offer the I-Thou relation as a haven for the wretched victims of automation, for those who have been deprived of work and excluded from great occupational collectives in American life. But from this Christianity we should not expect anything illuminating or clarifying on the problems of technology itself. In fact, such problems only serve to confirm the underlying suspicion of this kind of Christianity that technology is inhuman in essence and therefore inescapably anti-Christian.

Unfortunately those who advocate the gospel of personal love do not always relate themselves to the problems of the modern city. They cannot enthusiastically endorse this world, because it contradicts the kind of love in which they believe. At the same time, it seems too real and too enveloping for them openly to attack and condemn it in the name of love. What they do may be seen in many suburban churches today: they retreat into the family. For the family represents the only arena of private intimacy which still remains. It is therefore the only remaining sphere for which the gospel of personal love has any relevance. So it is that the American clergyman has become a family minister, calling on people in their family dwellings, preaching chiefly on family problems, hoping to resolve worldwide crises with family attitudes, and clinging to this island of intimacy with *not a single word of either blessing or judgment* to the urban world of technology.

IV

The direction of these remarks should now be quite evident. The prevailing personalistic notion of Christian love must be challenged, and challenged on two grounds.

First of all, it is simply not the case that city life dehumanizes people, that it violates and crushes their human sensitivity, saps their personhood, and in the end leaves them empty husks, with no personal reality except in their dream life or in their home life. Just the contrary seems to be the case. Individuals have their richest and deepest human experiences, not in relations of private intimacy, but when they share in some corporate enterprise, when they work as part of a larger whole. Far from depriving them of their humanity, these circumstances give a unique elevation to their lives. There they are needed because they have some kind of specialized skill, however crude. There their labor is part of a larger creative force—the company or department or profession—which reaches far beyond their own narrow sphere of life but with whose services and achievements they are identified. In this context, therefore, their "personal" failures extend far beyond themselves. Everything which they do has an expanded significance, not because of any exceptional performance on their part, but because of what the collective to which they contribute does. For that reason also the human relations which do occur there—the patience, the criticism, the support in adversity, but also the betrayal, the spite, and the envy—all these take on a larger, heightened meaning. They are points at which a person touches, not simply other individuals, but the life of a whole community.

In fact, compared to the dimensions of life that are nourished by the institutional world of work, people seem to find a lower order of intensity in their home life. It is very personal and very relaxing, but it is not as deeply gripping or as humanly challenging as the work-a-day world. Men today find it easier to turn their backs on their wives than on their jobs. The knowledge of this is a burden which every suburban housewife must bear. In spite of the cult of romantic love and family solidarity promoted by the mass media—and in this regard the church may certainly be regarded as one of the mass media—the housewife recognizes that in her world of the home her husband does not find the challenges and horizons which claim him in his work.

This is not to say that people can live entirely without some relations of personal intimacy. They do need home life and friendships. But this is to say with Karl Marx, and against Martin Buber, that a man or woman may be *more richly and deeply human* in his technological labor in an "impersonal" community than in his private world of intimate love.

A second ground for rejecting the gospel of personalistic love comes from the New Testament itself. For there we find a clear emphasis on four specific things.

1. The New Testament repeatedly describes love of neighbor as a *readiness to serve others* in their particular situation, a readiness to help them with their particular problem, to do good for them in the face of their specific concrete need. That is to say, love for the New Testament involves a real effort to do what is best for the other, to use the most satisfactory resources and to do so in the most effective way. There is no hint that only personal resources should be used, only resources that can occasion a personal I-Thou encounter. The New Testament never suggests that service is simply the expression of some gratifying experience of love. Love means a willingness and readiness to work to help another's need. It means turning away from the self and toward the other. It means becoming objective, becoming absorbed in finding the best that can be done for the other.

2. The New Testament repeatedly describes love as service of the *self* to neighbor. Love is not a matter of merely providing useful commodities. It means to give something of ourselves, to give what belongs to us and what is our own. But what is that specifically, in the face of the particular concrete need which burdens our neighbor? What I give of my own in my service is first of all my *time* and secondly my *creativity,* my technical skill, the best that I have for his need.

3. The New Testament repeatedly describes the love of neighbor as service to the neighbor in terms of his *concrete need*. Satisfying his physical hunger and thirst is not viewed as an occasion for something quite different, for an experience of intimacy. Just as the New Testament identifies the act of love with serving and helping, so it identifies the person loved in terms of his want and need. In other words, while Buber relates love to the richness of the other, to the way in which he fills the heavens, Jesus Christ relates love to the poverty of the other. Men are not yet sanctified and therefore they cannot yet be sources of true existence for each other.

A Christian is called upon to serve others perhaps without knowing them personally from the inside, or perhaps while knowing them only in terms of their greed and their ingratitude. Jesus never gives the impression that the simple concrete need which our neighbor suffers—his pain, his fear—is our legitimate concern only when it serves to produce a personal I-Thou intimacy between ourselves and him. The Christian is called by Christ to face, and work with, all the evil and wretchedness in the human scene, not because he finds in people some exalting value, but because he knows that Christ's victory has emptied that evil and wretchedness of its power and its seriousness. He works for his neighbor's needs, as a servant of the Lord who himself is victoriously bearing all human needs.

4. Fourth and finally, the New Testament repeatedly describes the love of neighbor as a service to the neighbor out of *obedience to God*. It is *not* the neighbor, and *not* the neighbor's need which authorizes our love and claims our service. Christian love is not a species of sympathy. God alone commands and claims us men. And what he authorizes and claims from us is that we actively serve the needs of others, in order to be a mirror of God's own service to man. Because his service to us is his creative action attuned to our concrete needs, to our need for daily bread and daily forgiveness, we in our love for one another should act in the same way. Because he gives himself in his service to us, so also should we with one another. And because he serves us, not in our richness and sufficiency, but in the desperate need of our poverty and evil, so also we should serve one another.

God's command to us through Christ and as Christ is not for us to act for the sake of intimacy, but for the sake of mirroring God's love to man's need. In the parable of the Good Samaritan, there is no hint of personal encounter. There is simply the emphasis on the Samaritan's astonishing liberality, as if he had a readiness to act in this way without waiting for an I-Thou encounter, in fact, as if his readiness were *impersonal,* that is, were grounded on, and were for the sake of, something other than his personal relationship with this particular wounded Jew.

So far as I give assistance to my neighbor in the name of Christ, I do so not to awaken his love and gratitude for me, but as a sign of the help which both he and I receive from God. My goal is service to him with respect to some particular need which torments him. It cannot be to bind him to me in intimacy. Such an aim is futile, because I am not real enough or rich enough to satisfy him; because my love is not wise enough or true enough not to be also a betrayal of him and a covert act of self-love. I can do nothing really good for him, within the perspectives of the evil and death which Jesus exposes. But by my assistance I can set up a sign of God's assistance. The nourishment of the relative forms of his life which I may give is only a sign of the nourishment for eternal life which God gives.

Such is the picture of love that may be derived from the New Testament. And if this picture is true, if the Christian love of neighbor is to be identified, not with personal intimacy, but with concrete creative service, then why cannot the world of impersonal technology be a perfectly legitimate form of the Christian life? Why cannot laboratories that analyze genetic structures, and corporations that produce clothing be a suitable form of Christian service? Such service does not require the presence of the other. It requires the disciplined focus of one's time and creativity for another's need. It requires that one expend oneself in gratitude and as a mirror of God's giving to men. Christ did not say that only the first-century Palestinian modes of service were an acceptable witness to God, or that only the twelfth-century monastic modes of service, or that only the nineteenth-century bourgeois personalistic modes of service. Paul's words in Romans 14 are directly to the point: Do not judge another about his mode of service. "Who are you to pass judgment on the servant of another? It is before his own master that he stands or falls."

The man who rides into the city, who works in some large office to distribute goods or to collect taxes or to process bills, and who may never see those he helps from one year to the next, is he really cut off from the life of divine service? Is he really trapped in some hopeless limbo of private dreams and public monotony? Is he excluded from performing his technological work under the aegis of Christ and with a Christian intention? Such a judgment is impossible. God's victory and grace do not cease when a man enters the city.

In the light of these points, we must reconsider the personalistic view of love and be much more severe in our judgment of it. For it has had the effect of making Christianity seem completely irrelevant for precisely that arena of life where men are most creative, where they live most deeply, and above all where their service to one another is most effectively affirmed. When the church indoctrinates its members with family-oriented sermons and with a personalistic view of Christian love, what else is it doing but abandoning their work life to despair? Instead of affirming and nourishing and guiding them in the areas of their dynamic humanity, this kind of gospel makes the mass world of technology seem completely cut off from the

Christian life. It means that Christ's promise of life has absolutely nothing positive to say to the deep problems that arise there. To be sure, even in the city the accidents of existence may confront a person with a situation that calls forth a readiness for personal relationship. But this does not happen often; and this certainly does not provide the substance of his concentrated daily effort. He knows that when he goes to the office or shopping center, he has to leave this personalistic gospel at home, and move into an impersonal world of collective identities and technical language.

V

Now in this connection a special word must be said about the campus ministry. For there the personalistic gospel proves particularly disastrous.

The university, just like the business corporation and the department store, is an impersonal world of technology. For the faculty their work is of a professional sort. They see themselves operating either the institutional tasks of their departments, or the technical research of their special fields. In this context a chaplain who is committed to the gospel of personal love soon finds himself perplexed and baffled by this university atmosphere. Unlike the pastoral minister who can retreat into the family circle with his I-Thou preoccupations, the university chaplain does not touch the adult members of that community at the level of their privately personal lives. He does not deal with them in terms of their wives and their children. He only confronts them in the world of their professional and corporate responsibilities. Therefore, if he tries to be privately personal in this world, if he makes it his Christian task to be a personal friend to everybody and to elicit the personal from whatever situation he enters, then he will only strike a sour note to the men and women around him. For they do *not* find the impersonal life of collective labor and creativity as embarrassing or as inhuman or as debilitating as apparently he does. They are thriving in their research and in their departmental teaching. They are performing a genuine, if only a relative, service to students, by training them in the execution of a technical intellectual discipline. They are puzzled and annoyed by the chaplain's dedicated intrusion of a privately personal note. It may happen that in their research a few members of the faculty may come upon serious problems of a religious or ethical nature. They may appreciate guidance on such matters. But the guidance which they require must be a part of that same technological and corporate world as the problems themselves.

In other words, if the chaplain today is to be of service in the university, he must become a technically equipped expert in some relevant but narrow area—whether that be giving counsel or doing the sacraments or exploring some particular sphere of theology.

VI

In my view, then, the first task facing the church—and the university chaplains—in our day is to recognize the human interchange of need and service which actually takes place in the modern city. Such recognition, however, requires a rethinking of the meaning of *service,* so that it is not limited simply to intimate giving, but may be executed in the life of collective labor. The church must make clear that working for a corporation and having a little role in a large enterprise which serves a vast body of people—that this is as much an operation of Christian service as the giving of a cup of water to some thirsty individual. The fact that no intimacy, no private personalness develops here does not make it any less Christian.

Once this is done, then the Christian can address himself to one of the real questions of urban life, one of the problems underlying and aggravating such problems as automation and genetic surgery. It is the problem which Gabriel Marcel calls the *misplacement of the idea of function* (*The Philosophy of Existence,* 1–3). In the city, individuals tend to appear, to themselves as well as to others, as nothing but an agglomeration of their functions. They look upon their bodies as a series of functional systems—the skeletal system, the nervous system, the reproductive system—each with its own demand for activity. So also they look upon themselves largely in terms of their social functions—as producer, or consumer, or voter, or soldier, or parent. Marcel emphasizes how everything in this functionalized world conspires to identify an individual wholly with his functions. As a result even his time is shaped in terms of functions. He plans his day to give so many hours to each function, so many hours for sleep, so many for pleasure and relaxation. In this world, even sleep and recreation are thought of as functions which must not be neglected any more than, say, the function of sex. The point is clear. Time is a matter of a functional timetable, a schedule. The details may vary from country to country, or from profession to profession, but what matters is that there *is* a schedule.

In this world it is natural that individuals should be overhauled at regular intervals like a watch, and given a physical examination. The hospital thus plays the part of the inspection bench and repair shop, where everything possible is done to keep this functional system that is a man or woman going as long as possible. There are moments, of course, when one's functioning stops, and these are very trying times. Think of the dreary image of the retired worker, aimlessly clipping his hedge. Or think of Sunday afternoon in a city, when the passersby have the look of people who have retired from life, because Sunday afternoon claims none of their functions. Finally there is the event of death. In this world death becomes objectively and functionally the scrapping of what has ceased to be of use, and must be written off as a total loss. Since at death men do become a total loss functionally, there is no point in having them occupy valuable space. Let us not bury them, therefore, but cremate them.

This is a sad and empty world not because there are functions, but because the functions are no longer the servants of *human need*. They themselves are taken to be life, as ends rather than means. Keep working, keep the timetable, and do not ask why. The body must function well. Why? So that the person may function well. Why? So that his business or office or family may function well. Why? So that the whole society, the whole network of city life may function well. Why? Function well for what? No one asks. This is the vacuity, the appalling emptiness in our city world of functions. They have eclipsed the needs which authorize and dignify them.

This functioning has a goal and meaning: the human anguish which it continually relieves and the human service which it continually channels. The Christian task in the city and in the university is to criticize this functional world, not for the sake of eliminating it or escaping from it into a haven of intimacy, but for the sake of laying bare the dimension of service which sustains it. In this regard the churches should champion technology as a service to human needs, and not as an end in itself. That is the fact which must be kept before the mind of the woman at the supermarket or the man at the office or the researcher in the laboratory. That is where the daily life takes on the form of Jesus Christ.

4

The Education of the Specialists

Written while McGill was professor of religion at Princeton, this essay was published in The Christian Scholar *in the Spring of 1966. McGill enters the debate about the relationship between Christian education and the liberal arts, contrasting humanistic (liberal arts college) and scholastic (research university) models of education. Continuing his critique of "personalistic Christianity," McGill contends that the humanistic emphasis on developing the whole person finds little support in New Testament depictions of discipleship. On the contrary, the Christian call to service may be better met by the specialized, technical education afforded by the research university.*

I. The Conflict

A conflict now in progress in the United States concerns the fundamental purpose of college education. On the one hand, there is the conviction that the college student should be introduced to scholarship. He should be instructed in-depth in a single discipline, should develop some practice in research techniques and investigative procedures, should master the basic literature in a field, and should learn the special, if limited, value of a technical vocabulary. In short, college education should strive to produce specialists, and should therefore derive its central, if by no means its only, content from the PhD program for graduate students. This may be called the scholastic conception of education.

On the other hand, there is the view that college education should be devoted to broadening and deepening the lives of its students. It should introduce them to the value-tradition on which our society is established. It should remove their provincialism, so that they learn how to appreciate alien cultures and strange behavior. It should expand their sensitivities, initiating them to the beauty of art as well as to the clarity of science. In short, by enriching their humanity, college education should aim to produce *leaders*, who will contribute a broadly sensitive and highly self-conscious awareness to whatever community they may serve. This may be called the humanistic conception of education.

At present the usual collegiate program in the United States represents a compromise between these two views. On the one hand, the student is required to choose a single department for concentrated study, in line with the scholastic theory of education. On the other hand, he must fulfill distribution requirements, in line with the broad humanistic view of education. But this is a very uneasy compromise on every campus, where there are enormous pressures to enlarge the major, to begin concentration in the sophomore year and to increase prerequisites for upper-class courses, and equally strong counter-pressures to establish a mandatory humanities program, to encourage bridge majors and to develop a more integrated program for distribution.

In spite of this compromise, the balance of control seems to lie at present with the scholastic forces, at least in the college programs offered by large secular universities. There the major dominates the student's academic program, and different aspects of the humanistic program are falling into disuse or are being dropped altogether.

The immediate source of this conflict lies in the completely different conceptions of the university that have been developed in Germany, with its total preoccupation with scholarship, on the one hand, and in England with its ideal of the scholar-statesman, on the other. But the conflict actually extends back through the entire history of the West. Think of the violent quarrels in sixteenth- and seventeenth-century Europe between those who championed logic as the key to knowledge and those who championed the study of classics and history. Think of the controversies in the twelfth century between the tradition of classical humanism and the new scholasticism. Think of Cicero's educational program, which made all study serve the development of oratory (for only through oratory could knowledge become publicly fruitful) and which opposed the bookish education provided by the philosophers. "Let those be ashamed," Cicero said, "who have so buried themselves in books that they can offer nothing for the common good" (*In Defense of Archias*). Finally, think of the conflict in Athens in the fourth century BC between Plato, who wanted to perfect the rational mind, and the Sophists, who placed education in the service of the social and political aspects of life.

In all discussions of this problem, it should not be forgotten that we are dealing with a conflict between two fundamental and incompatible ideals that have been in tension for twenty-four centuries. The question is this: should young people be given, before everything else, an initiation into *the life of intellectual clarity*, with all the disciplines and techniques that are involved? Or, before everything else, should they be taught how to *participate in the community life*—in its past by the study of classics and history, in its present by useful service, and in its future by far-sighted public leadership? If this level of the problem is kept in mind, then no total or easy solutions will be expected, and every proposal will be seen to entail some loss.

II. Christian Attitudes

Over the centuries this conflict of educational ideals has found Christians on both sides. It is difficult to say whether the church in its actual history has proved to be more concerned for an education that advances the life of the mind or for an education that brings enrichment to the life of the community. Scholasticism and humanism represent equally powerful Christian traditions, and do so even in both the Catholic and Protestant worlds of modern times.

In the last century and a half, however, while continental Christianity has tended to give full support to education in technical scholarship, just the opposite has been true in Protestant England and America. There, Christian leaders have conceived of higher education primarily in terms of the development of "whole persons" and the enhancement of the public life. In other words, there has been broad support of the humanistic tradition and massive resistance to the intellectualistic climate of *science*. In nineteenth-century England especially, the articulate Protestant Christians aligned themselves almost unanimously on the side of poets and artists, with their "humaneness" and "sensitivity" and social concern, and against the cold, ruthless, analytic, and dehumanizing objectivity of the scientist. One of George Gissing's characters expressed this familiar Christian sentiment: "I hate and fear 'science' because of my conviction that for a long time to come, if not forever, it will be the remorseless enemy of mankind. I see it destroying all simplicity and gentleness of life, all beauty of the world; I see it restoring barbarism under the mask of civilization; I see it darkening men's minds and hardening their hearts" (*The Private Papers of Henry Rycroft*, 268). All the qualities which the Sophists and Cicero and John of Salisbury and Thomas More feared in abstract thought—its way of alienating men from everyday life, its deliberate one-sidedness, its tendency to belittle moral and artistic values, its egoistic presumptiveness in seizing and analyzing everything—these were the qualities which the Christians of English-speaking countries saw facing them in science.

With the increasing role of technical scholarship in American higher education, this same protest is being raised by Christians today in the United States. Four points are often heard:

First, since God has set men in a world of manifold richness, it is argued that they have a clear responsibility to cultivate and appreciate *everything* valuable. No person is justified in "narrowing his horizons," in attending only to such things as he can master and manipulate, and in ignoring everything else. Life means openness to the whole—to all the unmanageable extremes of glory and horror and boredom. When, in order to shield his ego, a person withdraws into some cubbyhole and notices only what he can comfortably control, he shuts himself off from the staggering magnitudes which God intends for human existence. He is like Esau, exchanging his true birthright for a mess of pottage.

In the second place, it is pointed out that God has given to every person a marvelously complex nature, and that it is therefore his responsibility to develop *all* its latent richness. No one should become "one-sided," nurturing only a fragment of his resources. It is just as dangerous and culpable to disregard any aspect of the self as to overindulge it. Physical exercise and the social graces are just as important as intellectual accomplishment.

Third, stress is laid upon the fact that Jesus calls upon every man to live in *personal* relationships with his neighbors, as one free concrete individual helping other free concrete individuals. He should look upon each person as a Thou, never as an It. On this basis there are fundamental moral questions raised about the "professional," that is, the man who deals with people only through the impersonal facade of his technical work, and who therefore never considers them as whole persons with individual names,

The Education of the Specialists

but only as "patients" or "customers," as bearers of this disease or that charge account.

Fourth and finally, it is said that the unity of God and the obligation of the Christian to seek fellowship with all men requires him to look upon the world as a unity, and to work with an intellectually unified worldview that embraces the lives of all peoples. To let the minds of men break away from each other and retire behind the walls of narrow disciplines is both to do violence to the nature of God and to neglect the Christian task of keeping a common understanding with all of one's neighbors.

With this perspective in mind, Christian spokesmen have become the champions of a coherent and now familiar set of educational programs. There is first of all the campaign against university *departmentalism* and *specialization,* with all the divisive and stultifying narrowness which they involve. Proposals for a more integrated curriculum are constantly being advanced. Then there is the attack against excessively *technical scholarship* as such, which the PhD kind of education represents. It is felt that a college should deliberately incorporate the social and political and athletic sides of student life into the educational process—not merely to control these, as if they were dangerous distractions, but to affirm and cultivate their meaning for life. In this connection it is therefore felt that the curriculum should be less scholastic and more value-oriented, that it should "give the student a profound and comprehensive interpretation of human life and destiny" and so deepen him beyond the positivistic, materialistic, and technological worldview which now reigns (Arnold Nash, *The University in the Modern World,* 287). Finally the value of a more personal—and less professional—relation between teacher and student is emphasized. In the teaching situation, it is said, these two should meet, not just in terms of the teacher's subject matter, but as individual persons, conscious of and explicit about each other's many-sided wholeness.

There can be no question that a one-sided preoccupation with technical scholarship involves grave dangers and weaknesses for higher education, and that Christians have a definite responsibility to correct this one-sidedness. What is quite indefensible is the conviction that the spirit of Christianity is inherently anti-scholastic and anti-professional, that its personalism requires the Christian to support a humanistic education, and that churches today are somehow obligated by their Christianity to oppose the current trends in secular universities.

III. The Significance of Service

One important consideration that throws light on specialized education is the New Testament emphasis on *service to the neighbor*. Activities of *service* are clearly viewed as one indispensable form of a truly rich life. He in whom God abides will give of what he possesses when he sees his brother in need (1 John 3:17, 4:12). If he does not, then his faith is dead (Jas 2:15–17). Paul's admonition for men to be servants of one another through love, since such love fulfills the law (Gal 5:13), simply restates the meaning of Jesus' parable of the Good Samaritan.

The New Testament does not commend any and every outer act of service, however. What it is concerned about is *loving* service, which it specifies from three different points of view.

It speaks from the viewpoint of the one who serves, and there it focuses on his readiness to *expend himself* for another's sake, to give up what might otherwise be of value to him. Without this quality the service ceases to be an act of Christian love. Unless the person's very self is engaged in an outward movement toward the other, unless the other claims his time, his efforts, and his best resources, it is an empty game. Some commodity has changed hands or some skill has been exercised, and nothing more.

The New Testament also speaks of service from the viewpoint of the one who is served. And here its emphasis is on *suffering need*. It is a person's suffering which claims service from others, which defines their efforts and commands their dedication. Apart from need, service becomes nothing but a masquerade.

Finally, and most important, the New Testament speaks of service *from the viewpoint of God*. It maintains that service is valuable, not in and of itself, but as the form which human existence requires when it shares in the life of God himself. When through Jesus Christ men are reconciled to God, when they love him and trust him and obey him, then they live for their neighbors. "If any one has the world's goods and sees his brother in need, yet closes his heart against him, how does *God's* love abide in him? . . . Let us love one another, for love is of God, and he who loves is born of God and knows God . . . If we love one another *God* abides in us and *his* love is perfected in us" (1 John 3:17, 4:7, 4:12). To live in this way is to imitate Christ himself. His human existence from beginning to end was continual service to the neighbor because it was continually sharing in the divine life. It is the grace and love of God which give men this life of service, but on the human side this serving is the perfection and fulfillment of human life.

The Education of the Specialists

It is the form of man's true humanity, of the humanity which he has when he enters into fellowship with God and when his human existence attains its fullness.

Two points should be noted, however, in this New Testament description of service.

The New Testament does not insist that people must *first* measure up to some ideal of man, that they must *first* imitate some moral or behavioral or personality type *before* their service can be considered worthwhile. On the contrary, judging by the parable of the Good Samaritan, the value of service is measured wholly in terms of love, that is, in terms of the single-minded readiness with which someone *expends himself for* another's need. It is not conformity to some ideal type of person that makes loving service fruitful, but loving service which makes any and every kind of person fruitful. As an event of self-expenditure, service is no more natural for one type of human person than for another. There are no autonomous qualities to be acquired, which, when once possessed, will thereafter somehow make it *easy* for a man to lay down his life for his friends (John 15:13). The Christian community must be very careful, therefore, not to berate a person's service, simply because, quite apart from the actual service which he performs for others' needs, he does not meet some popular criterion of human types—for instance, he is not warmly personal, or he does not have broad interests. "Who are you to pass judgment on the servant of another? It is before his own master that he stands or falls" (Rom 14:4).

If the New Testament does not judge service on the basis of human types, neither does it do so on the basis of the benefit produced. There is no mention of a value-scale of services, with religious and spiritual help put at the top, say, then with assistance to interpersonal problems placed somewhat lower, and with the satisfaction of brute physical needs set at the bottom. On the contrary, Jesus speaks simply in terms of the urgency of the need *as seen from the other's suffering,* so that if food or drink or clothing are demanded on some occasions, companionship or encouragement or forgiveness or forbearance are required on others (Matt 25:35ff., 5:39–42). Again, therefore, the Christian community must be very careful not to judge service by some particular standard of success, and thus give recognition only to service which meets a certain class of needs—for instance, only to friendliness which relieves loneliness, or only to forgiveness which relieves guilt.

Third and finally, there is no protest in the New Testament against limited serving, no insistence on helping only the whole man rather than one or another of his limited needs. There is no suggestion that intimate friendship alone matters and that service only functions to establish personal relationships. On the contrary, in the teachings of Jesus, it is the *man as suffering* who holds the focus of attention in service, and when people help each other they are devoting their energies to what is demanded by the specific needs in a specific situation. In fact, because Jesus suggests that a person be modest in his claims to serve others, we might ask whether the desire of some Christians to serve "the whole man" is not imperial rather than benevolent.

The most obvious fact of our age is that technical knowledge and professional work constitute the *best* and *normal mode of service*. Of course, not all professional work is service in the New Testament sense, but the Christian who is called to expend himself in meeting the needs of his neighbors, should have no hesitation in doing so through a narrow and highly specialized professional career. He may not be concerned to increase the world's friendliness or to serve the whole man, but he is letting some suffering in others claim his best resources and his dedicated efforts.

IV. Education as the Advancement of Service

So far as young men and young women today seek to meet human needs by means of the techniques and instruments now available, then *they must have a specialized and technical education*. They must be trained precisely in the kind of discipline and narrowness provided by the college major. If the New Testament is correct, if men do not humanize service but serving humanizes men, then, so far as this technically impersonal and scholastic knowledge is a way for men to expend themselves for each other's needs, it is safely enriching. Fears about its impoverishing narrowness and inhuman professionalism are quite unfounded.

Specifically, there is no suggestion anywhere in the New Testament that proper Christian service requires on the part of the person serving either a personally friendly style or a deliberately self-conscious appreciation of the whole man whom he serves. There is no hint that, in addition to aiding the wounded man's broken body, the Good Samaritan also shared jokes with him, cultivated a sensitive appreciation for his marital difficulties, and tenderized the atmosphere around him with humane well-roundedness. At that level, he might have been an untalkative peasant. In fact, so far as Jesus presents him, the Samaritan shows just that single-minded preoccupation with one particular set of urgent needs which we find in the professional worker of today. There are no grounds therefore for fearing that narrow departmentalism will stunt a college student's humanity, and will somehow cut him off from a life of fruitful service. On the contrary, just the opposite is the case. The mastery of a limited field of study has become the basis for advancing the frontiers of knowledge (the service executed within the university) or for relieving the sufferings that beset men in their daily life (the service assisted by the university but executed by other institutions).

One might go further in fact, and question whether the broad liberal arts education developed centuries ago in England can be justified today in Christian terms. For that education was clearly designed to prepare men for a *special service*. The liberally educated man had the unique responsibility of being the articulate individual, who spoke to and for his community about the meaning of public events. Today the service of articulation is handled chiefly by the press, not by the college graduate, with the result that too often general education in the liberal arts is simply an exercise in indulging one's own interests, or in cultivating one's own sensitivities, and/or in finding distractions for one's own leisure. It is advocated, not in the context of a clear and urgent sense of service, but on the basis of the narcissistic principle of self-realization. It therefore has the danger of appealing to immature students who are worried more about themselves than about their neighbors' needs.

The conflict between the humanistic and scholastic conceptions of education might therefore be put in the following way: are men more fully humanized by a general awareness of community values, or by a life of disciplined service? The response of the New Testament to such an alternative is clear.

V. The Maintenance of Community

There is a second value in a specialized education today which makes it fruitful even for those who will not undertake professional service. Everyone in this age must consult and depend upon professional experts with technical knowledge. Whether it is plumbing or pediatrics, marriage counseling or securities analysis, the individual finds that precisely in those critical moments when circumstances carry him beyond his own depth he must rely on an expert. Therefore no arena of community life is so ripe for perversion as this. Here the expert is always being tempted to impose financial exploitation, psychological intimidation, or outright deception on ordinary people. And here ordinary people, especially when a crisis becomes destructive, are always tempted to be ignorantly resentful of the expert, or to overwork him abusively. The so-called "service industries"—government, education, medicine, etc.—now constitute over half the GNP (gross national product) of the United States, but they also absorb over half its IPA (intimate personal anguish). So far as the Christian is called upon to address sources of community tension, no arena more urgently claims his attention than the relationship between the client and the expert. Every single other community problem—from nuclear war to juvenile delinquency—is entangled with this one.

What a technical, specialized scholastic education does for the student is to initiate him into the world of experts. This will not solve his problems, but it may at least instruct him in the complexity and provisional character of expert knowledge, and may thus enable him to have a better appreciation for both the strengths and limitations of the professional workers on whom he will depend.

The Christian, however, who views community as constituted by service, has a special responsibility to recognize the human meaning and the human expenditure in the services which he receives. This is especially important in the world of impersonal professionalism, where this factor can be easily overlooked, and where, because a consulting physician does not know the patient personally, one forgets the human cost in years of study and in one-sided narrowness which lies behind the help which the physician actually gives. Therefore, an educational program which initiates people into the disciplines of cumulative specialized knowledge—that is, into a departmental major—may disclose the real self-expenditure and service that lie within the professional areas of life. A program in humanistic values tends to leave these areas in the dark.

VI. Conclusion

Therefore, from the Christian perspective of life as service and not self-indulgence, the current emphasis on technical scholarship cannot be repudiated by the church. To put this in a different way, Christian service must not be identified with the situation of *personal, I-Thou intimacy*. It can be

The Education of the Specialists

perfectly at home in the cold, impersonal, highly specialized and expert world of the modern city.

Yet this also imposes a specific responsibility upon the Christian churches. For if they begin to affirm the value of technical work, rather than to suspect it for its supposed inhumanity, they must also recognize the perversions of greed and domination which beset such work. They must affirm, not expertness as such, but the *service* which may be exercised through expertness. The churches, in other words, must keep reminding the college student that his *first* task is not to develop himself by means of a broad and well rounding education, but to begin assuming the adult responsibility of meeting the other people's needs. In selecting his courses, pursuing his major, and attaining his grades, his primary aim should be to become, not a full person, but an effective servant.

5

The Death of God and All That

This essay originated as an address McGill gave on multiple university campuses during the 1965–66 academic year as part of the Booth Ferris National Ministerial Recruitment Program. It was solicited for inclusion in the collection Radical Theology: Phase Two, *published in 1967. The "death of God" movement was making headlines in the mid-sixties, provoking animosity and anxiety in the church and academy alike. In this essay, McGill sympathetically interprets the major death of God theologians: Paul van Buren, William Hamilton, Thomas Altizer, and Harvey Cox. McGill's honesty about the prescience of these theologians is startling given McGill's conviction that theology is in service to the church. He agrees with their fundamental claim that we no longer encounter God as creator, provider, or redeemer. This "official God of the textbooks and the preachers" is no longer experienced as a source of power, thus "nothing happens in the churches." For McGill, however, this critique opens a return to the New Testament, where Jesus reveals a God who intensifies rather than alleviates the alienation that disturbs the theologians of the death of God.*

In speaking about the "death of God" theology, a person is on fairly reliable grounds because his audience will undoubtedly not know much about the subject. What I would like to do, therefore, is to get a picture of this phenomenon in contemporary theology. Most of my talk will be concerned with that, and at the end I will relate my own work to this problem. I speak to you as a theologian who does theology, and this movement is representative of the sort of problem that theologians worry about.

Now at the present time in the United States this death of God theology is, strictly speaking, a creation of magazines and newspapers. The representatives of this theology, so far as I know, did not know about each other until they had been named in an article in *Time* magazine. The most interesting thing about them, therefore, is that they are rather symptomatic of something. They emerged independently of one another with not identical but similar orientations. Three persons in particular stand out. The first is Paul van Buren at Temple University in Philadelphia; the second is William Hamilton at Colgate-Rochester Divinity School, and the third is Thomas Altizer at Emory University in Atlanta.

The fact they all start from is that God is unreal for most people today. Now note carefully, this is not a fact about God as such, but about people's experience of God. It's a Gallup-poll-like fact.

Van Buren's way of arguing this is a very suggestive one. He contends that for most people God is unreal because the letters G-o-d constitute a meaningless word. As the idea of some transcendent reality on which things and events are supposed to depend, the idea of God refers to nothing and hence is not even felt as a possibility for most people. It is meaningless in that sense. On what basis can van Buren contend this? It is because for so many people there are almost no situations in daily life where they feel that the name of God is absolutely required. They do not have to use the name. Their experience is such that there never seems to be an occasion where this name is the correct one and the only one. All their experience can be covered by other names. Now the significance of this rises out of the fact that a use of a word is usually required by what faces us. All words are made up. But the words which are living words are those that become identified with things in the moment of experience itself. Then experience seems to require the word and the word has the life of experience itself. From this point of view, dead words do not arise in the mind at the moment of experience; they are external to the experience. The mind must bring such words to the experience afterwards. Now in this sense "God" is a dead word. It is a word which people have to bring to experience after it happens; it is not a word that is drawn forth from them in their experience.

The Uncertain Center

One might think that there is one exception to this, one situation where the word "God" is required, and that is the church. Unfortunately the church is not, it seems for most people, a place where anything happens. It is precisely outside of experience, where one may get dead words to bring in later to experience if one is lucky. Therefore the claim that the word "God" has become meaningless is based on this usage fact, and out of this usage of the word van Buren comes to the conclusion that "God" is really meaningless. It is an outside word that has to be brought to experience and which may, but for most people does not, illuminate experience. There is nothing original in this; it is just another way of pointing to the familiar fact that in our age God has become silent, or in Buber's term God has become "eclipsed," or in Heidegger's term God is "absent." These are all ways of talking about this peculiar modern experience. What about this contention? Is it true? Not that there is no God, but that for people the word "God" is meaningless, that in people's experience there is no longer anything to correspond with this word?

I think it is necessary to become a bit clearer about the meaning of this word "God." The word "God" in terms of religion is any life- or death-giving power, any power that a person feels is capable of enhancing or crushing his life. Sex, war, penicillin may therefore be gods in this very special sense. Whether or not people call these powers gods, or whether or not there are organized institutions associated with them, is beside the point. Now for a god to be dead means that the god exercises no power over people's life. For a god to be dead means that whatever that name is associated with is itself to be decisive for its existence, yet people do not feel that their own existence hangs in the balance according as that god is kindly or wrathful. The god seems impotent, in other words.

All sorts of powers have served and do now serve as gods. What particular god is being talked about by these theologians when they say that people in America find God dead? It is, I think, the God identified by the religious institutions in this country; that is, the official God of the textbooks and the preachers.

Let me spell out this official God by three activities or modes in which his power is manifest. First, he is supposed to create everything that is; his is the power of existence and before this exhibition of his power the churchly response is thought to be awe. Secondly, he gives us the things we need for life. He is the power of Cornucopia, he is the good provider. He is good to us in the sense of our day-to-day lives and in this regard he calls forth our gratitude. Third and finally, he overcomes evil and especially the evil of the human heart, the evil of hostility and hate, and in this regard he requires our praise. This, as I hear it, is the God, the power being discussed today: the creator who establishes the universe, the provider who sustains life, and the redeemer who overcomes evil. Now let me return to the question at hand. Do people in fact find this particular God to be dead, to be impotent? I would say absolutely yes.

The cosmos is itself so unthinkable, the earth is now conceived as such a little corner of an almost unlimited and unknowable cosmos, that it is almost impossible for people to think of the creation of the universe. To say that the cosmos itself is created goes so far beyond the images we have of the universe and the images of our own place in the universe that I don't think this is a very functional assertion.

I don't think it points to an experiential ingredient. I don't think people experience the universe as a contingent arena which might collapse into nothing the way the Middle Ages did. The universe known to us is just an endless and unlimited complexity in which various things come and go. Therefore to say that there is a power that establishes the entire universe is to say nothing—nothing the mind can hold on to, nothing that echoes and lives out of something experienced by people.

As for providing, our provider, as we all know through our parents in terms of where the income comes from, and our food and everything else, is industry—General Electric, General Motors, they are the providers. They are hard enough to understand without bringing God in! The productive power of our experience is not associated with God. We certainly don't think that way. In so far as there is a kind of experience of productiveness, we think of a great factory, we think of a sexual event, we think of a football team—there is productiveness. There is energy exercised in fruitfulness. Throwing a bag of wind may not be fruitful, but it is a kind of model many people have of being fruitful. And therefore, when we say God gives—again, I just don't think it corresponds to the way people sense the productiveness of existence.

Finally, and most important of all, what about the overcoming of evil? What about God's redeeming power, God's victorious goodness? Well, if God exercises power by overcoming evil, I think most of us would have to say on the basis of the daily newspaper that he sure isn't doing his job. The concentration camps, the enormity of war, the misery of cancer, of nervous breakdown, which almost every family has gone through, simply make it seem like an incredible assertion that God is vindicating his power in our lives by overcoming evil. What we have to say is that most of us are very much aware that the last word is always death. All the assertions of life have for us a kind of dubiety, a kind of temporariness which makes ours a very sober age. In the face of all this we ask where are the sick healed so that we can see God's power, where do the hateful lose their hate and convert into love? And since most of us are not brought up in a hagiography, are not brought up with a sense of heroes or saints, the only heroes are the stars, the football players, or the intellectuals. It is hard for us to see and get a feel of the actual operation of a power that is spoken in the statement "God overcomes evil," so that, as a fact of modern experience, it would not be incorrect to say that this creative, this munificent, this redemptive God seems impotent.

Let me read two expressions of this awareness, one recent and one a century old. The first one is by an American poet who was also a vice president of a Hartford insurance agency—Wallace Stevens. He wrote this about 1951 and is speaking of the experience of having God disappear. He speaks as one who has this experience and is trying to express what it is like.

> To see the gods dispelled in mid-air and dissolve like clouds is one of the great human experiences. It is not as if they had gone over the horizon to disappear for a time, nor as if they had been overcome by other gods of greater power and profounder knowledge. It is simply that they came to nothing. Since we have always shared all things with them, and have always had a part of their strength, and their knowledge, we shared likewise this experience of their annihilation. It was their annihilation, not ours, and yet it left us feeling that in a measure we too had been annihilated. It left us feeling dispossessed and alone in the solitude, like children without parents, in a home that seemed deserted, in which the amicable rooms and halls had taken on a look of hardness and emptiness. What was most extraordinary is that they left no mementos behind, no thrones, no mystic rings, no text either of the soil or of the soul. It was as if they had never inhabited the earth. There was no crying out for their return. They were not forgotten of course for they had been part of the glory of the earth. At the same time no man seemed to be muttering a petition in his heart for the restoration of these now unreal shapes. There was always in every man the increasingly human self which instead of remaining the observer, the nonparticipant, the delinquent, became more and more all there

was—or so it seemed. And whether it was so or merely seemed so, it still left it for him to resolve life in the world in his own terms (*Opus Posthumous*, 206–7).

Stevens's voice, I think, is a voice that touches something all of us feel.

Now let me go back a century to that other great theologian, Henry Wadsworth Longfellow. This is a poem called "Christmas Bells," written in 1863 in the face of the Civil War. As you read it, keep in mind that third property of the official God—the ability to overcome evil.

> I heard the bells on Christmas Day
> Their old familiar carols play
> And wild and sweet the words repeat
> Of peace on earth, goodwill to men.
>
> But from each black accursed mouth
> A cannon thundered in the south
> And with the sound the carols drowned
> Of peace on earth, goodwill to men.
>
> It was as if an earthquake rent
> The hearthstones of a continent
> And made forlorn the households born
> Of peace on earth, goodwill to men.
>
> And in despair I bowed my head
> There is no peace on earth I said
> For hate is strong and mocks the song
> Of peace on earth, goodwill to men.
>
> Then pealed the bells more loud and deep,
> God is not dead, nor doth he sleep!
> Wrong shall fail, the right prevail
> With peace on earth, goodwill to men.

Although it was not what Longfellow intended, he could not have given a more devastating statement of the utter deadness of God. Having set up the problem, the only thing he could appeal to for God's aliveness is ringing church bells! If that is all his poetic imagination could grasp in the face of the death in the South in the Civil War, one can only say that in fact this is a most radical sort of disclosure of the utter impotence of God. You don't, however, have to go to Longfellow or to other poets to have a feeling of this. Go into the churches. Note the atmosphere of tired inertia, the sort of vacuum of complete powerlessness that sometimes overcomes one there. Nothing happens in the churches. There are no manifestations there, no theophanies, no revelations, no encounters with the power of life and death in such a way that the church becomes the most important and most power-laden place. I think for many of us the church functions in a rather different way—more as a place to withdraw temporarily from life, from death, from power. It is a place to withdraw in order to get a perspective, but a place therefore where it is important for nothing to happen and therefore a place where the only god one can let in is a god who is too impotent to bother you.

Thus you see this sense of the church as a place for withdrawing from life, and getting a perspective really covertly requires that the one thing you must keep out are the real gods who hold your life and your death in their hands. You get no perspective in their presence, you bow down! This new function of the church, therefore, as sort of a withdrawal arena for perspective is, in my view, the most decisive and the most communicative medium for giving the impression that the God referred to there is not power. All of which prompts me to say that the fact on which these theologians depend is true.

II

The next feature of their position to which I call your attention is somewhat more unusual. They take this popular experience as true. They accept and affirm this popular attitude. The official transcendent God is in truth dead, is in truth impotent. The word "God" is largely meaningless because God in fact is not real any more. Any "God" we men have to prop up is not God. The gods always vindicate themselves. They vindicate themselves as the sources of life and death, and if they do not so vindicate themselves then they are not gods and other gods have taken their place. These theologians take the fact of people's nonexperience of the divinity of this God as a kind of objective sign that in fact he is not operative. In fact he is dead, and therefore they insist he is to be eliminated from consideration. They are not saying, as many theologians say, "God has gone over the hill for a time,"

The Death of God and All That

"God is silent for our generation," with the hope that he may speak again. No, for them he is really gone.

Nevertheless, there is one feature of this atheism which is very distinctive. These writers will not dogmatically impose their view on the past. They will not dogmatically take the contemporary experience as the truth about all reality at all times. They are, like all of us, historically trained by modern education and trained enough to recognize that what is unreal for us today may not have been unreal for people in the past. This reservation and caution is expressed in the phrase which they prefer: "God is dead"—that is to say, he was once alive and is now dead. The analogy is to a dead person, like Napoleon. Those who knew Napoleon and were affected by him report to us about him though he is not available to our experience. He cannot be a living man to us. We know him only from the reports of those who did know him. It is similar in the case of God. These theologians say that to us it is as if he were dead and gone forever, but this does not allow us pompously to discredit the experience of earlier ages. We can only say in all honesty that once upon a time he was real and unavoidable and decisive for men. He is so no longer. The popular impression is true, and there is no arena of experience to which we can point, according to these theologians, and say "there, see, the transcendent God really is powerful, really is unavoidable and decisive for your life."

III

Finally, the third feature of these men is certainly the most exciting one. If they are atheists, they are atheists in a most peculiar way.

All of them are eager to get rid of this official God in order to revive religion! That is their peculiarity. This may seem very surprising, for isn't religion about God? Their contention is absolutely not. Or, more accurately, religion is about some god, but religion isn't about this God. As I mentioned, there are all kinds of gods, all kinds of powers of life and death, and to identify religion with some particular god is to misunderstand it profoundly. A dead god is the end of religion. God is, in a sense, therefore, as a name for something that has no meaning, killing such religions as there are. God—this transcendent, vacuous something—is killing Christianity! People go into churches, they hear about this empty zero called "God," it means nothing to them and neither therefore does all the rest of Christianity associated with that God. We must, these men say, get rid of *this*

God for the sake of the religious life. That is very unusual. It is also very modern, and I for one do not take the position that we have in these men simply the same old atheism of Marx or Feuerbach or Thomas Paine all over again. No, these death of God theologians are very, very religious, and when you hear them talk, hear their rhetoric, see the way they write, then you note that this is a religious phenomenon and that it is for the sake of religion that they think the unreality of God must be asserted and taken as the starting point. It is because of this single-minded preoccupation with religion, this concern for divinity in its authentic grandeur as a real power of life and death—it is because of this that these men are legitimately called theologians. If they are atheists, they are so only relatively speaking, only in relation to the official transcendent God. They are vigorous in their denial of this God out of a passion for some genuine divinity!

They differ, it seems to me, in what direction they expect men to look for the revival of their religion, for the recognition of real life- and death-giving power. One group—and this is a group which I think does not use the phrase "God is dead," but functions in a very similar way—is represented by Harvey Cox, who wrote a well-known book, *The Secular City*. He does not say that God is dead but simply that Christians should not talk about God. Well, you know in my experience the ones you don't talk about are those who have recently died. I don't want to misrepresent him, but it appears to me that he belongs in spirit if not in fact to this group. Cox's very powerful line is that we should stop talking about transcendence and talk about involvement. By transcendence he really means talk about a transcendent God. If you want to know about Jesus, about grace, about promise, about forgiveness, about the power of love, then get involved in the suffering of others, get hurt in the ordeal of service. This group of writers, of whom Cox is a representative, is really emphasizing the "where" of Christian reality, the "where" of divinity. This "where" is in the life and action and suffering of service, not in private prayer and above all not in the somber and impotent moment of a church service. No reference to a transcendent God is necessary or desirable because in the life of service God is met; he ceases to be transcendent.

He is not some abstract power who creates all the universe and provides people with happy lives. He is rather a different sort of power that works in the context of suffering service. This is a power that manifests itself more in modes of patience than in a full stomach, more in modes of endurance, more in modes of self-expenditure than in modes of thanking

The Death of God and All That

God for the list of all the good things you've gotten during the year. Cox insists the focus is where God's powerfulness is to be encountered, and that is not the church service oriented to some elsewhere God but in the act of life, of urban involvement.

Thomas Altizer is altogether different. He develops the kind of viewpoint you have in Arthur Koestler's novel, *The Age of Longing*. This position—and Altizer's is simply a contemporary way of saying this—is that the old God is dead and we now await the emergence of a new God, or better a new sense of the sacred, an experience of the sacred under a holier form that has nothing to do with the transcendent God. This is the subject of Koestler's novel. Men are longing for the restoration of divinity, but they are quite sure that divinity is not to be found in its old form of a cosmic God. Altizer feels that men must be taught to wait, and hence the great work of the theologian and religious person is not to try to give artificial respiration to dead gods but to alert people to let go of the dead gods, to be attentive to such movements and manifestations of the sacred as may emerge anew into our generation.

Van Buren, in *The Secular Meaning of the Gospel*, and William Hamilton in his writings, are different from Cox and Altizer. I find van Buren and Hamilton the most interesting of all. They maintain that the proper focus of a restored religion is already available. Its name is Jesus! Jesus should be the center of attention. That seems strange. How can we keep Jesus without God? Doesn't the Jesus presented in the New Testament stand there as God's Messiah, as God's revealer, as God's Son? Doesn't Jesus say the Son can do nothing of his own accord but only what he sees the Father doing? Technically speaking, abstractly speaking, this identification of Jesus with God is true. But what Hamilton sees so clearly is that this conjunction of Jesus and God is exactly what has been destroyed. His and van Buren's thesis is that Jesus is not and cannot be the revealer of God and the Son of God when the God most people have in mind is dead. That is just what Jesus is not—the revealer of a dead God, the revealer of a zero God, the revealer of a meaningless God! Absolutely not! So if God functions in this way, if God refers to some absolutely unthinkable and inexperienceable zero up in the heavens somewhere, then obviously he is not related to Jesus. Jesus is simply too potent with life- and death-giving power to be, so to speak, anesthetized with that kind of God. Jesus is far more real, far more potent, far more decisive than such a God. The fascinating proposal which Hamilton and van Buren pose is that men must choose between Jesus and God. If men choose God that is the end of their religion; at the level of religion they are just being slothful. They are just wanting to go to sleep, just living off the religion of people of an earlier age, just living by hearsay.

They should not be allowed to have concealed from them what in fact they are doing. What is fascinating about this challenge is that it is not unfamiliar in the history of Christianity. There have been earlier periods when the sacred in Jesus was felt to challenge the popular conventional God of the society. I would say that the God of my society has absolutely nothing to do with the kind of powerfulness I find in Jesus. What has occurred in these men which is rather rare is the proposal that Jesus requires us to abandon all theistic language, all language about God. That is the point, I think, where these men are misleading us, or more accurately following a strategy to wake us up. They all talk as if God were dead but they are all waiting for a new God. Their emphasis on God's death cannot be taken with the absoluteness of a full-blown atheism. They are not demolishers, they are gadflies. I think they must be understood in that context. The real test of them will be their ability to move out of the negative, out of attacking the dead God, and to say something positive. That will be particularly difficult since they have received so much publicity on the negative side. Their whole vocabulary has been on the negative, with the positive only very elusive, very latent. Whether they can develop a vocabulary for talking about the positive which is really free from the dead God—this is really their task. I would say at this stage that they have outlined their task, but they have not yet approached it. Be that as it may, all these writers—Cox, who stresses involvement, Altizer, who waits, Hamilton and van Buren, who point to Jesus—all these writers see the disappearance of God as a basis for the growth of authentic religion.

IV

My own position is not one of being quite so embarrassed about the language of God. I would like to repossess the language in a different arena. I am convinced that the official transcendent God is dead. That is a blessing because it allows us to get hold of the New Testament. I just think the New Testament is nonsense as the revelation of a transcendent God who creates the whole universe, who fills people's stomachs and gets rid of evil. I don't know what you do with Jesus! He's just a disaster with his crucifixion in that kind of gospel! It seems to me the point is that God's goodness in the New

Testament is not to give us what we need for a happy life in this world. That is not the message of the New Testament. The issue that I see raised here is *the power of God's goodness.*

Where is God's goodness vindicated in terms of power? The official, disturbingly middle class God tends to vindicate his powerfulness by what he gives us in our daily life in this world—how well we are clothed, how well we are housed, how full is our refrigerator. The morality of this God is to give other people good houses, good clothing, full refrigerators. That is the message of this religion, but it certainly is not the message of the New Testament. The New Testament has too much vinegar in it, too much death in it, too much realism in it to give support and clarity to that religion. I believe the direction theology must take is to focus on alienation between man and his world, alienation between man and his neighbor, alienation between man and himself.

Furthermore, it must see these, not as things which God is supposed to remove (the power to remove being the measure of his powerfulness) but as things which God intensifies. In other words, far from vindicating his powerfulness by improving man's life in the world, he does just the opposite. He vindicates his power by giving man life even when man is alienated from the world. *It is a gospel which speaks to the arena of death.* This is the kind of horizon, the kind of perspective, the kind of vocabulary which I find coming at me from the New Testament. What is the bread and wine for?—to celebrate the Lord's death until he comes. The sense of death, and not just physical death, but the death of human relationships, the death of ambition, the death of vitality, is a comprehensive image in the New Testament. It is in this image of death that the power of God is spoken of.

One technical term to describe this orientation, where God's power is vindicated, not by his ability to make the world full but rather by his ability to really open up for man in hope another world, is "eschatology." Therefore, I would align myself with certain movements in theology which really think that the language of God is not to be abandoned, leaving us with Jesus. No, the language of God is to be radically disengaged and transported from the not very well concealed theme of self-indulgence and contentment—an Elsie the Cow sort of picture—which creeps into the official God in a disturbing way. The arena of God's reality for man is not in his job or his full refrigerator or even his service to his fellow man, but in his death, where death is a far more embracing term than the biological cessation of life. There is where God manifests his divine reality, his actual powerfulness.

The problem raised by the death of God theologians is useful because it makes quite clear that in our age the theologian cannot mess around with academic irrelevancies. The most substantive question of all is just glaring at anyone—the subject of God. One has really to have a fairly strong stomach to be able to be a theologian responsibly.

6

The Radicals Are Not Immanent Enough

The following short piece appeared in 1968 in Theology Today *as "Critique II" ("Critique I" was by Gabriel Vahanian) of an essay by Albert Outler titled "The New Iconoclasm and the Integrity of the Faith." The "new iconoclasm" was Outler's description of radical theology in the 1960s, most especially death of God theology, a movement brilliantly summarized by McGill in the preceding essay, "The Death of God and All That." Outler argued that "whatever the new iconoclasm has done, in its efforts to shatter the 'traditional' answers, it has not yet succeeded in squelching the traditional* problematic." *Characteristically, McGill celebrates the challenges the radical theologians represent but suggests they are not being sufficiently radical.*

Let me begin with what I think is Professor Outler's total misunderstanding of the radical theologians. The one thing that always comes to me from the radical theologians is the affirmation or celebration of change. Process is good. Nothing is fixed, static, or frozen. Forms of thought and forms of institution have to be in transition, movement, mobility. Many should be adaptable, responsible, and open to new possibilities everyday. J. A. T. Robinson (*Theology Today*, July, 1968) has vividly expressed his profound antagonism to any form, attitude, or operation that refuses to change. And he makes very clear the basis of this antagonism. Anything static must be withdrawn into itself. The bishop, as all radicals, would yoke together, therefore, staticness and withdrawn, unloving, self-serving, self-enclosedness. And therefore he proposes an exploding, ever-changing church that participates in the flow of the world.

The point at issue is a perfectly familiar one. The radicals hold that the breaking and remaking of forms is the indispensable condition for the presence of life. True form is form that arises from and then dissolves into the vital flow. But the form that does not break holds back life and represses life. It would be like an eggshell that did not break. Or take milk as an example. At room temperature it is changing and going sour. We can prevent this only by separating the milk from its changing, by refrigerating it or powdering it. This is the way of slowing down its aliveness. And this is what many Christians do with their faith. This, in fact, is exactly how museums try to prevent the souring of art. We're always trying to save things by temporarily separating them from life, that is from changing. But at any moment, destruction may come suddenly, and then what happens is pressure.

Now, this very interesting sense of freshness and aliveness in our time repeats the old problem of authority and freedom. Authority represses, freedom is a source of vitality and change. What's interesting is the sense of life and aliveness as motion. And the consequence of this is that the only place to meet motion is in the present. Therefore both traditionalism, which wants to freeze present change to a past form, and utopianism, which wants to freeze present change to a future form, are enemies of life.

But the point is not just change, and certainly not just life as mere change. The point is that in change, or at least in some changes, men encounter a kind of magnitude, a kind of shine, a kind of intensification, in other words, a movement that corresponds to the biblical category of "glory." Genuine glory is most directly sensed precisely in the moment of change, when the form opens up and there is the unexpected movement. Therefore in the element of freshness and glory men must participate by just stepping into the flow.

For this reason, I really must question Professor Outler's suggestion that the focus of the radicals is repudiation, or iconoclasm, or cancellation. Their focus is celebration. And the whole point is that when the forms dissolve, we don't have to start all over again and build from scratch. The forms dissolve because out there there's real vitality. The removal of the forms does not leave a vacuum which men must fill. The point is not the removal, but the change, and the changing form is the presencing of life, of life with

The Radicals Are Not Immanent Enough

an intimation of glory. The point, in fact, is to repudiate nothing ourselves, out of our own self-enclosed, self-preoccupied forms, but to participate in and celebrate the life moving around us.

The source of change is always outside. The radicals want to do to Christian forms what sculptors and architects do to their forms. They leave them open so that the changing area may be internalized into the form. A glass building reflects the passing traffic. An open statue constantly changes and you see a window through it or suddenly a woman in a purple dress passes by. It strikes me that the "new morality" is an attempt to open ethical preoccupations to the sense of change and aliveness in the immediate environment.

The implication for the doctrine of man is clear. Man has no form, no ideal shape, but everything is fluid and man is flow as the world is flow. It seems to me, however, there is an obvious danger in the position of the radical theologians, and that Professor Outler's suggestion of a doctrine of man might compound the danger. They seem to be saying that life is flowing around me and my task is simply to let it take me over. I will step into the flow and be carried. In Bishop Robinson's phrase, "I will respond to the community when and as it occurs." But all this is very close to distraction, because there is no account of any inner nourishment in our development or inner growth of a facility for life. In fact, the way the radicals speak of change and life makes it seem as if its main function were to help me forget my own inner emptiness, my lack of power and vitality within myself. The radical theologians ask me to enter into the life of the world, but they do not see any growth of the principle of life within the person. Is there real participation or just spectatorship? Decadence and frivolity, therefore, constantly shadow this theological movement. In other words, if the task of man is for life, man should not just enter into life, he should become a generative source of life.

The radicals have not been immanent enough. They have not carried the celebration of vital change into the interior of man. If theology is to proceed in terms of a sense of life, a sense of change and of glorious freshness, it must consider the model of the athlete, who goes into training not for the sake of attaining some static external form but for the sake of having within himself a disciplined capacity to participate richly in the flow of life. The athlete is the New Testament image against all spectatorship, all decadence, and all frivolity. And the athlete knows how to use tradition for his training. I have no idea what this would involve theologically. There would have to be a clear understanding of life in order to know what disciplines to perfect. What is this life in Christ which consists of love, which redounds with glory, and which entails dying? What is Christology as a dynamism of life? This is what I mean by saying the task within which theology plays its role is the formation of man, but it is the formation of man for participation in and celebration of life. It is the intensification of his powers of action by training and discipline. In other words, "Onward, Christian Soldiers."

7

Is Private Charity Coming to an End?

This essay appeared in 1969 in a now defunct journal called Vanguard, *published by the United Presbyterian Church in the USA. The essay is excerpted from a paper McGill prepared for the "Amherst Consultation," meetings convened in July 1968, in Amherst, Massachusetts, by the Joint Exploration Team of the Episcopal Church, the United Church of Christ, and the United Presbyterian Church in the USA. The meetings were concerned with the "problems facing the church in the next generation." McGill observes in this essay that the most prevalent modes of Christian philanthropy have more to do with our own needs than with the needs of the deprived and the oppressed.*

What are the conditions for the fruitful human life? What are the minimal conditions necessary for a human being to be human at all?

A list has been compiled by Harold Lasswell, a political scientist from Yale, on the basis of a study of political life in a number of societies (*Power and Society*). He proposes eight conditions that are essential to a human life:

- wealth
- power

- deference (or respect)
- health
- enlightenment (as provided by education)
- skill
- rectitude (uprightness, or the fulfillment entailed in living morally)
- affection

One way to use this list is to say that in order for any person to have an adequate human existence he must *have access* to these eight conditions. Note that we have said "have access," not "possess." The point is not simply to possess these goods (wealth, power, respect, etc.) but to have them available in whatever way the society decides.

The Church and the Poor

All this has a bearing on the church, for the church is called to see that the hungry are fed and that the naked are clothed and that the wretched are comforted. The church—and by the church I mean the people of God, the community of believers—is commanded to see that all men have access to the basic conditions for human existence. Jesus' address on the Last Judgment (Matt 25) puts the whole weight of his redemption on this single point. The community and the individual will be judged not on the vigor of their churchmanship and not on the orthodoxy of their faith, but exclusively on how they helped and nourished Jesus himself when he appeared to them, not in the form of their pastor or bishop, but in the form of *their needy neighbor.*

"Then the King will say to those at his right hand, 'Come, O blessed of my Father, inherit the kingdom prepared for you from the foundation of the world; for I was hungry and you gave me food, I was thirsty and you gave me drink, I was a stranger and you welcomed me, I was naked and you clothed me, I was sick and you visited me, I was in prison and you came to me.' Then the righteous will answer him, 'Lord, when did we see thee hungry and feed thee, or thirsty and give thee drink? And when did we see thee a stranger and welcome thee, or naked and clothe thee? And when did we see thee sick or in prison and visit thee?' And the King will answer them, 'Truly, I say to you, as you did it to one of the least of these my brethren, you did it to me'" (Matt 25:34–40).

Is Private Charity Coming to an End?

Jesus' brothers, those he makes his own, are the poor, the sick, the sinful, and the deprived. These are the ones for whom he came and died. Because he has indeed made them his own, so far as we do to the least of these, his own, we do to him.

If we return now to Harold Lasswell's "eight conditions," we find that they are a useful catalog of what men need to be minimally human. These are the conditions, therefore, which the church should be passionately concerned to see that all men have available to them. But how?

Access by Work Alone?

The following description will indicate how people today have access to the kind of goods listed by Lasswell:

The foundation of everything is work by skill. In return for that work *money* is given. The most decisive mark of money is not so much the money itself, but rather the recognition of work which money entails. By virtue of that recognition a man enjoys a feeling of *rectitude*. The good worker is the dominant image of rectitude in our culture. Out of rectitude comes *deference* shown to that good worker. Money itself is able to provide *power*, *health*, facilities, *enlightenment* through education, and the means to secure more *skill*. In our culture today, then, access to these essential conditions of life depends on work and getting money by work.

Those left out of this description are the deprived—those who are excluded from the goods of life.

One can foresee grave problems arising in the future as the need for workers is seriously curtailed by automation. In a world where work is the taproot of access to the goods of life (health, education, respect), automation threatens to cut that root, increasing thereby the number of the deprived.

Can payment for work then continue to be the means of access to the conditions of life? What is the alternative? One suggestion that has been made is that access to these goods of life be considered a natural right. No one has to *do* anything to have access to health, to some wealth, to enlightenment and deference. Proposals regarding a guaranteed annual income flow from this perspective.

The Uncertain Center

From Almsgiving to Politics

A major question of strategy that will face the church in the last quarter of the century is one that is already upon us: *What will be the best form of charitable work?*

At present, the normal idea of charity is to contribute such money as one has available for the sake of the deprived. This is the pattern of Christian charity that tends to be most prevalent. One may give not only money, but one's property, or one's blood. Generally, however, Christians try to help the deprived have access to the goods of life by a practice of monetary charity. This pattern of personal charity goes back to ancient times when it was known as almsgiving. Each Christian gives what he can and Christians as a group gather their contributions together.

Today this practice is already becoming an outmoded form of charity. Why? Because of the existence of governmental agencies.

This can be dramatized in the simplest way by relating some figures. In 1967 the largest almsgiving type of operation in the United States was the United Fund and it was able to collect $600,000,000. This amounts to $3.00 for every man, woman, and child in the country. By contrast, state governments spent $7,832,000,000 on welfare in 1967, or 15 percent of the entire budget of all the fifty states. The United States Government Department of Health, Education, and Welfare spent $11,739,000,000 or 8 percent of the national budget, and this outlay was second only to the expenses for national defense. Thus through assistance given by governmental agencies in 1967 there was spent for the deprived $497 for every man, woman, and child in the United States.

In the next thirty years the indications are that the government will be playing an even larger role in welfare, and hence the volume of assistance will continue to increase. If private charity is now a relatively small enterprise, this will become even more the case.

The question facing the church, therefore, is a simple one: *What new mode for participating in the work of charity can be found?* And the answer is clear. In the coming decades the church must learn to use its energies to affect the decisions of governmental agencies. The Christian passion for nourishing the deprived can lead only in this direction. The Christian community must enter the arena of political pressure groups, influencing Congress when it forms its welfare budget, influencing national welfare agencies and their policies, keeping an eye on the committee that handles the welfare funds for each local county.

Is Private Charity Coming to an End?

For the individual and the Christian community, the days of charity by the gift are drawing to a close; the days of charity by the vote and by the pressure group have now begun.

There are, however, two obstacles to the church's moving firmly in this direction. Two pervasive ideals stand in the way.

First, there is the normal desire that charity be the exercise of one's private virtue. Whether or not my giving helps others is almost secondary to the principle that it should be personally and distinctively mine, in my name. We do not connect charity with a governmental decision about tax funds, but rather with a personal check, a care package with one's name as the sender.

But there may be too much self-indulgence in this habit of ours in regard to charity. Charity is essentially to help another, not to indulge in our own virtue. If, as is now the case, governmental agencies are pouring billions of dollars into welfare, then the Christian's task is to see that this money is properly channeled and efficiently administered. The Christian's task is to see that by means of these resources the poor are fed and clothed, even if we cannot put our own name on the service rendered.

There is a second obstacle, and it is even more subtle. It is the capitalistic belief in the fecundity of money. In the description given above the meaning and not simply the utility of money becomes clear. Money is that which generates power, gives access to health, and is the key to education. Furthermore, by virtue of interest, money is able to beget money, to make money.

In a middle class country such as the United States, the church on the whole has adopted unwittingly this outlook in regard to money. The church has tended to measure the help that a Christian gives to another person in terms of money, as if money were the measure of good. This is a very deep notion in the imagination and not simply in the intellect of American Christians today. They do not feel they are helping others unless their gift can carry weight in monetary terms. To tell Christians in our country that the most important thing they have for the poor is their political power—their power to affect political decisions—is to speak a language they do not yet understand.

An urgent education task faces the church in this regard: to enable each person, each parish, and each hierarchical structure to realize that what it has for its Lord, insofar as its Lord stands before it as the poor, is political effort. And woe to those Christians who through sloth or pride or indifference fail this call (Matt 25:41–46).

Above All, Dignity

There is another problem that faces the church in its service to the deprived. Consider once more the eight conditions that Lasswell names. There is now going on a shift of emphasis as to which of the eight is the most important.

In the standard view held by the affluent in America, the poor should be given *goods* and *services*—that which money can buy. But it is already clear that the deprived of the world are no longer primarily interested in goods and services. It is dignity, *deference*, that has become first and foremost in their minds.

How do the deprived secure deference today? Again, the standard middle class way to secure deference is by work that brings income and bestows rectitude and respect. But work does not bring goods and services for the poor today. The government does. In this new situation the deprived have found a new way to secure dignity by participating in the decisions of the government that affect them. And how do they do this? By political pressure—Black Power! For the poor today, the first blessing is dignity, and the way to dignity is not to receive it as a gift but to seize it by the exercise of political power. Then government and political structures must take account of them, consult them, come to terms with them on decisions that affect their lives.

This means that what the church must seek for the deprived in the next decades is a place in democratic decision-making. Political activity is therefore not only *how* the charity of Christians should operate (that was the first point), but political activity is *what* the church should *seek for the poor*. The dole is not going to be tolerated either by black or white poor, or by underdeveloped countries abroad. For while the dole may provide goods and services, it takes away dignity, and people today will not pay that price. Participatory democracy is what is at stake everywhere, and this will continue to be the case for the rest of this century.

8

The Ambiguous Position of Christian Theology

This essay was originally prepared for a conference held at Princeton University in 1968 on the occasion of George F. Thomas's retirement as Chairman of Princeton's Department of Religion. The theme of the conference was the study of religion in American colleges and universities. Other presenters included William Clebsch, James Gustafson, Victor Preller, and Krister Stendahl. Of all McGill's published essays this is the longest and most polished, no doubt because he wrote his dissertation on a similar theme. It includes not only an argument for the inclusion of the study of religion in secular institutions, but also a genealogy of the development of theological/religious faculties, treating them as counterparts to reigning secular critiques of religion. The essay constitutes a remarkable précis on theological method, one that helps us see how McGill was able to do theology so fearlessly and faithfully.

To speak of the discipline and teaching of Christian theology within the faculty of arts and sciences in a modern "secular" university is to broach a very complicated problem.

On the one hand, Christian theology seems to be fundamentally at odds with the kind of intellectual discipline to which the faculty of arts and sciences is committed. It proceeds from a posture of belief, not from the critical, open posture of neutral reason. In a way quite consistent with this perspective, certain principles or orientations are simply taken by it as given and thus considered to be beyond judgment by the free play of man's native intelligence. Furthermore, in proceeding from this posture of belief, Christian theology belongs within the sphere of a religious community. In theologizing the theologian serves the special interests of the church; otherwise, he would not be doing Christian theology. In this way he obstructs one of the aims of the faculty of arts and sciences, for this faculty seeks to free human reason from the control of special interests, practical institutions, and ideological communities. Within the total life of a university, such theology may find an appropriate place in one of the professional schools, which are designed precisely to help disciplined rationality serve the needs of practical communities. But within the arts and sciences, theology appears incongruous.

This is one side of the situation, but there is another. Some faculties of arts and sciences, within their departments of religion, actually provide instruction in Christian theology. And by that I do not mean instruction simply in the philosophy of religion, or in the history of Christian ideas, or in the "religious factor" in Western thought, but instruction in the analytic and constructive work of specifically Christian theology. Certainly without any intention of identifying themselves with the interests of the Christian church, and without any thought of compromising or even modifying their ideal of critical rationality, these faculties nevertheless employ Christian theologians, grant them tenure, and compete against professional divinity schools for their services by making them unconscionably lucrative offers.

Such, in brief, is the confused state of affairs at present affecting the place of theology among the arts and sciences. In the following remarks I shall attempt to sort out some of the elements in this complex picture.

Religious Truth

Perhaps the most important point to note is that, in some respects at least, the problem of Christian theology is but an aspect of the problem of the study of *religion itself* within the faculty of arts and sciences. For it is in their preoccupation with *truth* that all religions pose such difficulties within the

The Ambiguous Position of Christian Theology

academy. We must therefore consider the peculiar features of truth within the sphere of religion.

Let me characterize religion as the human response to those superior powers from which man sees himself and his communities deriving life and death. In this sense, religion does not primarily pertain to a certain set of objects defined in terms of their own natures, but rather to a mode of relationship between man and that which has his fulfillment or destruction at its disposal. This characterization of religion is certainly not final or completely comprehensive, but it does identify a feature conspicuous in all religions and one that is fundamental for the problem at hand.

1. A religious attitude on the part of an individual or a community entails the judgment that such and such a thing or power or presence does in fact have some kind of control over human life. The word "life" may have too narrowly biological a connotation; we might better say "control over the fulfillment or impoverishment of human existence." Obviously, such a judgment can never be a matter of indifference. What is at stake is the attainment or the loss of life itself. For a community to orient itself toward realities that have no authentic power while ignoring those that bring life and death would be folly and perhaps fatal folly. For instance, if full life comes through the clarity of understanding, so that the power of intelligibility is the authentic life-giver, then submission to the forces experienced in sensuality would be debilitating and ultimately destructive. On the other hand, if expanded sexuality is man's way of participating in true life, then monogamous marriage may simply be the way of living death.

Concern for truth is therefore absolutely central in religions—concern, not for any truth, but for truth regarding the sources of life and death. In other words, in religions truth is not a matter of satisfying the intelligence but of fulfilling existence. To be sure, this religious way of construing the human situation may be wrong. Perhaps the powers over life and death do not lie beyond man, to be received from certain supernal realities. Perhaps these powers lie wholly at his disposal and under his control. Perhaps the fullness of life is simply a matter of improving his moral character, or turning aside his hostilities, or releasing his suppressions, or improving his machines, or purifying his drugs, or merely manipulating the right bits of genetic information. But insofar as the human situation appears to be religious in character, in the particular fashion just described, then the truth-question is central and decisive. The quality of a person's existence is seen to depend on that which is not himself, that which is beyond him, that about which he must learn by being attentive to what is *extra se*. Such attentiveness is identical with a preoccupation with truth. In religions, therefore, the question of life and death is seen as a truth-question, as a matter of judging truly about reality.

In religions the truth-question itself becomes part of the religious venture and is not something preliminary or detached. An element in being nourished by the gods of one's personal and communal existence is knowing them and thus being able to live "properly" in relation to them. Therefore, pursuit of this kind of truth is urgent, since a beneficial relation to the gods depends upon its success. In moments when knowledge of religious matters becomes confused, this sense of urgency produces a deep uneasiness, even anguish. In moments of insight and assured knowledge, it comes to expression as advocacy. Because his own and his community's life and death may be hanging in the balance, no man can deal with religious truth without feeling the impulsion toward either uneasiness or advocacy. The one impossible attitude is what medieval writers called *curiositas*. To consider the gods as if they were not gods, to approach the powers which are thought to have control over life and death with an attitude of curiosity, that is, in abstraction from urgency, apart from any religious relationship, as if the fulfillment or destruction of one's own life were not at stake in this consideration, is nothing but self-deception. For departments of religion the posture of advocacy has always been a matter of distress. These departments sometimes act as though their reason for being could be fully justified once they disinfected themselves of this posture. Advocacy, however, has its roots, not in the peculiarities of individual temperament, but in the urgency of the subject matter which these departments study.

Christian theology, at least the kind of theology that poses a problem in the faculty of arts and sciences, pursues the truth-question precisely within this kind of religious framework. It responds to what it takes to be disclosures of the authentic source of all power over life and death. It understands its own pursuit of truth as in some way constitutive of a fruitful, rather than a destructive, relation to that source. It shares the urgency which is inseparable from the religious attitude, and whether it has the form of apologetic theology or confessional theology or kerygmatic theology or dogmatic theology, it is always informed by either uneasiness or advocacy.

Whether the Christian God might be considered in a nonreligious way—that is, not at all as a god who holds sway over human life and death,

The Ambiguous Position of Christian Theology

but as a necessary explanatory hypothesis, say, or as a factor in cosmic history—remains open. Nonreligious theology is often pursued. But for our purposes it is religious theology which poses the difficult problem.

2. The matter of life and death refers to the self in its actual existence. This actual existence is not primarily biological. It is constituted of hopes and memories, of daydreams and nightmares, of intelligent insights and covert symbolizations. In these various dimensions every actual self experiences an endless sequence of fulfillments and deprivations, and does so in ever new and unexpected situations. Some disastrous circumstance, some unforeseen enormity, some suppressed hunger or unappeased wish grips the self, and all the careful strategies it has developed for handling the sources of life and death now become useless and discredited. The religious orientation of previous moments has been complicated and challenged by the impact of reality, either from outside the self or from within and behind the self.

Take a native New Yorker and set him in the African jungle. He will not know how to identify the source of his nourishment or where to perceive the signs of danger. He will not even be able to tell what life and death will be within himself in this new world. This kind of upheaval is experienced by a work-oriented man who is suddenly dismissed from his job and by every person emerging out of young adulthood into the unfamiliar contours of middle age.

But dramatic change of this sort does not occur simply in the lives of individuals. It is a significant feature of community experience as well. A sustained drought makes a mockery of a people's long loyalty and deep identification with the land. A nation that has never lost a war becomes demoralized when its military power is successfully challenged. The American democratic way of life proves incapable of handling the complexities and ambiguities and long-term horizons of international leadership. In such situations it appears that the beliefs and rituals which previously aligned concrete existence with the powers of life and death in a successful manner become confused or inadequate when confronted with new circumstances.

This fact of existence should lead us to recognize that at the religious level *the truth-question is never closed*. The gods who seemed so clearly to have control over a people's life and death yesterday now become impotent and irrelevant. No reality has so clearly, so universally, and so unavoidably manifested its lordship over all life and death that every new experience at the level of actual existence immediately confirms that lordship. To be sure, people may use the term "God" to refer to something so abstract, so devoid of any manifestation in contemporary existence that it is unaffected by the shifts and surprises of concrete experience. But by the same token all that then remains to them is a god void of all religious significance, who stands in no relation to the concrete actualities of life and death. So far as anything has been experienced in some sense or at some level as having real control over some dimension of life in an individual or community—that is to say, so far as anything is taken as religiously important—people will discover that its status is questioned, complicated, or challenged by later experience.

The life of every community is deeply affected by the uncertain character of its religious truth. Some societies accept this uncertainty as one of the essential features of divinity. Polytheism, for instance, assumes the existence of innumerable unknown gods that the people have not yet encountered but that may suddenly appear tomorrow. Dynamistic religions expect the extraordinary to erupt in new modes and at new places, and Hinduism emphasizes the inexhaustible capacity of divinity for assuming new forms. These might be called "open" religions. But even "closed" religions, which believe in a final and decisive disclosure of the realities of life and death, recognize that this disclosure is not yet fully appropriated, that the truth-question keeps becoming confused even for believers, that some kind of darkness—the darkness of *maya* in Buddhism, say, or of sin in Christianity—allows people to be distracted by unreal gods and to refer authentic life and death to powers that do not in fact hold sway.

The consequence of this unsettled character of religious truth is obvious: it means that *change* is inherent in all the forms and expressions of the religious attitude. It is not the case that, at the level of the actual religion of actual people, there is some fixed entity called Islam, for example, and that the history of this religion is a record of the maintenance, the compromising, perhaps the corruption, but also the repeated recovery of this fixed entity. There is no such thing as a fixed religion. No person anywhere has discovered a source of life and death that is immediately and unavoidably decisive in every situation. All religious judgments, therefore, are constantly being shaken and transformed by new frames of reference. And because these new frames of reference bring with them new dimensions and new experiences of life and death, every reaffirmation of a god followed yesterday really entails a change in the understanding of that god.

The Ambiguous Position of Christian Theology

Transformation in religions, then, is not a matter of external compromise and infection; it is an inherent and essential property. Not only does religion have the posture of truth as its central preoccupation, but it also has the *problematic* of truth as its fundamental dynamic. In the extreme case this transformation may entail the conscious and deliberate abandonment of an entire fabric of religious forms and the turning to new gods and new rituals. Usually, however, it involves an ever-shifting sense of the actual identifiable content of authentic life and, therefore, a changing expectation of how the god will concretely reaffirm his lordship over the forces of life and death. Thus a single religious orientation, which at one time follows a world-renouncing, sacramental way toward a trinitarian God, can at another time, while committed to the same Lord and guided by the same Scriptures, seek the perfection of worldly possibilities for suffering men.

The uncertainty of truth at the religious level has been very central in the history of Christianity. The Jews had expected the Messiah to be God's agent in closing the truth-question in religion once and for all. "For in the last days it shall come to pass that I will pour out my Spirit upon all flesh, and your sons and your daughters shall prophesy, and your young men shall see visions and your old men shall dream dreams . . . and I shall show wonders in the heavens and on the earth" (Joel 2:28–30). The Lord of all life and all death shall become unavoidably manifest. The earliest Christian community saw Jesus as the bearer of this decisive event, for the blind see, the lame walk, lepers are cleansed, the deaf hear, the dead are raised, the low are exalted, and the hungry are filled with good things. Yet the momentum of disclosure begun in Jesus was not completed. The *parousia*—the decisive, unambiguous, and universal "presencing" of this God as the authentic Lord of life and death—did not occur.

The Christian community has always been caught up in the same problematic of truthfulness as other religions. It is always being perplexed internally by shifting experiences of apparent life and apparent death. It was shaken at first by the prospect of antinomianism, then by the prospect of persecution, and after Constantine by the prospect of acculturation. In fact, the theological doctrines of the Christian church have been established precisely because the truth keeps becoming unsettled in the concrete life of Christian people. According to one Protestant tradition, for instance, the Christian community is one that is constantly falling into arrogant forgetfulness. It cannot, therefore, let itself be measured by any agent or any order or any historical moment from within its own life. It must allow itself

The Uncertain Center

to be recurrently reformed by that which stands beyond it—in short, by the claims of the Scriptures. On the other hand, according to one Roman Catholic tradition, moments of uncertainty and confusion are too concrete, too contemporary, too immediate to be dispelled by statements made in the past and preserved in writing. Over and above the Scriptures, the Christian community must have an infallible living voice to remove uncertainties, and this God provides through the office of the Pope.

This problem of uncertainty is not just a feature of community life, however. Every individual Christian must wrestle repeatedly with the question of religious truth. That is why he develops faith to hold on to that which he does not yet see. That is also why each Sunday he seeks a revindication of God's life giving power, a re-presenting (*anamnesis*) of God's victory in Christ in the liturgy of Word and Sacrament.

However far Christians may want to advance beyond the "old" dispensation of the Jews, and however rhetorically they want to stress the fullness of the revelation given in Jesus Christ, they still cannot break out of the condition of recurrent uncertainty and tension and change in which all religious truth stands. A hiddenness remains. It is not without reason, therefore, that in the New Testament the word "revelation" is reserved for that final unavoidable disclosure which has not yet occurred. And it is not without reason that in the Schweitzer school of theology the delay of this final disclosure is seen as the decisive fact that has shaped Christianity through every period of its history.

In the Christian tradition, the pursuit of the question of truth takes the form of theology. This not only means that theology is grounded on and shaped by the religious attitude. It also means that the activity of theology is enveloped by the religious problematic. The religious truth with which Christians seek to be identified keeps becoming obscured. Christian theology thus can never proceed from and can never attain a final form for its truth, a form that is persuasively valid for all peoples everywhere. No insight, no assertion, and no belief is immune from uncertainty at the religious level.

For this reason it cannot be assumed that past theologians have completely taken care of certain doctrines, that in these areas it is simply a matter of repeating their work, and that, if the contemporary theologian wants something to do, he must find a doctrine not already "covered." The theologian can never adopt the posture of Alexander the Great looking for new worlds to conquer. Not a single fragment of Christian truth has been

The Ambiguous Position of Christian Theology

conquered so securely that the theologian can take it for granted and need not constantly listen for obscurities and confusions in people's understanding of it, at least at the religious level. Every act of theological reflection begins with a *questio*.

What the theologian finds true in others' work must also be true in his own. Nothing he can say will at any point carry Christian awareness out of the circle of recurrent confusion. He works with seriousness, because he expects his efforts to be successful. He expects actually to penetrate through a particular religious confusion and to attain a clarifying insight regarding Christ's lordship over life and death in some specific area of existence. But he knows that such success will be provisional and that his insights, far from forestalling further obscurities in the future, may themselves become the source of new confusions in the face of changing situations.

Not for one moment, therefore, can the Christian theologian detach himself from the *problem* of religious truth and pursue other tasks. He cannot turn away to some other order of problem, for example, to the problem of building an intellectual system out of a number of individual truths that may be taken as settled. He cannot turn from the church and ask himself about the views of non-Christians toward Christianity—as if the difficulties regarding Christ which plague non-Christians were not simply pale reflections of the truth-question that constantly breaks open at the very center of the Christian religion itself. In Christianity what is uncertain is the very center, the viability of Christ as Lord and Savior. That viability becomes obscured at ever new points as changes occur in an individual's or a community's awareness of life and death. That Christian theology cannot detach itself from this religious problem poses a severe difficulty for the faculty of arts and sciences.

3. If religious truth—the truth about the sources of life and death—becomes confused, how can this confusion be removed?

Normally confusions are dispelled intellectually by the mind taking initiative and bringing into view from its vast storehouse of knowledge some datum or some principle or some analogy which dissolves the obscurity. Where uncertainties of a religious sort are concerned, however, this is exactly what cannot be done. Such uncertainties arise because the actual sources of fulfillment and deprivation in experience have become blurred. People have difficulty in making out which god really counts. Therefore, to remove this difficulty is not a matter of thinking better. It is a matter of the authentic source of life and death being revindicated as such in their lives. Its action upon them must be perceived anew so that they may again have a taste of the actual life or death which they believe to be at its disposal. Without this *concrete vindication* the confusion will remain, at least religiously.

The religious attitude finds control over the powers of life and death not finally at man's disposal and, therefore, also not at the disposal of his desire to resolve religious confusions. Gods cannot be made to come out and show themselves as gods whenever devotees so wish. If men could dispose of their religious confusions by such efforts, that would simply mean that the problem had ceased to be of a religious kind and had been transferred to another frame of reference.

Religions do resolve their religious uncertainties in a religious way. That is, when the sources of life and death become obscured in some area of existence, the authentic gods are *invoked* to show themselves. The difficulty is not solved by men. It is referred to the gods themselves, and men wait for them to deliver such impulses of life or death as will exhibit the truth.

This act of referral and waiting is rarely as dramatic as the contest between Elijah and the priests of Baal. But this basic structure has always been present. Over time rituals of invocation and referral are developed within every religious tradition as it is embroiled in religious uncertainties; it is expected that the authentic god will again affirm himself to the people as the true source of life and death for them and will thus revindicate his power and dispel their confusion.

No exception is presented within Christian theology. For all their conceptual precision and concern for rational proof, theologians do not themselves have the means of disposing of the confusions which they face. Such matters are not academic. They depend for their clarification upon the actual re-presencing of the lordship of Christ. Theologians must therefore align themselves with the means of grace and be responsive to the illuminations of the Spirit. The complete dependence of the entire Christian life on Jesus Christ pertains just as much to the process of theological clarification as to deeds of charity. And if the theologian does succeed in his work, if he exhibits religious (not intellectual) truth with a restored clarity, this achievement will be manifest in the attitudes of the people actually oriented toward Jesus Christ. In short, the Christian theologian belongs to his religious community both in the processes and in the fruit of his work.

Such, then, are three important features of religions. First, they consist in a particular attitude about truth in the matter of life and death, namely, that life and death are received by man from beyond himself. Thus all religions convey what they hold to be authentic and fruitful knowledge about the sources of life and death. Second, the flux of actual experience results in confusion about this knowledge; therefore, it must be constantly recovered in fresh forms. Third, this restoration is believed to be carried out, not by man, but by the revindicating action of the sources of life and death themselves. If Christian theology stands at odds with the faculty of arts and sciences, it does so because it is a religious activity and thus necessarily embodies these three features of religions.

The Antagonism to Christian Theology

By tradition the faculty of arts and sciences has been identified by its subject matter—the arts and the sciences. This has come to embrace, first, the study of the languages, writings, arts, and other self-conscious modes of human expression; second, the investigation of natural phenomena; and, finally, the study of man himself and his sense of the world by means of philosophy, history, psychology, and so forth. As to methods and goals, however, the faculty of arts and sciences has no fixed direction. There is no ideal paradigm by which its activities in various universities can be judged. The intellectual aims and procedures of faculties change according to what use is made of their work and according to what methods prove most fruitful for the purposes at hand. In one age the study of the arts and sciences may be pursued in order to serve the Christian church and its theological inquiries. Then the liberal arts become the handmaid of theology. In another age an arts and sciences education may offer the best preparation for political leadership. In still other circumstances this education and knowledge are thought to provide the fullest development of human power, the most effective way for mankind to gain mastery over itself and its environment and for the individual to realize his latent capacities.

Recently, however, there has flourished a somewhat different view of what the faculty of arts and sciences should be, a view that has been—and still remains—decisive for the status of Christian theology. As its model for responsible inquiry, this view looks to the kind of detached and critical reasoning which was first developed by the new physical sciences in the seventeenth century. It maintains, therefore, that one condition is absolutely necessary for genuine understanding, and it insists that only an intellectual enterprise which fulfills this condition can be legitimately included within the faculty of arts and sciences.

This primary condition is that true knowledge must arise from *autonomous inquiry*. Reasoning must serve only its own demand for clear understanding. Accordingly, it must keep itself free from entangling alliances with ecclesiastical communities or nationalistic ventures or commercial interests. On this view, the search for truth begins when reason poses *its own questions* about the object of inquiry. These are not questions which have their roots in the practical life of social groups, but rather questions which the mind finds pertinent to its own endeavor to comprehend. Further, the search for truth is advanced, not when the mind has recourse to long-accepted principles or to religious beliefs or to wish-fulfilling values, but when it formulates answers that are entirely at the service of its own rational requirements. And, finally, the search for truth is completed when reason, in order to justify its answers, can provide probative evidence that will be intelligible to any rational person. All reliance on esoteric knowledge or external authority to support the truth is excluded.

In recent times this condition of autonomy has been widely adopted by faculties of arts and sciences as the proper norm for their activities. They exist, it is maintained, to seek understanding of the arts and the sciences in complete independence from all external claims, which is to say, from all the claims that may arise from nonrational impulses within the scholar and from all those that may be imposed on his thinking by his social environment. We find the presence of this norm of independence everywhere in the modern university. There is, for instance, the practice of tenure and other such procedural stratagems by which these faculties attempt to resist control by the church money or the corporation money or the government money that supports them. For the individual scholar there has developed the now universal demand that he secure the PhD degree and in that way give evidence of his ability to pursue a lengthy technical inquiry without once being subverted by any nonrational, nontechnical interest.

The true autonomy of reason, however, requires more than this independence from extrinsic forces. Beyond social institutions and personal emotions, the mind may also become falsely imprisoned by one of its own momentary insights or by the impact which some object happens to make upon it at one particular time. Reason, therefore, must also keep watch over its freedom even in the course of its own work. That is to say, it must learn to review its own attainments continually and to submit them to the criticism of others. It must refuse any hint of dogmatism. It must insist on seeing its subject matter from various sides, letting the knowledge gained from one approach be qualified by and integrated with the knowledge gained from others. In short, reason must maintain what is called "critical distance" with respect to its own achievements.

Today we have a shorthand term to convey this elaborate notion of the faculty of arts and sciences as the citadel of rational autonomy. The term is *scholarship*. When a faculty measures its attainments, promotes its members, and assesses the work of its students in terms of their scholarly competence—that is, their competence in pursuing an objective, methodologically self-conscious and self-critical inquiry, their competence for formulating rationally urgent questions, for finding rationally satisfying answers, and for providing rationally probative evidence—then this faculty has defined its essential function as the exercise of autonomous reason.

The adoption of this ideal of rational autonomy by the faculty of arts and sciences is the chief reason why, over the past two centuries, the entire domain of religion has become alien to this faculty. For the religious attitude, in one of its essential features, involves man's seeing himself in relation to powers that prohibit any trace of autonomy. When men come to realize that their lives and deaths depend on the movement of enormities that lie beyond their control—that is to say, on the movement of gods—then the posture of scholarship, with its detachment, its leisurely and many-sided inquiry, and its critical distance, is neither possible nor desirable. Above everything else, man in the religious situation must be attentive to what stands beyond himself. He must be ready to respond immediately to any signs that the impulses which nourish his life are about to wax or wane, that his own existence may be moving out of fruitful alignment with these decisive powers and into a position where they cease to nourish him and become destructive. The whole of a man's existence is thought to be at stake here. He has no vantage point, therefore, to which he can withdraw in order to rationally examine and observe the gods. There is no safe center from which he can direct questions at them. As gods, they are related to him only in ways that exclude objectivity and distanced consideration. He does not judge them; they judge him. His life and death depend on movements that are utterly beyond his competence, for they issue out of the depths of these inscrutable powers.

Religion thus requires a very demanding attitude of attentive responsiveness, an utmost willingness to follow the movement of God or the gods.

The Uncertain Center

In religion—and in any intellectual discipline that partakes of the religious attitude—truth does not mean a knowledge that satisfies the demands of reason, but a knowledge that is fruitfully responsive to the movement of the gods.

Turning now to the other side of this issue, we can see clearly that religion represents a fundamental enemy of truth as conceived from the standpoint of autonomous reason. For the religious attitude is not simply a purveyor of erroneous assumptions or false information or faulty inferences. From the perspective of rational autonomy, it is wrong through and through to its very essence; it is an intrinsic perversion of the human capacity for truth. Instead of opening man to the real world and liberating his awareness with authentic knowledge, it closes him off from the world. By its very concern with the question of man's own life and death, it fosters in him a narrow, egocentric preoccupation with himself and encourages him to judge everything from that perspective. The exhortation that men should be willing to lose the world in order to gain their own souls perfectly expresses the self-absorption which the champions of rational autonomy find inherent in the religious attitude and which they decisively reject.

In order to exhibit the essentially closed and untruthful posture of religion, the rationalists of the eighteenth century emphasized the role of fear in the religious attitude. Religions arise, they said, because men feel themselves in the grasp of unknown powers, powers utterly beyond the control of their paltry strength and the ken of their crude perception. They find themselves helpless and ignorant. Naturally, therefore, they are filled with fear. The gods with whom religions people this world are expressions of this fear. Because men can pray to these gods, however, and perhaps appease them, religion also provides men with a way to cope with this fear. According to this analysis, then, religion exists first to foster a fearful attitude toward the world and then to allay it.

The force of this rationalistic account lies in the recognition that fear is the most claustral and defensive of all human emotions. In maintaining that religion was grounded on fear, the eighteenth century rationalists were simply trying to exhibit how thoroughly closed this attitude is. How, they asked, can religion be based on an openness to the real, how can it be capable of any rational truth whatsoever, when it insists on seeing man's basic situation as one of ignorance and helplessness—that is to say, as one of dependence on uncontrollable powers—and therefore demands an

The Ambiguous Position of Christian Theology

attitude of fear? The catchword for describing religion in these terms was "superstition."

Today this negative judgment upon religion has become more subdued. There is less talk about ignorance and more about mystery. The term "awe" has replaced the word "fear." Myths have been rehabilitated, and no one now speaks of superstitions. Yet nothing we have learned about religions in the last hundred years challenges the fundamental accuracy of this description. In the religious attitude men do conceive their existence, at least in its final dimensions, to be at the disposal of superior and undomesticated powers and see it, therefore, as something of which men will always be somewhat ignorant and always somewhat fearful. Such a vision of human existence cannot be neatly integrated with efforts to attain truth through the discipline, the autonomy, and the detachment of scholarly reason.

In the course of the nineteenth century this ideal of rational openness became widely influential in the faculties of arts and sciences. Their methods and their criteria for legitimate investigation and competent personnel fell increasingly under the dominion of this ideal. Consequently, religion, both as a viewpoint from which to teach and as a way of life for which to teach, was more and more excluded from these faculties.

This process of excluding religion constituted a long and bitter struggle, a struggle not only against religion in general but, above all, against the religion at hand, against Christianity. This new autonomous rationality did not, after all, have virgin territory to conquer. The Christian religion had a controlling hold on every single area of learning, and the new perspective had to fight every step of its way against these entrenched interests.

The theology advanced in defense of the Christian religion in this struggle was not a neutral, detached, purely rational kind of theology, but a thoroughly religious theology, that is, a theology shaped by and dedicated to a belief in Jesus Christ as the sole Lord of life and death. Through the work of its theologians, the Christian religion sought to limit the autonomy of reason and subordinate intellection to the requirements of a religious posture. Theology directly challenged the commitment of autonomous reason to truth.

The course of this struggle has long been over, but the memory remains. The condemnation of Galileo and the opposition to Darwin which Christian theologians sponsored continue to be recalled. Thus each new generation has exhibited to it the lack of truth, the fear-ridden closedness, and the essential enmity against autonomous reason that allegedly characterize the Christian religion. Yet it is not simply the echo of these great public events that continues. For, in fact, every faculty of arts and sciences that is over a hundred years old still carries the marks of that struggle within itself, and long after local incidents and personalities have been forgotten, there remain deeply implanted the quite justified *feelings* of hostility toward the theological aspect of the Christian religion.

To suggest that religious theology be pursued and that religious theologians be trained under the auspices of the faculty of arts and sciences is therefore to reawaken this conflict between two incompatible modes of truthfulness. Irenic claims that such conflict is unnecessary, that Christian theology and a faculty devoted to scholarship really share a common ground or pursue a common belief in reason, are simply false. Scholarship does not measure truth according to the degree of its participation in the life-giving power of Christ. And the Christian theologian does not submit the religious issues of life and death to the judgments of his own autonomous, self-critical, and publicly verifiable reasoning. There can be no question of appealing to fair-minded tolerance in the interests of "giving the Christian faith a chance in the intellectual world." Nor is there any point to the contention that Christian theology, in its subservience to the beliefs of its religious community, merely exemplifies the way in which all rational inquiry depends on fundamental assumptions. The religious sense of dependence on lordly powers means that in theological reflection the moment of responsive submissiveness has a positive and fulfilling significance that is quite unknown in good scholarship. No amount of clever intellectuality in theology should be allowed to conceal this difference.

The proposal to bring Christian theology under the aegis of the faculty of arts and sciences, then, makes visible once again the tension between religion and the posture of autonomous rationality.

The Establishment of Departments of Religion

The recent establishment of departments of religion must be viewed in the light of this tension between religion and autonomous rationality. For these departments did not arise out of a purely neutral curiosity about a new field of learning within the faculties of arts and sciences. The question of their establishment was never wholly separated from the conviction that religion

The Ambiguous Position of Christian Theology

as such is not the way of truth and that the Christian religion in particular has been the most formidable enemy to the development of rational truth.

Departments of religion represent the positive attitude of objective, scholarly reason toward religion. Without once forgetting its fundamental opposition to the claims made by the religious attitude, the advocates of autonomous reason have never imagined that their only responsibility was to repudiate and discredit religion. On the contrary, they were bound to take religion with utmost seriousness for two reasons.

In the first place, religious truth involves not simply a posture of attentive responsiveness, for it also has a content. It consists of ideas about the divine and the world, about human origins and human destiny. If autonomous rationality is to vindicate itself as the way of truth, it cannot ignore all this content. If it claims to provide the mind with an open and luminous relationship with what is real, a relationship not dependent on the action of superior forces but available simply through the subjective action of the rational power that lies within man himself, then it must demonstrate its capacity to discover and validate the truth of "religious" matters. It must undertake a positive program to bring the content of man's religious awareness under its own judgment and to show its effectiveness in this decisive area.

Second, the way of reason would be false to its own nature if it were to adopt a purely negative and repudiating attitude toward the sphere of religion, for such an attitude of closed hostility has always been one of the major faults of the religious posture. What would be gained if reasoning were simply to substitute for the closed intransigence of Christian dogmatism an intransigence of its own toward everything religious? Autonomous rationality has not claimed that it possesses a certain content of truth which is infallibly correct and that any conflicting content ought therefore to be suppressed. It simply maintains that its method of arriving at the truth yields such clear, reliable, and objective knowledge that no defensive repudiations are necessary anymore. It is in this same spirit that it ventures upon the study of religion, for the advocates of rational autonomy have always wanted to penetrate and understand this whole region of life and, in fact, to understand it so profoundly that even religious men will be compelled to admit that autonomous reason provides the best access to the truth of religious matters.

But how can this inquiry best be carried out?

The Uncertain Center

We may take Renè Descartes's approach as typical of one procedure. It is fascinating to observe in his work how subtly and yet how thoroughly autonomous reason establishes itself in the area of religion.

He makes it clear that he thinks of truth only as that which can be accepted by autonomous reason. The only things which he will consider to be true, he says, are those ideas which are completely clear and perfectly defined to the rational intellect, or which can be inferred with absolute certainty from such clear ideas. Anything confused or obscure, anything on which the least doubt can be cast—in short, anything which does not satisfy the mind's own inherent demand for satisfying knowledge—will be rejected as if it were absolutely false. This criterion eliminates the entire domain of religion, which by his own account (*Discourse on Method*, Part I) concerns those matters that are wholly beyond the capacity of human knowledge.

Proceeding in this way, and beginning with a clear idea of himself as a thinking being who lacks perfection, Descartes immediately establishes therefrom a secure and unshakable knowledge of God as the being with all perfection and as the source of all the reality and truth in the world.

It is at this point that the full significance of Descartes's purpose becomes evident. For it now appears that he is not interested simply in satisfying his mind. He uses the truth secured by his mind to inspire the whole concrete existence of living man with an attitude of confident openness toward the world. As he explains it (*Discourse on Method*, Part IV), because reasoning has shown that everything real and true in human experience proceeds from a perfect and infinite being, men may be assured about their judgments, so far as they are based upon clear and distinct ideas, and about the world which their judgments assess. In short, by the use of autonomous reason, men not only may satisfy the demands of their minds but may also escape the oppressive feelings of dread and uncertainty about the human situation and may release their energies for a confident engagement with the world. It is no wonder, then, that Descartes can exclaim: "I have every reason to render thanks to God, who owes me nothing yet who has given me all the perfections I possess" (*Meditations* IV).

This familiar Christian theme of God's unmerited goodness must not conceal from us what Descartes is here doing. Having set aside the truths of religion as wholly beyond the grasp of thinking, he then shows how autonomous reason can establish some of those very truths entirely out of its own resources. He first authenticates the foundation on which religion

The Ambiguous Position of Christian Theology

rests—the awesome idea of an utterly perfect and utterly infinite being. And then, on the basis of that idea, he lets his reasoning show how proper it is that men take an affirmative attitude toward the world and toward their own subjective judgments. Finally, in this setting, he exhibits the free graciousness of God to men and thus validates the claim which God makes upon their thanksgiving. In short, reason in the writings of Descartes does not criticize the religious posture. Rather, by its own light it establishes the content long associated with religion and purports to do so with a subjective persuasiveness far greater than anything provided by religion itself. Precisely for that reason it will presumably be more effective than religion in generating the basic religious emotions of awe at God's infinite perfection and thanksgiving at God's unmerited goodness.

In this aspect of his work Descartes may be seen as representative of one positive approach which autonomous reason may take to religion. In seeking to understand religion, that is, in seeking to bring the religious aspect of human experience into the orbit of intelligence, this approach examines the fundamental tenets of religion—for example, the existence and goodness of God—and tries to reconstitute these in its own terms, judging them according to how well they satisfy the mind's demand for rational clarity.

This procedure has flourished for three centuries after Descartes, usually under the name *philosophy of religion*. In it man is viewed primarily as mind, and religion, therefore, is regarded as one of his ways of groping for a full cognitive knowledge of reality. But religion is an inadequate way, it is maintained, and man can fulfill the aim of his religious life only by applying the disciplines of autonomous rationality to religious questions.

This thesis has been formulated in various ways. According to the deists, for instance, religion fails because the natural reasoning by which every human being knows the one same universal truth about God and human destiny becomes mixed with the products of irrational fear—with magical practices, with an authoritarian priesthood, and with deified heroes. Autonomous reason brings out the true content of religion by removing all this excrescence and exhibiting religious truth, not as true in a religious way—that is, not in terms of the life- or death-bringing action of divinity—but as true rationally, in terms of its power to grasp and satisfy the demands of autonomous reason.

According to someone like Hegel, on the other hand, nothing in religion is to be eliminated as false or superstitious. It is inadequate, not because it represents a mixture of fragments of falsehood and bits of truth, but because in religion men express the truth about the Absolute through the imperfect medium of concrete sensuous things. In all their rituals and myths, their holy objects and holy places, people manifest their true awareness of the Absolute. But, for Hegel, this mode of expression is not an adequate medium for conveying the truth of ultimate reality. Men therefore can fulfill the inner intention of their religious consciousness only if they transform their religion into philosophy and grasp the truth about the Absolute in purely rational terms, devoid of concrete events and physical images. Hegel assigns to autonomous reason the task of teaching men to carry their most fundamental questions beyond the areas of the concrete life, where the life giving powers wax and wane. It must help them to *think* the non-concrete content of their religious pictures and to replace the certainty of religious faith—faith in certain concrete events or actions as manifestations of divinity—with the certainty of self-conscious knowing.

Within the study of the arts and sciences, the approach of the philosophy of religion came most fully into its own in the nineteenth century. While the religious theologians seemed entrammeled in the quagmire of dogmatism, scripturalism, and denominational self-justification, the religious questions of God and man were being successfully clarified by autonomous reason. Why shouldn't any practitioner of such reason, any scholar in the arts and sciences, whether his specialty be Hellenic archeology or vertebrate zoology, be able to speak out on the true—that is, on the rational—meaning of religion? And so in the nineteenth century many chose to do so.

By the turn of the present century, however, there came into being a new awareness of primitive religions and of the religions of the ancient Mediterranean. It was then that the whole enterprise of the philosophy of religion itself began to be seriously questioned. For in its preoccupation with the views held by religions concerning God and the world, this approach failed to grasp the peculiar way in which religious men see themselves *related to* these beliefs. The new study of less advanced and less rationalized religions showed clearly that religion is not primarily a cognitive effort to understand the world, that myths are not erroneous explanations of natural phenomena, and that the effort to prove the existence of God to the satisfaction of reason—the nerve center of the philosophy of religion, for if this point is not settled, the reasoning mind has no grounds for even considering divinity—is either entirely absent or quite peripheral in actual religions. Accordingly, it became obvious that the philosophy of religion did not understand the human side of religion, the motives and the attitude toward reality that operate here. And hence it did not succeed in gathering religion into the domain of autonomous reason. Instead, it made the religious posture a mirror of its own rationality and only overcame the problem of religious truthfulness by ignoring it.

In response to this crisis there has arisen a much more rigorously descriptive and inductive approach to religions. There has been no change, however, in the fundamental project: rational autonomy is still held to be the only guarantor of true openness and, therefore, the only reliable means of securing the truth. In dealing with religion, the scholarly mind is expected to ask its own questions, to seek answers satisfying to it, and to establish those answers on the basis of publicly available evidence.

But this new descriptive approach is more modest and indirect than the philosophy of religion. It does not simply look at a religion's views of God and man in order to judge of their truth or falsity. It tries to suspend the modern Western rationalistic preconceptions about what constitutes reality and how men should think and act. It tries to let every element in a people's religious behavior stand forth in its own right—their legends, their rituals, their sacred officials, and their holy days. It wants these to disclose what meaning they have, not for the philosophic quest of Western man, but for the people who believe in them. It moves to grand generalizations only very slowly, almost with reluctance.

The success—or, better, the promise—of this descriptive approach in recent years has led to the establishment of departments of religion within faculties of arts and sciences. To put this in another way, in view of the failure of the philosophy of religion to handle the immense range of data about religion that is now being accumulated, that is to say, in view of its failure to comprehend the whole truth-posture of religion within the more radiant truth of scholarly reason, some faculties of arts and sciences have looked to the new descriptive approach to achieve this goal. Accordingly, they have set up departments of religion.

Obviously, many interest groups, including an important segment of the Christian community, have out of their own motives sought the formation of these departments. The very real influence of these groups may be seen whenever departments offer courses on Catholicism, say, or Judaism, covertly oriented to the needs of believing Catholics or Jews. The philosophy of religion is also usually represented in courses within the departments of religion. As faculties of arts and sciences have made the decision to form these departments, however, they have not been interested in providing young people with instruction in the faith of their choice, and they have expressed no strong demand that philosophic clarity be achieved on religious matters. What they have expected is that these new departments will study something of the variety and history of human religions and will do justice, in whatever way reasoning may find best, to the almost unmanageable range of phenomena in religious behavior.

If we survey the actual work of departments of religion and look below the sometimes rather confusing surface of their course offerings, we find that the descriptive approach does indeed dominate the scene. An unremitting effort is made to avoid any one-sided preoccupation with the local religions of the West. Even when competent personnel cannot be found, departments still try to give some instruction about Eastern or primitive religions. There is a general willingness to get along without a particular methodology and certainly without a definition of religion. Philosophical analyses jostle happily along in the company of sociological and phenomenological studies. The subject matter is felt to be too complex, too pluriform and many-sided, to permit any broad theoretical generalizations. As to vigorous scholarship, departments of religion today almost universally stress the value of historical sophistication. This emphasis simply follows from the recognition that every religious phenomenon belongs within the matrix of life of some particular place and time. By requiring historical skills, departments are able to demand of their descriptive work the highest standard of accuracy.

The faculties of arts and sciences have made it quite clear that their departments of religion are to be agents of rationality and not of religion. These departments are expected to exclude all confessionalism, all advocacy and indoctrination. They are not to represent any particular religion or even religion in general. They are not to let reason become the instrument of some faith, nor allow the religious posture to hold sway. They are to show how the power of descriptive reasoning can penetrate and understand the phenomena of religion. In short, they are to proceed by the same canons of competent scholarship as every other department in the faculty of arts and sciences.

In this climate it is obvious that Christian theology in the religious sense still has no place in a department of religion. Its posture of faith and its preoccupation with life and death as mediated concretely through an

The Ambiguous Position of Christian Theology

incarnate God and a religious community remain at odds with the commitment to reason that is still voiced in faculties of arts and sciences.

Nevertheless, because of their descriptive approach, present-day departments of religion frequently do set aside a place for what is often called "Christian theology." This situation corresponds very closely to what happened to theology during the nineteenth century when the philosophy of religion flourished in the arts and sciences. At that time many Christian theologians accommodated themselves to the prevailing approach. They investigated how well various Christian beliefs could be reconstructed on the basis of natural knowledge, without making any reference to special revelation or to life-giving events at the concrete level. Although they themselves were believers, their work, which came to be known as philosophical theology, was very eagerly accepted in the world of rational autonomy. For it completely ignored the religious problematic of life and death and examined the truth of Christian teachings from the quite nonreligious perspective of rational cogency.

In a similar fashion, departments of religion as they exist today also have need for a certain kind of Christian theology. If they wish to describe so theological a religion as Christianity, they must present the theological aims and insights of the important theologians who have shaped the Christian awareness. They must have "historical theologians." But these theologians are no more called upon to wrestle with the problems of religious truth than were the philosophical theologians of the last century. They are asked by their departments, fundamentally, to be intellectual historians, to explain what Tertullian or Jonathan Edwards may have thought, but not themselves to take up these theological questions in all their religious urgency.

The Attraction of Theology

The fact remains that Christian theology in the strict sense has been included in certain departments of religion. Some theologians have been appointed, not as philosophers of religion or as intellectual historians, but as believers who conduct rational inquiries under the control and for the sake of their beliefs. Notwithstanding the traditions of scholarly research and autonomous rationality, some faculties of arts and sciences prove not to be averse to the presence in their midst of minds that work within the religious problematic, that let their thinking be wholly responsive to the life- and death-giving power of the divine, and that therefore serve the interests of the religious and not the rational posture. To be sure, the outer forms of scholarship are insisted on. Any theologian appointed to a faculty of arts and sciences is expected to attain the technical competence entailed in the PhD degree and to have a certain command of historical knowledge and historical methods. But there seems to be a certain relaxing of the rationalistic demands which would have been made upon him previously. The legitimacy of his activity does not depend on his avoiding the religious pursuit of theological questions or on limiting himself strictly to those matters that seem evident to natural reason.

On this basis it would appear that the tradition of rational autonomy is being questioned today within faculties of arts and sciences. The rejection of the religious posture is less assured than it used to be, and this hesitancy indicates that the basic purpose of these faculties is again under question. When described in this way, however, the situation is made to appear far more clear-cut and self-conscious than it actually is. Behind the tentative steps now being taken here and there to include Christian theology in departments of religion, there lies a variety of concerns, none of which is decisive in itself and all of which together do not constitute anything like an explicit challenge to the tradition of rational autonomy. Yet their presence clearly points to a certain blurring in the sense of purpose that controls the arts and sciences. The problem of fundamental goals has thus begun to be raised at the heart of the university.

Let me indicate briefly the three concerns which are most frequently voiced by those who support the inclusion of Christian theology within departments of religion. It should be remembered that I am not considering the views of religious groups or of seminary graduates or of anxious parents. I am interested exclusively in the ways in which the presence of Christian theology is justified in terms of the overall responsibilities of the faculty of arts and sciences.

1. The most important factor is simply the character of theological writing actually being done today. No member of a faculty of arts and sciences can escape some engagement with the work of contemporary theologians. Their ideas are discussed everywhere, and some acquaintance with Buber or Niebuhr or Tillich has become the normal mark of a literate person.

When a faculty member reads this theology, however, what he encounters has none of the obvious irrationalisms which he has been taught

The Ambiguous Position of Christian Theology

to distrust. There is nothing closed or defensive or compulsively doctrinaire in this enterprise. Instead of a mechanical repetition of dogmas and authoritarian proof-texts, he meets intellectual insights that ring true far beyond the precincts of the churchgoing religion which he may have known. Instead of subservience to narrow ecclesiastical interests, he finds all kinds of questions—even skeptical ones—explored openly and at times with a seriousness that seems almost unfair. There can be no doubt that these writers are religious: rational clarity is not their overriding criterion for the truth. But from within their religious perspective, they are able to shed light on a whole variety of problems in a way that autonomous reason finds strangely satisfying. The religious factor is decisive but nevertheless not altogether obstructive.

The impact of this kind of theological literature on faculty members in the arts and sciences should not be underestimated, for it has raised a doubt about the simple and straightforward manner in which theology had been judged. This faculty has its primary allegiance, not to certain views about what reason can or cannot do, but to every intellectual enterprise that does in fact yield clear and compelling understanding, however unlikely its credentials or fragmentary its achievements. From this point of view, it has not been difficult for some faculty members to suggest that the nonsectarian and anthropologically self-conscious theology now in fashion might well have a place among the arts and sciences.

2. Among the highly educated class there is present today a new feeling of urgency about religious questions. This has nothing to do with the revival of any particular religion. It seems to be connected rather with a loss of confidence in the competence of rationality to provide answers in this area. After several centuries of liberated rationality, there are many who feel oppressed by the weight of religious uncertainty, that is, uncertainty about the real source of life and what might be judged its authentic character.

This mood is not a matter directly pertinent to faculties of arts and sciences, though it does reflect on certain claims made for the autonomy of reason. But it is the sign of a new sense among intellectuals of the importance and the irreducibly religious nature of religious matters, and this in turn has deeply influenced the technical work in various departments in the arts and sciences. It has become apparent that religious beliefs and the religious posture may be far more deeply present throughout the whole scope of human life than was previously suspected. Far from being a crudely primitive way of groping for the truth or a set of special actions that are universally recognized as religious, religion now appears as a vital perspective that gives shape to man's political life at one extreme and his works of art at the other. Once the full urgency of the religious question was perceived, it was easy for literary critics and political scientists to discover its influence in great novels or political revolutions.

For numerous faculty members in various departments, this discovery has drastically changed the bearing of religion on their technical work of scholarship. No longer can it be dismissed as merely the consciousness of religious institutions or reduced to purely rational terms. The demands of their subject matter have required them to consider the religion pertinent to their data—usually Christianity—in terms of its own urgency and according to its own sense of truth. For this purpose the presence of Christian theologians in the faculty of arts and sciences has seemed both useful and appropriate. After all, if religion has such a profound bearing on the most creative and the most communal aspects of human life, and if theology breaks beyond ecclesiastical forms and is willing to think into the mysteries of life-giving power at this deep level, it can be excluded only at the price of intellectual impoverishment.

3. Finally, serious questions may be raised about the descriptive approach which now prevails in departments of religion.

In contrast to the professional schools, it is said, the faculty of arts and sciences considers knowledge only with regard to its truth and falsity, not with regard to its practical effectiveness or its public acceptability. The descriptive program in departments of religion is criticized on this ground. For religion is not a "thing." It is a tissue of attitudes and judgments about reality. A faculty of arts and sciences cannot fulfill its responsibility here simply by *describing* what religious people believe and how they act. After performing this necessary first step, it must then go on and raise the truth-question. It must itself enter into the problems which activate religion and must judge those religious judgments. In adopting the descriptive approach, departments of religion have proved far more successful than the older philosophy of religion in coping with the immense volume of data. But they have paid a price. The approach lacks the seriousness which gave the philosophy of religion its commanding stature. It avoids coming to grips with the question of truth. Or, rather, with the limited aim of securing a true account of a particular religion, it ignores the more obvious fact that

The Ambiguous Position of Christian Theology

each religion is itself an account of reality which must be considered on the merits of its own truthfulness. Specialists in these departments sometimes offer the ludicrous spectacle of being more interested in what other specialists think about a religion than in what that religion itself actually thinks.

The call for Christian theology to be established as a corrective in this situation does not represent any conviction about the truthfulness of Christianity. It is simply suggested that Christian theology would be the most effective enterprise for getting the truth-question off the ground again, for reminding everyone that all religions are preoccupied at their very centers with the question of truth and falsity and that no faculty of arts and sciences can afford to forget this fact for one moment.

What are we to say about these three reasons for including Christian theology within a department of religion? They certainly involve no religious conversion to Christianity on the part of faculty members. Of more significance, they do not grow out of any self-conscious ideology about the meaning of scholarship in relation to life. The only fully stated ideology one ever hears in the faculty of arts and sciences is the familiar theme of critical reason, rational autonomy, and "sound scholarship." The interest in Christian theology, however, betrays a new and not well-articulated reservation about that ideology. When it comes to the religious dimension of human life, is the old ideal of autonomous reason a proper model for successful inquiry? Or does this involve a pose of such detached objectivity and a commitment to such narrowly rational satisfactions that it proves unrealistic and fruitless in this area?

On the matter of the place of theology, the overwhelming impression in the faculty of arts and sciences, then, is one of confusion—not the confusion of two perspectives in conflict, but the confusion of a habitual self-understanding in the process of erosion. The place where that confusion is manifested most fully is the department of religion. Is religion to be drawn into the domain of rational clarity and transmuted into terms that are satisfying to reason? Departments continue to maintain programs in the philosophy of religion. Is religion to be described in all its phenomenal complexity, without pressure for hasty judgments about truth or generalizations? Departments provide a large battery of descriptive courses. Or is the religious posture to be allowed to maintain its kind of truth-seeking, subordinating the rational demands of reason to the life-giving claims of some divine power? There are departments which offer work in Christian theology. Given this incredible troika, it is a wise departmental chairman who avoids policy discussions.

That religious theologians are being given professorships indicates how deeply this confusion extends beyond the department of religion to the whole faculty of arts and sciences. It almost seems as if, in its commitment to deal with religion, this faculty finds that it has a tiger by the tail—a tiger which has broken free from the cage of rational philosophy and has overcome the tranquilizing of phenomenal description. Some faculties, of course, are kindly appointing Christian theologians to hold on to that tail!

9

The Crisis of Faith

The following is a transcription of a lecture given in 1973 or 1974, preserved as part of the Thesis Theological Cassettes series. To my knowledge it is the only surviving voice recording of McGill. According to the introduction on the cassette tape, McGill delivered these remarks "at an ecumenical school of Christian studies sponsored by a number of churches in the Tallahassee, Florida area." "Why do more and more people find Jesus unimportant, or irrelevant, or unbelievable?" McGill asks. With his characteristic technique of inversion, McGill shows that among middle class Americans, only the person who finds it difficult to believe in Jesus is actually encountering Jesus.

Let me make a distinction between two ways in which we might think of the crisis of faith. This phrase may refer to the fact that many people today cannot find anything to believe in, anything on which to stake their lives, anything because of which they can feel confident about the meaning of their own existence, about the purpose, or the goal, or the value of their lives, and their country's life. They look out upon the world and find nothing to trust, nothing to believe, nothing to value. They have only themselves, and alas, they know better than others how impotent, how flimsy and boring and inadequate they are. Such people find themselves in a crisis of faith.

The Uncertain Center

Now the phrase "crisis of faith" also has another meaning. Here it refers to the difficulty which many Christians have to believe in Jesus Christ and the new life or the new vision that he brings. Here we are dealing not with the crisis of faith in general, but the crisis of Christian faith. Why do more and more people find Jesus unimportant, or irrelevant, or unbelievable? Why do so many who go to church wonder if Jesus has much to do with their lives? Why do many who preach from the pulpits and lead congregations carry the painful suspicion that the one who they serve and through whom they worship, Jesus of Nazareth, may really have very little bearing on the real needs and anxieties and terrors of our life today? It is this crisis of Christian faith which will concern me now.

If you are at all familiar with the sort of discussions about Christian faith in our day, you will probably have come across one very popular way of approaching this topic. This way looks at the manner in which the church talks about Jesus and the kind of beliefs that the church has about Jesus and decides that this way of talking and that these beliefs make Jesus too old-fashioned. As usually presented in the churches, so this argument goes, Jesus is simply out of date. For instance, when we read about Jesus in the New Testament, we find that he is reported to have done many miracles. However, most of us today have never encountered a supernatural miracle ourselves, nor can we easily imagine anyone performing them. That is to say, miracles seem to have been the way earlier societies responded to events which we in our society approach scientifically. When our children are sick, we do not look for a miracle; we look for a well-trained physician. Therefore the portrait of Jesus in the New Testament as a miracle worker makes him seem remote and old-fashioned.

Or consider another example. The New Testament, and many Christian churches, have spoken of Jesus as the incarnation of God, the enfleshment of God. Jesus is God come down into our human situation. Now this belief was natural and inevitable in a past age when people saw the world full of transcendent realities taking on physical form—angels appearing as wise old men giving us good advice, or devils appearing as sensually arousing men and women pandering to our lust. In this context, God also would deal with us by becoming a person. But today in our society, people do not interpret the world in that way. Today therefore, the idea that Jesus is God in the form of a human person seems rather queer, rather puzzling. According to this view then, the crisis of Christian faith for people today

The Crisis of Faith

arises because Jesus is presented in these old-fashioned ways—in ways that have not kept up with the changes in our culture and in our society.

Now, I personally do not accept this viewpoint, for it seems to believe that the crisis of faith is due to the way in which Jesus is presented to us. In short, it is simply a problem of packaging. Jesus is hard to believe in, and hard to relate to, because he is packaged in old-fashioned ways. If we could put him in a new, up-to-date package, then we could believe him. Now I consider this kind of argument both naïve and shallow. The crisis of faith is deep and serious, but it does not arise because the church fails to make Jesus relevant, because it fails to put Jesus in modern, up-to-date ideas, because it fails to make Jesus important to our daily lives.

The crisis of faith arises because our daily lives are completely at odds with Jesus. He is not irrelevant to us; we, in our social and personal values, are irrelevant to him. The person who finds it hard to believe in Jesus is exactly the person who is beginning to know Jesus. Jesus is not a prop for American middle class values, or a helpful guide for American middle class conscience, or a consolation for American middle class anxieties. The crisis of faith is a valid, a healthy, and an inescapable discovery—not that Jesus is at odds with us, and ought to be changed, but that we are really and truly at odds with him. And whoever does not find Jesus a threat, or a disturbance, or a bafflement, anyone who finds in Jesus a confirmation of up-to-date values and a reassurance of social ethics, is, it seems to me, running away from the real Jesus, and is simply believing in a Jesus that that person has fashioned in his or her own image.

But why is this so? Why is our daily life fundamentally at odds with the teaching and the life and the love of Jesus? What I would like to do this evening is to examine one important, one very fundamental aspect of our daily lives, which Jesus consistently condemned and repudiated, not only in his teaching, but in his own existence. It is a way by which, I hope, you will be able to sense why a perceptive person, upon confronting the church's talk about Jesus, should feel a crisis of faith. The important, valued aspect which I have in mind in our daily lives is what I call the strategy of possessions. What highlights this problem is a very clear theme in the New Testament, a clear theme in Jesus' life and his teachings. It is the theme of receiving and giving.

For many of us, we think more of Jesus as teaching us how to give. But if you look at the New Testament, you will find that Jesus is much more concerned with teaching us to receive. Jesus lives as someone who constantly receives, who has no embarrassment about receiving, and he calls upon all people to do the same. It is not the case that we are supposed to receive once and from then on after that live off what has been given to us. The theme that seems to come through in the New Testament is that we constantly receive from beyond ourselves. We receive from God ultimately and from the world immediately. And we receive anew every morning. We receive all things anew—the air, our food, our friends, the world. And that is why, it seems to me, for Jesus, and for the New Testament, gratitude is always a fundamental feeling.

It is not gratitude for what we once upon a time received, and now own. It's gratitude because we are constantly receiving. And part of the theme of the New Testament is to teach people to receive, to acknowledge their receiving, and to be joyful of their receiving. And the name in the New Testament for this positive attitude toward daily receiving is gratitude. And gratitude appears everywhere in the existence of Jesus and the life of those around Jesus. Only those who are free to be needy are free to be grateful. And one can only be grateful to the extent that one is willing to receive and willing to turn from beyond himself or herself to another.

In Jesus' life and teaching, there's also the other theme of giving. And here, Jesus makes it disturbingly clear that the giving which he exemplifies is a giving which involves giving away what we need. Now this is very threatening to all of us. It's not our extra time, not our surplus blood, not our unbudgeted money—Jesus has no concern for that kind of giving. He never tolerates it, and he just rejects it. The rich man who gives from his surplus is ignored compared to the poor woman who gives of what she needs. Jesus in his own life exemplifies a giving that does not fear, because of giving, to enter into neediness—the giving away to another of what we need so that after we have helped someone else, we must ourselves call out for help and existence. But again, this kind of giving is only possible for a people who are not frightened of being needy. And if in your heart you have the least fear of need, then you can only give to people of what is surplus, and to that extent your giving will have nothing to do with Jesus.

Now with these rather startling and very clear themes in the New Testament in mind, let us look at our own lives—the life that I have, that perhaps you have, and that certainly our whole American society teaches us to have. One of the outstanding facts of our way of life is fear of need—is the dedication to possessions. And for that reason, society in the United States stands in profound tension with the life and the teachings of Jesus.

The Crisis of Faith

In the United States wealth is not just a fact. It is a state of mind. It is a central and taproot value. At point after point in our daily lives, we show how convinced we are that we have solved the problems of human existence by the technique of having—by encouraging individual freedom, by giving talent-oriented education, by seeking out the natural resources in every continent, by exploiting those resources with the full productive power of technology, and by training people not to accept their deficiencies but to secure a variety of riches for every need. The American way of life has been marked by extraordinary confidence. Therefore, we should not really speak here of a technique of having, but of a gospel of having. Gospel means good news. And for much of America, wealth is the good news—that which will save us and redeem us from all evil. The wealth of money, the wealth of scientific knowledge, the wealth of social diversity, the wealth of individual opportunity, the wealth of military power, the wealth of international prestige, the wealth of God's unreserved goodness to us: America the beautiful toward which all history moves.

Now let me ask this. Suppose that Jesus Christ does represent the truth. Suppose it is the case that neediness is not just an unpleasant accident that happens to befall some people because the world is evil, but is the essential and fundamental human condition. Suppose that each of us is authentically himself or herself only so far as we are willing to be needy, willing to identify ourselves with need and not possessions at our very center. Then the gospel of wealth and the search for possessions cause a person to dissociate himself from his own neediness. He's embarrassed about his neediness. He puts on nice clothes and hides his neediness. This means that he loses touch with his real self and with his own true humanity. For through the technique of having, a person is only aware of himself as dealing with and managing life by his possessions. But if a person is essentially needy and if his humanity consists in taking on his own neediness and becoming one with his neediness, then he cannot be a person at all by acquiring possessions. He can only become alienated from his true self, and become a non-person.

Possessions, and especially intellectual and religious possessions, never drive us into ourselves for a shocking reassessment of ourselves. They never require us to come to terms with and take on our essential poverty. They only cut us off from ourselves. Therefore, so far as the educational system of the United States works to give people knowledge, it only works to cut them off from that central ignorance about their own existence which is their true condition every day of their lives. And churches that try to persuade people to have faith, or to have love, are really no better.

As I see it then, the crisis of faith in our society arises because most Americans believe in possessions. They are mentally terrified of being needy. They live by their possessions. In times of trouble they cling to their possessions for help, and they educate their children to seek possessions. They come to church in the natural hope that Jesus will help them with their possessions. They think that he represents a God who is good because this god has given them their possessions. They think that he calls for a love that wants all people to have possessions.

But this is not Jesus and it is impossible to make Jesus fit into this rich man's world. Jesus does not direct us to that god for the possessions which he gives us. He directs us anew each day to turn to God and to our neighbors in neediness and in gratitude that our neediness is met ever anew. Jesus does not tell people to measure their happiness by how well they possess, but how readily they receive and how readily they give—that is, on how readily they are able to be needy. Our hope, I think, therefore must be that the crisis of faith in our churches will grow worse and that Jesus' warning against our possessions may be heard more clearly

10

Structures of Inhumanity

This essay, published in 1975 in a collection titled Disguises of the Demonic, *took shape as McGill's contribution to the 1973 Lowell Lectures at Boston University School of Theology. McGill, and also Radu Florescu, John Karefa-Smart, and Ann Ulanov, were each invited to offer "mature efforts to meet the challenges of demonism on a serious level." Further developing a theme from* Suffering: A Test of Theological Method, *McGill here provides a phenomenological account of "the demonic" alongside a genealogy of belief in the demonic. He christens a "new demonism" that is replacing the humanism we no longer trust. Thus the Christian who reads the New Testament discovers she is now living in a world strangely congruent with the biblical language of demonic principalities and powers.*

I

At the present moment witchcraft and Satanism are enjoying a mild popularity in the United States. It seems to me that these are simply faddish archaisms, and as such they will not concern me here. What I do want to consider is the demonic as a quality in the world of our contemporary experience. For this purpose I will use the term "demonic" in a very precise way, to refer to any transhuman powerfulness that is experienced as negating human life and human values. We should note the two elements in this definition.

The Uncertain Center

On the one hand, I shall use the term "demonic" to designate what is encountered as a transhuman powerfulness. The essence of the demonic is power over the human situation, power to change, to control, to have disposal over the existence of people. But the demonic is not just any kind of powerfulness. It refers to such powerfulness as seems to come from *beyond all human agency*. We are familiar enough with the force that one person can wield over another person, that one group of people can bring to bear on another. We know only too well the degradation, the oppression, the exploitation, and the cruelty to which people have subjected one another in every age of human history, and not least in our own day. So far as power seems to emanate from a recognizably human agent, we are not involved with what I am calling the demonic. Demonic powerfulness is experienced as surpassing the whole horizon of human activity. It releases a destruction, or it opens up a magnitude, or it cuts through to a depth, or it involves a finality that no individual or corporate human agency could possibly attain.

In the traditional representations of the demonic in the West, we find that it is shown as operating in either of two ways. Sometimes it crushes and violates with overwhelming force, and, as such, may be associated with events of disease or insanity, famine or flood. In this mode the demonic is represented as a giant or a dragon, full of brutally destructive violence. At other times the demonic is experienced as securing its mastery over human beings, not by crude force, but by subtle insinuation, by playing on the weaknesses and perverse wishes of the human mind and thus seducing people to give themselves over into its power. In this mode the demonic is represented as a wily serpent taking on the appearance of a lovely woman or handsome man, manipulating and enslaving the human ego by means of enticing forms. In either mode, however, as terrifying or as seductive, the demonic signifies a powerfulness from beyond the human arena that ruthlessly dominates the lives of people.

Powerfulness, then, is one of its features. Its other feature is destruction of human life and human values. That is, the demonic, as I am using the term, belongs to a dual way of experiencing the world. It designates an agency that executes its powerfulness in an inhuman or antihuman way, in an evil way.

This awareness of duality developed in the West out of the Christian frame of reference, and is not found in many other traditions. In ancient China, for instance, transhuman powerfulness was identified especially with the power of wind and of water, and was commonly represented by the dragon. This powerfulness had no special association with destructive or antihuman activity. It could shatter, but it could also nourish and bless human life. It did not function at all within a duality-structured experience. Similarly in the mythology of Greece the *daemon* was an inferior divinity, sometimes an individual person's protective guardian and at other times the source of ill fortune.

By contrast, the Christian perspective has always been characterized by duality. For it trains people to see Jesus Christ in a theandric way, as the God-man in whom God's will and power are actualized for humanity. Approached in this manner, Jesus Christ stands forth in extreme opposition to destructive and antihuman powerfulness. In him God does not dazzle or overwhelm or intimidate, does not compel or degrade or exploit. In him God's powerfulness appears as serving and nourishing rather than as dominating. There is a striking saying to this effect in the Gospel of Luke. The disciples began arguing about which of them would be the greatest and Jesus said to them: "In the world kings lord it over their subjects, and those in authority are called their country's 'Benefactors.' It shall not be so with you. On the contrary, the highest among you must conduct himself like the youngest, the chief of you like a servant. For who is greater—the one who sits at the table or the servant who waits on him? Surely the one who sits at the table. Yet here I am among you like a servant" (22:25).

The contrast here between two kinds of powerfulness—one that dominates and the other that serves and nourishes—characterizes the whole Christian perspective. This duality came to structure the experience of many peoples in the West, who therefore developed a sense that a certain kind of powerfulness always exercised itself in an evil and destructive way, in opposition to the will and way of God. To this the word "demonic" came to refer.

Yet not all evil is demonic, not all represents the action of transhuman forces. Alongside of demonic evil stands human moral evil, the evil that is understandable within human terms—the wrong decision, the selfish goal, the hardhearted response. The demonic designates the destruction of human life and values that cannot be attributed to the moral self-conscious decisions of human beings. It is a term required by those occasions when people find themselves victimized by transhuman energies and structures.

Such is the meaning of "demonic" as I will use the term. I have stressed the experiential element, because I have no interest here in the demonic as a postulate for self-conscious explaining. It is certainly the case that many peoples have appealed to Satan or to devils in order to provide an explanatory cause for diseases or insanity. With this I have no concern. As I look at contemporary experience, it is not the demonic as a deliberately formulated explanation, but the demonic as a quality of destructive powerfulness encountered in the world that I wish to investigate.

II

It is an obvious law of nature that life feeds on life. All organisms need nourishment and have to derive it from other organisms. From this perspective, diseases in the human body are perfectly natural phenomena. They involve certain organisms supporting themselves within the body in such a way that the balance of one or another biochemical operation is upset and the bodily functions are impaired. Normally the body maintains life by its own natural vigor and adaptability. The presence of disease marks a debility in the body. The body fails to have enough vigor to nourish these other organisms while sustaining its own life, or enough adaptability to control and limit their presence. If we think of the organic realm as a network of mutual nourishment, then disease is a perfectly natural event, in essence no more abnormal than any ordinary meal which we enjoy.

It is an extraordinary thing that most people in the United States today do not look upon disease as a natural phenomenon—that is, as an instance of an operation that belongs naturally and universally to all life. On the contrary, as people imagine a disease, they tend to experience it as terrifyingly *abnormal*. In fact, in all popular accounts of disease *abnormality* is always the dominant theme: disease represents, not a life-affirming process, but something life-negating, something disordered, destructive and anti-natural. If workers in the medical professions do not always share this viewpoint, they nevertheless depend on it and encourage it in their quest for government funding and social power.

I wish to call attention particularly to three features of the prevailing sense of disease. First of all, disease is commonly thought of as an event of destructive power. There appears in the body some kind of harmful energy, some organic dynamism whose essential mark is to upset and destroy our life-processes. We commonly think of a disease taking over some part of our body, as if it had an energy of its own and by that energy could master one of our organs or tissues, negating the life that is in them. We often think of diseases as capable of spreading, or being characterized by a kind of drive to extend their destructive possession of our bodies.

What we are dealing with here is an experience patterned by duality. Contrary to all the testimony of science, disease tends to be pictured as a kind of anti-natural, anti-life energy. That is, cancer is taken as the paradigm of what disease really is, a spreading, devouring, life-destroying form of vital energy.

The opposition between the scientific understanding of disease and this folk view is a matter of some importance. The scientific interpretation is not concerned with how a sickness may be experienced by a patient, but only with its symptoms, etiology, and explanatory categories. Therefore it is exactly what the scientific approach disregards that the popular view takes as its central datum: the characteristics of a disease for the patient who actually endures it. And from that perspective diseases do seem to drain away our energies, to impose an ordeal of pain, and to make us feel as if we were being ravaged by some destructive energy. In other words, while the duality notion, which opposes disease-energy to life-energy, makes little sense from the perspective of biological explanation, it does articulate a crucial element in the actual experience of sickness that the scientific view must in principle disregard.

Destructive powerfulness is one feature in the contemporary folk view of disease. There is a second feature for which scientific studies have been chiefly responsible. This is the notion that disease comes into the body from outside. "Germs" or "bacteria" or "viruses" become the vehicles which carry this destructive energy into the human system. The whole idea of "infection," in fact, reinforces the view that a disease is somehow an outside energy that invades some part of the body and works dynamically to gain control of it.

For the popular viewpoint this coming-from-beyond-the-body does not express simply a matter of physical place. It carries the meaning of that which is alien, of that which belongs to a very different and incompatible biological framework. Disease does not come into the body from "outside" in just a spatial sense, but also in the sense of coming from *beyond*, from another realm and order, from outside that whole fabric of nourishment and life-support systems in which the body is favorably embedded. In other words, in this sense of "outside" there reappears that duality notion which sets the evil energy of disease in fundamental opposition to the good energy of life.

What emerges from this analysis is the way in which the popular notion of disease fulfills the characteristics of what I am calling the demonic. Illness is a matter of some quite alien powerfulness penetrating into our body and there exercising its energies with purely destructive effects.

There is, finally, a third feature of the contemporary situation which confirms this analysis in a curious way. Here I have in mind the striking but prevalent feeling of vulnerability before disease. Today it is not common for people to rely on the natural power of their bodies to preserve them against disease. They act as if their health were in a fragile and impotent state and unable to endure the least infection—that is, as if the demonic powerfulness of disease surpassed any defensive energy that their own bodies could naturally bring into play.

What people do, then, is to prop up the uncertain ability of their bodies with artificial supports, with vitamins, pills, drugs, and inoculations. They do this all the time, even when they are supposed to be healthy. When a sickness does appear, they do not dare to let it run its course while they depend on the body's own resources to overcome it. They seem convinced that the body has no adequate resources. Medicines or injections or surgical operations are necessary. So transhumanly powerful are diseases believed to be that we can "fight and overcome them," as the physicians like to say, only if we put into our bodies some equally transhuman counteractant. In our day there is something definitely obscure and occult about medicines. The fact that we are now quite prepared for them to produce dangerous side effects shows how conditioned we have become to the demonic character of the entire situation. In my view the fact that people show extraordinary pessimism about their own human resources in the face of sickness represents the most important sign that in this area they feel themselves subject to a demonic kind of powerfulness.

The patterns of experience which we find associated with disease are also in evidence in many other areas of contemporary life. Consider the way in which people have come to picture the character of war. There was a day when war was accepted as a normal instrument of national policy. It was conducted by men and controlled by men. It called forth the profoundly human virtues of courage and honor, and it was pursued for the sake of genuinely human values. In view of the overwhelming power of present-day military weapons such an attitude seems incredibly remote.

Structures of Inhumanity

Modern weapons produce such massive and thoroughgoing destruction that their use cannot in any way be justified in terms of the advancement of human goals or the enrichment of human life. They are too dreadful to be agents of proper human activity at all. It is therefore widely believed that anyone who would deliberately undertake massive war must in some way be insane. That he must have lost his human ways and fallen under the spell of the same destructive forces that he releases. War appears as the intrusion of some kind of transhuman and antihuman monstrosity into the human scene.

As something transhuman, it obviously cannot be dealt with by means of humane and rational measures. The impulse to war on the part of any nation is not really something that can be gathered into reasoned discussion. Just as in the case of disease, the only reliable counteractant to the threat of war is the use of instruments of equally massive power. Demonic powerfulness can be contained and turned aside only by equally monstrous power. Therefore, there can only be one reliable defense against war and that is the power of war itself.

It is rather eerie to watch how in the United States this demonic sense of war underlies the rhetoric of the government's military policy. Since no sane nation would undertake war today, a sane country such as ours (so the reasoning goes) could only maintain its military establishment for the purpose of dealing with the barbaric insanity *of other peoples*. Hence in the United States—one of the most militaristic of all states and the supplier of militarism to countries all over the world—the military is called the *Defense* Department. This is not just pious and deceptive hypocrisy, a gloss behind which all kinds of aggression can be conducted. This name echoes the conviction that war is a transhuman demonism, which decent people only undertake in order to protect themselves against war itself, in order to provide shelter for the weak and fragile humanity of ordinary life.

At the other end of the scale from international conflict, consider how people tend to picture the hazards which may threaten their own individual lives. If the gas furnace explodes, if the car goes out of control, if the airplane crashes, these incidents are called "accidents." This term is much less innocent than it sounds, for it not only carries the meaning that such disasters do not result from any deliberate human doing (that is, they stand outside the range of human purpose) but the term also means that they belong to no order of purpose at any level of reality. Neither the intentions of some God nor the movements of some positive destiny are available to set these incidents in a context which gives them meaning. At every level they are accidents, irrational and absurd and detached from all significant purpose. That is to say, in these disasters people find themselves in touch with a totally disordered powerfulness that stands wholly outside the human order and in that sense is essentially demonic.

Even within the strictly human sphere incidents can trigger the contemporary sense of the demonic in diminished ways. Think of the ordeal of trying to cope with a bureaucratic process on which you depend in some way, but which suddenly fails to deal with you. For instance, perhaps the welfare check does not arrive. You go through the usual procedures in such a case, but they do not bring results. So you stand in line. You talk to an official. You are sent somewhere else. You sit in a crowded office. You finally talk to another official. You are told to come back the next day. You come back and are sent somewhere else. The devastating thing in such experiences is the discovery of the implacable nonhumanity within what appears to be a perfectly human process. The reason for this is obvious. In a bureaucratic system each worker is responsible only for executing a step *within the process,* and his or her attention is allowed to focus only on the process as such. As for the people that the process is supposed to serve and benefit, responsibility for them lies with no individual worker but only with the process itself as a whole. In fact, that is how the process is defined and justified in the first place: people are not served by responsible individuals but by the whole organization. If, in your case, the system fails, there is no one to take responsibility for you. Each functionary whom you visit will check only on that segment of the process that rests with him. However, because the total process is so complicated and the errors within it can be so subtle, so arbitrary, and so unexpected—a confusion of names here, a slight mistake on the IBM card there, a faulty instruction somewhere else—it is extremely unlikely that you will ever find the right worker to ferret out the source of your difficulty.

In this kind of experience there is no outburst of obvious violence. One meets, instead, an exasperating absence of any rational or humane address to one's problem. The process empties one of any human reality, and the feeling of being crushed by a subtly inhuman and inflexible powerfulness can be severely intense. For people who are prone to experience the demonic in the world, the same sense of helpless victimization will easily come into play here.

Structures of Inhumanity

This survey of various areas of contemporary experience—disease, war, accidents, and bureaucracy—indicates the presence of a belief in a demonic powerfulness, a powerfulness too great to be controlled by human resources and essentially destructive of human life and values. At present this belief is in a very primitive stage. It has little self-consciousness. It has no mythology associated with it. Cancer and war are the effects of a powerfulness that has no name and no form. Rationally we have to argue that for every activity there must be an agent. Yet in these experiences no effort is made to identify the agents which are working through this destructiveness. Life is felt to be threatened simply by strange forces that lurk beyond the circle of familiar existence, waiting to break in.

To associate this awareness with the old beliefs in a personal devil and in demons that have horns, tail, and cloven feet after the fashion of the satyrs in Roman mythology, is a profound confusion. For the people of earlier times were able to identify destructive powers with the grotesque ferocity of animal vitality. Satan was a monstrous dragon. St. Anthony was attacked in the desert by various wild and savage beasts that howled and brayed and sniffled, and attacked him with their horns and paws and teeth. A higher level of sophistication in the ancient world found its supreme experience of destructive powerfulness in terms of a deliberately malicious will. Then Satan was represented as a fallen angel.

For people today neither of these forms has much relevance. In the machine world of modern mass society, there is simply no encounter with powerful animal vitality, and the human will even of the most powerful leaders seems lost in the movement of vast forces beyond calculation. What is a mere dragon compared to the hydrogen bomb? How can a malicious will be taken with final seriousness in the face of the nightmare of overpopulation, where the most precious of all values—life itself—turns out to be, by its very vigor, a source of terribly inhuman destruction? For our age the demonic does not—and cannot—wear these old forms, but appears rather as a formless and impersonal dynamism that seizes upon us unexpectedly in the cancer cell, in the auto accident, in the cascade of napalm bombs, or more subtly in the impersonality of bureaucratic systems on which we depend.

With this sense of the demonic now in our midst, I find it no accident that newspapers and television programs offer us pictures of the mangled human body with almost liturgical regularity. To view a child in Vietnam burned with napalm or a bloodied corpse twisted inside a wrecked automobile is not to see simply a remote and unlikely oddity. For many people these pictures help bring forth their own sense of the essential human condition, of mankind caught under the impact of a destructive powerfulness which is totally antihuman and before which the human form is pathetically impotent.

We should note one final aspect of this contemporary awareness of the demonic. It profoundly colors people's attitude toward final things, toward the largest and farthest horizons to which their minds can reach. In theology this is called "eschatology." What appears often today is the belief that if we extend our gaze beyond the human sphere we will find no meaning, no value, and no life. We will find only the kingdom of the demonic. In other words death as the violation and extermination of life becomes the sign of all final realities. The human venture is a mere bubble in the chaos of blank and pointless power, and eschatology is a thoroughly negative arena. A passage in Thomas Wolfe's novel, *You Can't Go Home Again*, expresses this sense of ultimate things.

> There came to him here an image of man's whole life upon the earth. It seemed to him that all man's life was like a tiny spurt of flame that blazed out briefly in an illimitable and terrifying darkness, and that all man's grandeur, tragic dignity, his heroic glory came from the brevity and smallness of his flame. He knew his life was little and would be extinguished, and that only darkness was immense and everlasting. And he knew that he would die with defiance on his lips, and that the shout of his denial would ring with the last pulsing of his heart into the maw of the all-engulfing night (epigraph).

Many people today have such a sense of the demonic as ruling reality that in honesty they can only look upon ultimate things with this kind of despair.

III

Let me now turn to the question of how people cope with this sense of the demonic, how they actually gather this into their lives and let it shape their behavior. We must recognize that the entire cultural tradition which we carry at present stands totally opposed to this experience. It denies the existence of anything like the demonic. Let me briefly characterize this tradition, so that we can appreciate how threatening everyone finds the new awareness of the demonic.

Structures of Inhumanity

The tradition which has long prevailed can be summed up in one principle: the world is favorable toward our humanity. Are we human beings creatures of reason? Then the world is rational. It is so constituted that its nature is in harmony with our subjective reasoning, and it actually makes itself available for our reasoning. If something is not rational, if in its essence and action it cannot be understood and cannot be enveloped in some context that explains it, then that thing does not exist, and anyone who believes that it does exist is simply the victim of superstition.

Are we human beings creatures of creative projects? Is making and fabricating the nerve of our humanity? Then the world is indeed receptive of our projects. It waits to be worked upon with our creative energies and to be gathered into our human projects. As the young Karl Marx insisted, nature is there to be humanized by our labor. The raw materials of the earth, the soil, the plants, the animals, the planets and stars exist for no other purpose than to serve the creative projects of the human race. But what about the other viewpoint? What about, say, the American Indians who refused to use the land because they believed that it belonged to the plants and the buffalo? By such an attitude they showed themselves to be subhuman and unworthy of life, or at least unworthy of being related to the land. But perhaps natural resources are limited. Perhaps the world prohibits the pursuit of some projects that are valuable and important for human life. Not at all. That is irresponsible defeatism. Nature is made for our human projects, and if one area of nature were to fail us, then human ingenuity will learn how to tap the resources in another area.

Are we human beings creatures of love? Is our highest humanity found in the service and affection and honor with which we can relate to one another? If that is so, then according to this tradition human beings are made to love and to be loved by one another. Is there an innate destructiveness and aggression in human beings, so that in taking on the attitude of love and in thus putting ourselves at the disposal of other people, we only pose an irresistible temptation to them to manipulate and exploit us? What a dreadful notion. Is there an innate fear within human beings, so that the closeness and oppressive claims of love always seem an intolerable threat? Preposterous. Since to be human is to love, then human nature as we actually find it must be made for loving and for being loved.

Such are three versions of the tradition that has long pervaded our culture. It is the tradition of humanism, which believes that the world around us favors and supports our human aspirations.

The Uncertain Center

The experience of the demonic, as of an essentially and implacably antihuman powerfulness in the world, stands in opposition to this humanism. The tension between these two perspectives deeply affects the various ways by which people today cope with their experience of the demonic. Let me distinguish three such ways.

1. The first way might be called the state of dissociation. Most people simply live with these two viewpoints coexisting in their minds. There is the educated part of their consciousness, pervaded by humanistic triumphalism and full of bold confidence about the world and its support of all our human values. But alongside this they also carry an awareness of cosmic evil, of enormities in the world before which all human values are as nothing. Many people vacillate between these two states of mind, perpetually torn by this contradiction.

2. A second way might be called the attitude of submission. A few individuals refuse to exist in this schizoid condition. For them the humanistic tradition seems like a lie, a deception that has left them completely unprepared for the terrible demonic forces which they find threatening their lives. In anger they want to sweep away the lie of humanism. They want truth, and truth requires them to become the agents of, and the witnesses to, the demonic powerfulness which they find ruling existence.

In his novel *Dr. Faustus,* Thomas Mann gives an extraordinary portrayal of this nihilistic passion. For Leverkühn, the hero, life to its very core is absurd and chaotic. Therefore he is in violent reaction against the prevailing humanistic belief that the world has order and meaning. Beethoven, he is convinced, was mistaken. Therefore he undertakes his plan to compose a piece of music that would take back and "unwrite" Beethoven's Ninth Symphony, that greatest of all musical celebrations to the harmony between man and the world. This monument to prevailing humanism is false, he believes, and must be revoked.

3. There is also a third attitude, which I would call the way of courage. Here, people move beyond humanism altogether. They do not hold onto it in a schizoid fashion, nor do they violently attack it and shatter it in submission to destructiveness. Instead, they start by accepting the demonic character of reality fully and, living primarily out of courage, work to resist the demonic and to maintain a sphere of human value for as long and as well as possible, without any illusions about—or even reliance on—the world. As one who articulates this attitude we think immediately of Albert Camus. Yet it is instructive to realize that the old Norse culture shaped all human life in terms of the necessity of courage. Judging by the Icelandic Eddas, these people had a pessimistic eschatology. While the present order of existence was, they believed, maintained by the gods, a great dragon lay encircling the earth. According to the prophecies, the day would come when that dragon would rise, would destroy the gods, and would engulf the earth in sea. All things godly and human would then vanish away. The prophecies of the ultimate power of the demonic also disclosed that this final convulsion would begin on the day when the great wolf, now prowling near the gods, would attack and kill the god Odin. Therefore, in order to preserve the order of the world for as long as possible, it became necessary to restrain this wolf. The dwarves were called in to make an unbreakable leash, and this they did, fashioning a thin silk-like band from the roots of a mountain, the breath of a fish, and the sound of a snowflake. But the wolf, ever suspicious, would not let this leash be tied around his neck unless one of the gods placed his hand within the wolf's mouth as a pledge. The god Thor offered his hand. The leash was tied around the wolf's neck, and it held him so that he could not break it. That is to say, the world order was preserved for a while longer. But this was secured only at a cost, for the god Thor lost his hand.

These Norse stories reflect a way of life which has no trace of triumphal humanism and which seeks to maintain human values in a world where the demonic is ultimate, where the last word can only be defeat and disaster. In that situation one lives by courage and by sacrifice. One knows that the order and stability of daily life are fragile and temporary, and that in the struggle to preserve them against destruction, sacrifices such as Thor's are an accepted necessity. By contrast with this Norse attitude, it is sobering to recognize how little courage is fostered in the upbringing of children in this country. Since people here are not trained in courage, we can appreciate how helpless and terrified they must feel when they become aware of the world as a demonic realm.

IV

Let me consider this contemporary experience of the demonic from a Christian point of view—that is, in the light of the biblical witness to Jesus Christ. In recent centuries Christianity has been strongly affected by the prevailing humanism, with the result that Christian theology has tended to ignore the demonic completely and to take *human* wrongdoing as the primary form of evil. It has claimed that the world is good, nature is good, and that the only blot upon God's magnificent creation is the sinful human will. It therefore has looked to Jesus to purify the human spirit of its wrong choices and perverse desires, confident that once the mind and heart of humanity were cleansed of sin, all would be perfect.

It is rather a shock to discover how far such a viewpoint is from the entire biblical perspective. For the Bible does not have a primarily moral understanding of the human situation, as if people's lives were decisively shaped by the daily choices which they make. Instead it understands the present human condition as a drastic loss of all genuine moral life. It views sin religiously and not morally. We can appreciate this if we distinguish two aspects in the biblical account of sin. On the one hand, sin constitutes a repudiation of the Lordship of God by humanity. In their existence people refuse to acknowledge God as the basis of their life, as the origin of their good and as the goal of their striving. But this repudiation of God does not mean that they take God's place and themselves rule the universe in his stead. The world is full of agencies and dynamisms that completely transcend the reach of human reason and the control of human power. According to the Bible, what is actually entailed in the repudiation of God is a submission to these other enormities. They are not gods, only beings created by God, but they impose themselves upon people as if they were gods, as if by their power they were the lords and disposers of human life. In the Bible these are occasionally identified with Satan and the demonic. They may be enormities of nature or of society. They may be uncanny occult impulses from beneath the earth or heavenly forces that rule the stars. In any case sin is that repudiation of God which subjects humanity to the control of these forces. And their rule is necessarily destructive. This is because of the biblical conviction that life depends essentially and universally upon a right relationship to God. When humanity cuts itself off from that relationship, it becomes subject to forces and enormities that can only bring destruction.

Thus we can understand why, from this biblical perspective, sin is not merely a series of wrong moral choices, but is a religious event. When people turn from God and move into the control of destructive enormities, they fall into a dreadful servitude. They lose touch with the only ground for their effective freedom. Their existence is enveloped by intimidating powers and by the destructive finality of death. Every moment of life thus becomes entrammeled with the threat of the demonic. Free choice—the authentic choice which grows out of the absence of fear and out of assurance

Structures of Inhumanity

in the ground of one's own honor and vitality—such free choice completely vanishes from the human scene. No moral freedom is possible because, having lost touch with God, the entire structure of human existence finds itself victimized by demonic enormities.

From this biblical perspective, then, it is simply not the case that the human mind and will are the only sources of evil. In the event of sin, humanity discovers a disorder in the cosmos far beyond its own horizons. It discovers magnitudes in the world that also seem to repudiate the Lordship of God. It discovers the demonic. In the Old Testament the overwhelming imagery for the demonic world, where life is cut off from God, is impotence, sickness, and sterility. Everything is in a state of dissolution. There is much violence, but because the agents of this violence are not rooted in God—that is, in authentic reality—their apparent strength is a delusion which can exist only for a time. The demonic forces that assert their own glory instead of the glory of their creator—and the sinful person who, because he is cut off from God, must order his life to these demonisms—may flourish and display their vigor for a time. But their strength does not spring from reality itself; instead, it is artificial and abnormal. The Old Testament therefore often identifies this demonic and sinful activity with magic and whoredom. For these designate actions that seem to be full of strength, but in fact are hollow and barren and essentially vain. The Old Testament actualizes the cosmic dimensions of sin by developing a whole geography for the world into which sin moves people. Sinners find themselves inhabiting a desertland, full of fiery heat and severe winds, where their thirst for refreshment is always unappeased. They have no road and no goal, and therefore soon become lost. For how can there be any real direction of their existence in a land the essence of which is confusion and disorder and trackless waste? This geography is a metaphor for the world of dreadful sterility and victimization in which people who have become cut off from God eventually find themselves.

The New Testament is not so picturesque in its language, but is equally emphatic. As revealed in Jesus Christ, God stands forth as one who has nothing to do with absolute power, with a power that can produce square circles, or smash kingdoms, or dissolve a universe. As encountered in Jesus Christ, God's power is that which nourishes and orders, which heals and rectifies. In Jesus Christ, God does not assert himself over against the world at the expense of the world, but affirms and reconciles the world to himself at the expense of his son. By comparison with Jesus Christ, most of the powers which people worship as God are intimidating and degrading, are in fact demonic. For the New Testament, as for the Old Testament, sin means bondage to destructive powers—above all to the decimating power of death. Even sin itself, according to Paul, is a power which masters and controls us and over which we have no control. "I am a slave of sin," Paul writes. "It is no longer I who performs these actions but sin that lodges in me" (Rom 7:14,17).

We thus find in the Bible two important themes. First of all, the condition of sin is really a condition of terrible victimization. There is no trace of humanism there, no belief that the world is favorable to present human values. On the contrary, people find themselves subjected to inhuman powers from which they cannot escape—powers in nature, powers in society, powers beyond the horizon of present experience. Second, this whole realm of inhuman power and victimization is cut off from God and therefore, in spite of its appearance, is really impotent and sterile. It is a dissolving and debilitating powerfulness. It has no rootage in authentic and effective vitality. In this realm a destructive power may thrive for a time, but then it disintegrates; it becomes a specious pretense. Throughout Christianity, Jesus Christ is seen as exposing the pretense of all demonic powerfulness, including the apparent powerfulness of death, and as doing this because of the way his existence was rooted in the power of God.

I have been speaking in a rather abstract way. Let me point out the crucial role of the demonic in the work of Christian service. Humanism has taught us to expect that service to our needy neighbors, to suffering children, to enslaved prisoners, is bound to be successful. Suffering and despair will be eliminated by human caring. This is obviously false: the children continue to cry, the prisoners continue to grow weaker, the poor continue to die. At this point the humanist flees. Taught to relate to suffering for the sake of removing it, he is shattered when he discovers that his service can no longer help. When the patient's death is inevitable, the physician disappears and leaves him to the nurse. When the reform of welfare fails, the social activist turns away to another and more manageable project. In other words, humanism is not prepared for the demonic which confronts us in our suffering neighbors. Our age is full of the wreckage of humanistic projects that wilted before the demonic.

Anyone who has ever dealt seriously with human destitution, who has served in hospitals or in prisons or in impoverished villages, knows perfectly well that the most severe problem is not the hardness of human

Structures of Inhumanity

hearts but the intransigent and obscure forces that manipulate circumstances, intimidate leaders, and frustrate service. To go out and serve the needy without being able to face up to the terrible powerfulness of the demonic is folly.

In this connection I would remind you that two very different approaches to the demonic are presented in the Gospel accounts about Jesus. There is one way of exorcism, where demonic powerfulness is driven away and people are liberated from bondage to disease or insanity. But this way is not given great attention. It does not carry any crucial value. In fact the New Testament makes absolutely clear that no one is going to exorcise the demonic out of this world. On the contrary, demonic inhumanity will increase. The present power and pervasiveness of demonic forces in the world is too extensive to imagine that they will be removed by exorcism.

The other approach is the way of the cross. Jesus calls upon people to take up his cross—that is, in some sense to enter into the arena of demonic suffering rather than to flee from it. This is the approach that receives primary emphasis in the New Testament. But what is this approach? What does it mean to take up Jesus' cross and to let oneself be attacked by inhuman dreadfulness?

The fundamental issue at stake here is the mode in which we discover the Lordship of God as an actual fact. It is easy to mouth the creed about God being almighty, but in the face of the powers that seem to rule this world such a belief remains unreal. Where and how do we actually discover for ourselves, as the truth of our own existence and of the existence which we share with our fellow humans, that the Father of our Lord Jesus Christ is indeed the only authentic power in all reality?

The only place we really discover this is where we are being attacked by demonic forces. It is one thing for God to rule by removing these dreadful forces from the scene, in the manner of exorcism. It is another thing for him to vindicate his rule precisely when, and as, these ferocities are in full activity. But what does it mean to say that he "vindicates" his rule at the very moment that the demonic displays its power in full force? What does this vindication amount to? As I see it, this is one of the meanings of Jesus' death. For on the cross Jesus did not submit to the demonic—that is, did not act as if it, and not his Father, were the master of his destiny. He refused to fear, to defend himself, to imagine that this dreadful destructivity had any final power over him. In short, while on the cross Jesus was sustained in his human way, in his confidence in his Father and in his compassion and care for those around him. God vindicated his rule in Jesus, not by removing the powers of destruction and death from him, but by maintaining in Jesus that supremely human condition of trust and love even while these powers worked their fullest.

To be sure, our lives may suddenly be delivered from suffering by an unexpected drug, by a political revolution, by a change of circumstance. Such blessings are not to be disdained. But the deepest discovery of God as the Lord of life will occur decisively only as he proves able to sustain in us the humane strengths of trust and love while the demonic is at work. That is how I would understand the significance of Jesus' command to take up his cross.

Yet an odd thing happens very often. We may be most unnerved, most severely tested, most profoundly assaulted by the enormity of the demonic when victimization is imposed, not on us, but on others whom we cherish. That is when we are most tempted to despair of God, to let anger or panic possess us, and then to turn away from those very persons who suffer in order to preserve our own sanity. To companion another who is dying without withdrawal, to continue working with the poor after all resources have failed, to maintain one's trusting and one's loving when the forces of demonic inhumanity seem to be in full control—as I see it, that is what it means to take up Jesus' cross. This is what it means to be with and to serve the neighbor, not with triumphal humanism, but in his name. This dimension of service, however, only begins when one is willing to endure the impact of demonic enormities.

Let me conclude with reference again to the Norse legends. Because defeat and disaster stood at the last horizon, courage was the indispensable condition for every moment of life. The Christian perspective does not share that ultimate pessimism. It does, however, see the taking on of demonic suffering as an essential part of the love of neighbor and of the knowledge of the power of God. Courage, then, becomes a primary form of Christian faith. The contemporary experience of the demonic points us to this need for extraordinary courage.

11

Suffered Under Pontius Pilate

This "theological brief" is an example of the "case method" approach to theological education. It appeared in Christian Theology: A Case Method Approach, *a book structured around nine fictional cases, each of which is paired with a clause of the Apostle's Creed that is thought to connect to the case in some way. McGill was invited to respond to a case titled "Ben Phillips Dies—Funeral Today;" the "suffered under Pontius Pilate" clause of the Apostle's Creed is supposed to guide McGill's reflections. According to the fictional case, we are to imagine Ben Phillips, an African American who pastored Midville's Fourth Baptist Church in the early sixties and from that position rallied Midville's African American population to the civil rights movement. His leadership had been noted by Martin Luther King, Jr., who would later call on Ben to assist him in other cities. Ned Turnball, a white pastor from across town, became acquainted with Ben Phillips through the Midville Ministerial Alliance. Ned observed Ben's gradual decline as the "victories" of the civil rights movement failed to accomplish racial equality in Midville. Ned last saw Ben, who had stopped attending the meetings of the Midville Ministerial Association, drunk and voluble at a party. Shortly thereafter, Ben was killed in an automobile accident, putting an end to his days of bitter disappointment. Ned had been asked on the spot at Ben's funeral in the Fourth Baptist Church to "make some remarks." Had he known he would be so asked, he would have skipped the funeral. What was he to say? McGill's response to the fictional case is notably all that he published on the issue of race.*

The Uncertain Center

The case of Ben Phillips confronts us with the destruction of life—with death—in three different modalities. There is, first, the systematic, centuries-old oppression of black people, against which Ben Phillips directed his life. This is the living death of starvation, sickness, destitution, and degradation. Second, Ben's own vitality has withered away before the realization that all his efforts have failed, that the killing power of the white establishment remains undiminished. Ben knew that, when measured by its results, his life of dedicated service "wasn't worth the trouble." He sank into despairing alcoholism. Third and finally, the automobile accident ended Ben's life completely.

Ned Turnbull's task—and ours—is to bring Ben's life and death into the light of the existence of Jesus Christ.

As Ned discovers, this is not an easy task. For Jesus throws upon our existence a strange and difficult light and overturns our basic assumptions. Nowhere is this more striking than with regard to the significance which the New Testament and many of the Christian traditions attach to Jesus' death. The New Testament is quite emphatic that Jesus' death is not an accident, is not a disaster, and is not primarily the work of evildoers. On the contrary Jesus' death is viewed as life affirming, as the essential and indispensable event in the way in which God through Jesus brings renewed life to humanity. So crucial is it, in fact, that all those who would attain that life are called upon to "take up his cross," that is, to pass through the kind of dying which occurred in Jesus. That death is God's way of bringing us to life. Until we die that death we will not find the fullness of life.

How can Jesus' death—how can any death—be life-giving?

In his various letters Paul develops one view. Paul finds that Jesus lived his life constantly and comprehensively in the posture of *thanksgiving*. He did so, according to Paul, because in all ways and at all times he knew that he was receiving his reality from God. God was the ongoing basis and origin of himself, of all humanity, and of the whole cosmos. In other words, in all his life-acts Jesus did not live on the basis of an identity which he possessed. His identity, his being, was constantly coming to him from God's loving activity. There was no moment and no regard when, to himself or to others, he was simply the reality which he possessed, simply his own self. Always and in all ways he was receiving himself from God. At his center was not his own act of having and holding on to his own reality. At his center was God's activity of giving him himself, God's parenting activity.

Jesus' center, then, was no longer in himself but in God. To know Jesus properly is to know him as he knew himself, namely, as constantly constituted from beyond himself. According to Paul, through Jesus we are to understand ourselves and one another in exactly the same terms. "What have you that you did not receive?" Paul asks. Nothing, not even ourselves. "If, then, you really received it as a gift, why do you take the credit to yourself" (1 Cor 4:7)?

From this vantage point Paul easily identifies that fundamental perversity which marks human life. This perversity is rooted in the tendency of people to live, not on the basis of the activity of God, but on the basis of their own capacity to have and to hold on to some bit of reality as their own. Whether or not they think that God once gave them their reality makes no difference. They now relate to themselves by the technique of having, and not by constantly receiving themselves, as a gift from God. They find their identities within the circle of their own beings, in terms of that reality which they imagine belongs to them. For Paul this being by virtue of possession is the essential form of human evil, and all the monstrosities of oppression and envy and anxiety in human life arise from this.

In terms of the new kind of identity which is actualized in and through Jesus, death loses its sting, its ultimate power. For death does indeed empty us of everything within the circle of our being. It kills our bodies and our souls. It ends our possessed being. However, if our reality is continually constituted, not by what we can hold on to as our own, but by something wholly outside of us, that is, by God's activity, then the death which dispossesses us of all the reality which we have does not reach to God and does not destroy the root and basis of our being. As Paul writes, whether we live or whether we die, we belong to God through Jesus Christ (Rom 14:8).

People have learned to live perversely, to live out of themselves, on the basis of their own reality. They do not take on this new christic kind of identity with magical suddenness. Their growth in this new identity is a slow and convulsive process. In this process death plays a crucial and climactic role. For as long as people do possess some bit of reality, it is never brought out how much they may be clinging to that bit for their being. Only in relation to their dying, only in relation to the end of all their possessed being are they liberated from every secret impulse to have and are perfected in their life of pervasive thanksgiving. The whole of the Christian life, so far as it seeks to uproot evil, is a willing movement toward death, a practice of dying—of dying with Jesus—a learning to live in thankful receptivity and not by the technique of having. Only at death are we purified of every strategy of being by possessiveness.

Jesus' resurrection represents the entrance of human existence into a domain liberated from all having, where therefore God's bestowing activity is manifest in all things and through all things. Resurrection does not mean that the dead get back what they lost through death; resurrection is not the reinstitution of having and the reappearance of perversity. Only the dead in their destitution, only the totally and thoroughly dead who have willed their dispossession and loss of all having—only they are in the condition to enjoy the fullness of the life of constant receiving. The resurrected are the dead as such, those who have nothing of their own possessing but who are alive wholly from God.

The life of Ben Phillips is marked by the oppression of many blacks—an ongoing death—and by Ben's own despair and death. These take on an unexpected significance in the light of Jesus.

The oppression of black people by the establishment is not some momentary forgetfulness or some accidental failure of love. That oppression brings to light the essential character of the technique of having by which the middle class lives. Middle class existence is now tyrannized by that technique. Because the people of the middle class live by holding on to themselves, holding on to their possessions, holding on to their achievements and holding on to their kind, they cannot be receptive at the center of their beings and therefore they are cut off from love. The energy of possessing carries inescapably within itself the anxieties of greed, envy, domination, and exploitation. The degradation and destitution imposed on the blacks is an outer expression of the savagery which middle class people have executed upon themselves by their enslavement to possessiveness. Therefore, to resist middle class oppression, as Ben Phillips has done, is to oppose, not just some bad people, but that style of life which carries all the energy of evil, and which Jesus, with his life of radical receiving and radical giving, sought to eradicate.

As we consider Ben's working life, we must remember that the horizons of Jesus are not the horizons of middle class affluence. Because of its seeming power and arrogance and secure self-contentment, the establishment can hypnotize us. Entranced by its illusions, we come to believe that any blacks who are cut off from affluence are cut off from life. This is not so in the horizons of Jesus. For there the technique of having is itself exposed as the essential lie, the fundamental sickness, the nightmare of destructive

Suffered Under Pontius Pilate

conflict and isolation. In the struggle against oppression the aim is not to enable everyone to possess and to share in that sickness, but to enable human existence to receive more freely and to give more freely.

Even while the struggle against oppression goes on and at times seems hopeless and futile, those oppressed are not separated from the Lord of life. Though cut off from having, they are not cut off from God. And within the horizons of Jesus, their dispossession is not without its meaning, its capacity to humanize, its role in the reordering of human existence to the love of God. Precisely because, through the positive significance of death in the perspective of Jesus, a newness of life may grow in the most terrible darkness, because even there people learn to become more fully receptive and more freely self-expending, that growth gives them the power to continue the struggle against oppression.

Where were the voices reaffirming this vision to Ben Phillips in his despair? Where were the neighbors to sustain him in his process of undoing and dispossession, in the movement of his life into the shadow of the cross? Who reminded him that the Christian way is not simply a series of outer victories over the social environment but also an inner breaking and emptying where new dimensions of fellowship and humanity come into play? Who will tell us that his self-offering, his risking of himself against principalities and powers wholly beyond his power, and his being broken on the rack of their crushing immovability—who will tell us that in all this Ben advanced along the way of Jesus that many of us never reach?

Obviously Ned Turnbull will not tell us these things. Ned apparently knows nothing of the positive meaning of death, has never realized that death belongs part and parcel to the overcoming of evil and the perfecting of love. Because the practice of dying has not been at the heart of his ministry, because for him death has never been an essential element in the transformation of human existence, when he comes to the funeral he obviously will have nothing to say. Ned is probably a middle class minister, that is, a minister of the technique of having. In that perspective, Ben's death—like Jesus' death—can never be anything more than a senseless accident.

The approach of the Christian community of Christian individuals and of Christian ministers like Ned Turnbull to the positive meaning of death does not occur at funerals. It occurs in the midst of life. It grows out of the realization that what we cling to as "life" is itself the most subtle death, is itself that which separates us from God who is our authentic life. The realization that our enemy is not out there in the waiting cancer or the speeding automobile, but is the very life to which we cling with passionate intensity—this realization comes to us from the existence of Jesus. By our daily encounter with Jesus' kind of life, the secret possessiveness that lies at the heart of our will for life may become apparent to us. Only then may we also realize that the death which ends our possessive existence, the death which empties us of everything we possess as our own may itself be liberating and not simply destructive.

In all sermons and in all counseling, the Christian minister seeks to foster these realizations in the community to which he or she carries responsibility. It is a difficult calling in middle class America, because there the belief in one's *own* being and one's *own* name and one's *own* possessed reality is so deeply entrenched. To discover the arrogance, the exploitive inhumanity, and the godlessness of that possessiveness is what the Christian venture is all about.

12

The Religious Aspects of Medicine

This essay, which appeared in print only shortly before McGill died in September 1980, was written in 1977 during McGill's participation in a study group on "Religious Studies and Medicine." The group was one of five study groups sponsored by the Institute on Human Values in Medicine and funded by the National Endowment for the Humanities. McGill's group was made up of ten people—five scholars of religion and five medical practitioners. They met for five two-day meetings between December 1976 and December 1977. McGill presented this essay at the second group meeting. The essay is vintage McGill, employing a phenomenology of religion to show that contemporary medicine, far from having to determine whether or not it should consider religious categories, is already our culture's primary way of invoking and placating the forces we believe are most determinative of our lives. Medicine, that is, is one of the places to which the holy has migrated in this supposedly secular age. A transcript of a unique conversation between McGill and his colleagues follows this essay, along with McGill's personal statement of interest in the work of the study group.

This essay seeks to identify in a clear way the religious aspect of the health professions. This is not a simple task for two reasons. On the one hand, it is not easy to identify the "religious" aspect of human living in an accurate and comprehensive way. This means that all such identifications have a provisional character and require constant modification. The reasons for this difficulty and this need for correction will be discussed shortly. On the other hand, the religious aspect does not seem to operate alongside other components of human life; it penetrates them and is in turn penetrated by them. Therefore certain qualities of religion make it difficult not only to identify its intrinsic character but also to secure a clear and fixed understanding of its bearing on other dimensions of life. As we shall see, both kinds of difficulty arise from the same source.

A Phenomenological Approach to the Study of Religion

In the twentieth century the present state of reflection confronts us with two very different kinds of inquiry. Religion is an activity of the human consciousness, but the activities of the human consciousness are today being interpreted from two very different points of view, that is, with regard to two opposed features of consciousness. In the short compass available here I can elaborate only one of these viewpoints.

We all recognize that, as one of its most obvious features, consciousness is aware of things. To be conscious is always and everywhere to be conscious "of." Through sight I am conscious of the tree outside my window. In boredom I am conscious of a quality of static emptiness. When I have an idea, a concept—for example, when I realize by my own insight, and not just by taking someone else's word for it, that power tends to erode and corrupt human faithfulness—I am aware of a general condition, an "essence" or "universal" that works in and under the surface appearance of many things. When I have daydreams (or "nightdreams") I am conscious of a fantasy world. The procedures for examining consciousness in this way are called *phenomenology. Phenomenon* means "that which appears."

In one direction phenomenology seeks to describe accurately whatever stands before a particular activity of consciousness, a particular awareness. This procedure rejects the belief that humans are truly aware only of sensible objects, with all other content of consciousness being "made up" by the mind; or the belief that humans are only aware of general ideas and become conscious of everything else only through general ideas. Because the only access of our consciousness to reality is consciousness, we must oppose all efforts to give favor to one or another of its aspects. In sensory perception, are we aware of sensible qualities, or of an isolated object, or of an object in the foreground surrounded by a field which we make into a background? And whichever one of these possibilities is indeed the case, what particular bearing does it have on various other dimensions of our awareness as persons with living consciousness? How does absence stand before awareness—the absence of a loved one, the absence of something hoped for, the absence of an amputated hand? What stands before consciousness has so many modalities of presence, engages awareness in so many ways and at so many levels, that its description is an extremely delicate enterprise.

In the other direction phenomenology seeks to attend to the full range of activities or awarenesses in the consciousness. The isolation of thinking from other subjective activities becomes a danger, because in practice, thinking is always accompanied by feelings and wishes, even when it is struggling against feelings and wishes. In this direction phenomenology has discovered how powerfully certain pervasive *moods* can affect the flavor and character of a person's awareness—the mood of boredom, or anxiety, or hope.

This general approach has developed extensively a phenomenology of religion, that is, a study of the religious attitudes in various peoples. The reason for its continuing attention to the religious aspect of experience becomes clear when we realize that through their religions people are related, not to any particular object, like God, or to any particular activity, like magic or prayer, but to whatever is most decisive for them, whatever carries the maximum of significance. Because a religion involves consciousness with whatever it regards as final or maximal or ultimate, the phenomenologist finds consciousness peculiarly revealed in and through its religious activities.

We no sooner introduce the matter of religion, however, than we must consider the other view of consciousness which marks our age. Phenomenology looks upon consciousness as the mode whereby anything becomes *present* for human engagement. That is, consciousness itself is taken as the arena where things become evident.

Why might it not be the case, however, especially in terms of anything which a person sees as having the greatest significance or impact, that his or her consciousness works to deceive? Is consciousness really a realm of straightforward evidence, where a person lets appear whatever steps before him or her? Or is consciousness one of the devices that is used to effect deception? This latter possibility now goes under the name of *false consciousness* because it wrestles seriously with the possibility that the hunger of consciousness for awareness may be secretly motivated by the desire that something else be kept hidden from consciousness. I am intensely aware of A precisely in order to keep my attention from B. In this view consciousness functions to deceive, because it appears so directly open to anything and everything. Its apparent openness, on which phenomenology counts, makes it a very effective instrument for deceiving. Of course, in no area of life do people feel a stronger wish to deceive than in the meaning or arena which they take to be most important.

Against the views of consciousness by phenomenology, then, stand the views of *criticism*. I use this term for any attitude that is critical of the apparent openness of consciousness and which sees behind consciousness an activity that causes this apparent openness to be deceiving and false. For us in the West today, Immanuel Kant, Karl Marx, Friedrich Nietzsche, and Sigmund Freud have developed very different "criticisms" which portray consciousness as hiding and therefore as deceptive.

Yet every child quickly discovers this truth, especially in reference to whatever he or she finds most significant, that is, as we might say, with reference to his or her religion. The awareness of how subtly we humans may and do deceive each other and ourselves has always been a central concern in every major religious tradition. The more we treasure something, the more we become defensive against threats to it, and the more our act of treasuring may itself be our flight from some unpleasant truth which we would rather not face.

In the remarks that follow I shall be working primarily out of the approach of phenomenology, but the question of criticism and the deceptiveness of consciousness cannot be ignored, at least in connection with religion.

Types and Dimensions of Religion in Everyday Life

One of the elements in religion is its preoccupation with the powers believed to be decisive for the exalting or the threatening of human existence. At a certain stage these powers are called gods, but the gods appear very late and not universally in the history of religion. What seems to be decisive is a concern for various kinds of powerfulness, and especially for such powerfulness as is believed to magnify or injure human life.

Because every human existence proceeds within and depends on an environment, the working of these powers involves the environment in one way or another. It may be the power of fertility in the local soil, or it may be power on which the entire cosmos is founded. In any case the existential concern for those kinds of powerfulness which may exalt or threaten human life always finds an environment included within its horizon.

Religion might be characterized as a twofold project. On the one hand, it is the activity of identifying, understanding, and teaching others the character of these decisive powers. On the other hand, it is the enterprise of orienting human existence appropriately in relation to these powers, promoting a proper way of participating in those that are favorable and maintaining a proper avoidance of those that are harmful.

It is important to understand how the word *power* is being used here. The term does not designate some hypothetical cause of an observed effect. The question at hand is not what causes religion, as if religion were some property of a thing called consciousness. The habit of treating consciousness as if it were a thing in the world on which various causalities fall is a misunderstanding. Far from being a thing effected by causes, consciousness is a mode of existing to which things step forth into manifestness. Causes are among the conditions that become manifest to consciousness.

The question, therefore, cannot be what causes the effect of religion in consciousness, but rather what is present to consciousness. Religion is not an effect but a particular set of activities in relation to something made present. The term *power* names what appears in correlation with the human attitudes labeled religious.

The term *power* is particularly useful in connection with the concern for the exaltation or enervation of life. Life here does not indicate a process or a potency observed from the outside, for which various stable conditions may be assigned as necessary. Life here denotes life as concretely lived. And in concrete experience life as actually lived has the qualitative character of rise and fall. The necessary biophysical conditions on which life depends do not constitute life in its actual ebb and flow. They are a necessary but by no means sufficient condition for life. The social and psychic components of our existence are decisively involved in the experience of the life force in us which qualitatively rises and falls. When *life* is used to designate the quality of lived experience as more or less, when it becomes a way of characterizing the quality of existence for a human being with consciousness, then life in that human is correlated with the presence before consciousness of an enhancing or threatening power. This powerfulness operates in the world; it thereby becomes manifest before a person's consciousness; and finally it also activates that person's consciousness and life force from the inside, so to speak.

Among the many typical experiences which help to constitute a religion, that of being healed is one of the most important. Healing occurs in a religious perspective because a favorable, a health-giving powerfulness comes into play in relation to a condition where it had been absent, where some kind of destructive or debilitating powerfulness had held sway. This movement of human existence from sickness to health represents an instance of what in some religions has come to be called *salvation*. When people fall ill, whoever cures them is their savior. Healing pertains to that operation of power which produces salvation. Just as in the Christian New Testament Jesus' power to heal was taken as a decisive mark of his status as savior, so every successful physician is regarded as someone who bestows salvation.

Religions in this sense vary enormously from one age to another, from one generation to another, from one society to another, from one class and occupation to another. The efforts to classify and order this variety have been extensive.

For our purposes we might distinguish between two general types of religions. There are the so-called high religions which construe all decisive power for human existence as centered in a transcendent reality or domain. Jewish and Christian monotheism would be two instances. Such religions not only believe that there is one God and no other, but they also strive to orient life properly to the power of that God. Since no other powerfulness is considered decisive, since no other can bless or curse life in any deep and final way, therefore the effort to align human existence to any other powers is believed to be misguided.

Over against these high religions stands a second type. This type does not involve any radically transcendent domain. Rather, decisive powerfulness is read directly out of the impact of immediate experience. Different situations and different places are discovered to entail very different kinds of powerfulness (different "gods") and to require very different orientations.

The Religious Attitudes Toward Medicine

These two types of religion are both current in the United States today, and they set the practice of medicine in very different religious perspectives.

The Religious Aspects of Medicine

For the high religions like Judaism and Christianity medicine does not have a decisive religious significance. The bodily life which medicine tries to protect and sustain within the horizons of everyday life is not believed to be life in its decisive form. Authentic life depends exclusively on and is constituted exclusively by a proper relation to God. All other human conditions commonly called "life"—married life, the economic life, social life, bodily life—are themselves secondary. So far as any of these is properly related to God, then indeed it too becomes a form of genuine life. However, so far as any of these arenas of human existence is not properly related to God, then no matter how exalting it is in terms of immediate experience, in truth it is not alive in any authentic sense.

For the high religions medicine is a subordinate and secondary enterprise, not directly concerned with what is decisive for human beings, but attentive to some of the provisional, nonfundamental forms of life. In this perspective, since the corporeal world is not the decisive source of powerfulness for exalting or destroying human existence, the medical effort to assist humanity in its vital engagement with the corporeal world is also not decisive.

Let us now turn to the other type of religion—the religions of immediacy. Here medicine takes on a much more decisive religious significance. Characterizing this religious attitude is a delicate matter.

At the center of one conspicuous attitude toward medicine in the United States today stands the conviction that death in the biological sense represents some kind of profoundly catastrophic mutilation of proper human existence. No human should die. Death is thoroughly and unqualifiedly antihuman. It is an outrage, a powerfulness which has an absolutely decisive bearing on human existence, but which, when possible, must be totally avoided.

In this perspective the practice of medicine represents an effort to protect life from the decisive power of death and from the injuries and illnesses which may lead to death. In other words, the proper orientation toward death is that of avoidance. As such, medicine is an important religious activity.

The practice of medicine in this perspective is properly controlled by an unqualified resistance to the antihuman powerfulness of disease and death. That is its religious function. This particular function is reflected in two features of contemporary medicine.

Because death is believed to be an extraordinary and final powerfulness in this perspective, the medical personnel who are commissioned to resist this power directly have their religious character reflected in almost every aspect of their work. The wearing of distinctive uniforms, the avoidance of personal interaction with patients, the stark decor of waiting room and hospital, the huge machines that maximize the sense of alien powerfulness, and the carrying on of all communications in a language quite unintelligible to and removed from ordinary experience—all these features become proper from a religious perspective, as reflections of the fact that medicine struggles against a decisive and ultimate powerfulness, and that engagement with this powerfulness necessarily must remove medicine from the everyday domain.

From the viewpoint of the patients, all this seems quite proper. Since death is seen as abnormal and extraordinary, then those who struggle directly against death should work outside the arena of normal experience and normal expectations. Therefore, because medical treatment cannot be discussed with patients in terms of their own experience, from their viewpoint it is essentially occult, like the death it opposes. That is, it involves a knowledge which the ordinary patient finds secret and incommunicable. On the same basis, all medical treatment seems to bring into play those operations of nature which lie beyond ordinary experience. But this, according to the *Oxford English Dictionary*, is the meaning of *magic*.

Physicians usually do not notice this aspect of their work. They believe that their activities are required by clinical experience and grounded on scientific rationality. They do not realize how much of their effective authority in relation to their patients is religious in character. This authority is derived from the absolutely ultimate powerfulness of death which medical practice seeks to resist, and this authority is properly actualized by the possession of what, from the patient's viewpoint, are occult (that is, transnormal) knowledge and magical (that is, transnormal) agencies.

In this perspective death is seen as essentially and comprehensively antihuman. For that reason the medical struggle against death and disease places its practitioners in the most extremely antihuman of horizons. And for reasons that have not yet been investigated, medicine has chosen to fight this antihuman power, not with the cultivation of the humane (courage, charity, compassion), but by the implementation of nonhuman agencies (drugs, scalpels, X rays). In this conflict between the nonhuman agencies which may protect people against death and the antihuman power of death, the persons being "treated" are often considered to be passive. In the term now in vogue they are *patients*, that is, they are passive recipients of activities from outside themselves, and not agents.

Naturally, when treated in this way by medicine, patients feel very inhuman. But this inhumanity can be seen as justified. For it is not medicine itself, but the disease and death against which it struggles that sets patients in a radically depersonalized and inhuman domain. It is disease and the prospect of death which create the unqualifiedly antihuman situation. Within that grim situation all medicine is fated to move.

Human Mortality

The whole attitude that I have just described, where religion is an orientation not toward the transcendent God, but toward whatever powers immediately seem to present themselves, and where death is believed to be the final powerfulness which affects a person—this attitude is held by many people in our time. This way of thinking about death, however, depends on not accepting another view which alters everything.

The prevailing attitude looks upon life as an intrinsic property of any person and therefore views death as happening to that person from outside. *Death*, therefore, is the name for that decisive powerfulness which is able to overcome the life that each of us properly is.

But suppose that death is not an alien outside threat that may strike us at any time. Suppose that dying is a native property of every human. A person does not die because something harmful obtrudes into his or her otherwise positive vitality, though this may happen. Dying is a feature, or a property, of everyone's own being. My death is a possibility that comes out of myself, not from an outside intrusion into me. When I die, there may at that time be the intrusion of a blow or a germ or a bullet into me, but that is not thought to be the significant feature of my dying. That is only secondary. Death comes essentially from my being, and, should a medical doctor help me to avoid something which might be a fatal intrusion into me, that would not change my basic relation to death. In other words, "mortality" is not seen as one of the circumstances that will befall a person. It is one of the features of a person's innermost being.

If one goes along this path, something further must be considered. When death is seen as that which strikes a person from the outside, it is primarily an event which occurs at some particular time and at some particular place. It can be photographed. But when death is seen as a property of every person's own being, it is not primarily an event in the circumstantial sense. The death which occurs at a particular time and place is not the aspect of death with which I primarily wrestle. That more essential aspect of death is a dimension of myself.

With this sense of human mortality, death ceases to be an alien powerfulness from which we try to protect ourselves and ceases to be that which elicits our religious intentions. As a dimension of ourselves, our dying, like the other aspects of ourselves, only pertains to our way of being related to some kind of powerfulness.

It is striking how broadly modern American medicine tries to avoid seeing mortality as an intrinsic property of every human being, and how emphatically it views death as something that only happens because of some circumstantial event that befalls us. That is, medicine vigorously maintains death as a crucial religious focus and itself as a provisional savior from that enormity.

McGill experienced a heart attack on the journey home from presenting "The Religious Aspects of Medicine." Notice of this event reached the study group at its third meeting some months later, provoking a conversation which is included in part below. One member of the group suggested that this conversation was the "clinical counterpart" to McGill's paper.

McGill: At the conclusion of our last meeting I had a heart attack, so I was out for eight weeks. It happened at the airport.

William Marine, Professor of Medicine, University of Colorado: You mean just after I left you? You still had about two hours before the plane was to leave.

McGill: It was about twenty minutes after you left me.

Marine: Would you tell us about it?

McGill: Well, I had shortness of breath and thought I had bronchitis. I was walking over to the gate and had almost gotten there when I had a terrific pain in my chest. I put my suitcase down and sat on it for about forty-five minutes. I'm not a physician—my imagination went like wildfire—but that's different from really knowing what was happening. A fellow came along and I asked him to check in my bag. I went very slowly to the plane, and I had no further pain. I got to the Boston airport and my son took me to the Peter Bent Brigham Hospital, and I was put in intensive care. And then an odd thing happened. After three weeks arrhythmia developed. It went on for four days with absolutely no clue about its cause, and then one evening, for reasons I don't understand, they failed to give me some obscure pill. That evening as they tested my heart the arrhythmia decreased. But nobody knew that they hadn't given me the pill, and the next morning the pill came back and the arrhythmia reappeared. Then it occurred to me that for the next three times I wouldn't take the pill. The arrhythmia began to disappear, and then I told my physician.

Sr. Alice O'Shaughnessy, C.S.J., practicing internist, Long Island, NY: You treated yourself, then? That's very castrating to the M.D.!

McGill: Well, my doctor is good. He isn't convinced that medicine is the only answer. He's open to more than one dimension of his patients' lives.

Donald Shriver Jr., Professor of Applied Christianity, Union Theological Seminary: Now that it is over, do you think that you learned something from it all?

McGill: I learned a lot about my relations with my children. Telling them what my death would mean and especially hearing their sense of what it would mean for them.

John Bryant, Director, Office of International Health: Have you slowed down any?

McGill: Yes, I guess so. I don't take on certain responsibilities.

Shriver: Did any new reflections on *religion* come to you while you were lying in intensive care?

McGill: I have always been absolutely convinced that my death was one of the most crucial elements in my destiny. Death is something that's mine. I never think of my death as something that befalls me because of cancer or a heart attack. My death is the climactic event of my own personal biography. So this illness did not introduce me to something that I felt was alien to me. In that sense it didn't alter my horizons. But it certainly did for my children.

Thomas McElhinney, Director of Programs, Institute on Human Values in Medicine: How old are your children?

McGill: Twenty-three, twenty-one, and sixteen. My wife's father died, so the children rather early in their lives had that experience of death. But it was nothing compared to this.

Shriver: Did you find yourself going over some of the issues that our group has raised in the midst of the experience? What about the paper you wrote for the last meeting?

McGill: You know, it's very striking that the intensive care world is staffed by the most reserved of all the health care professionals. Judgments are cautious, and the claims to knowledge are very relative. It was very strange.

Shriver: They make conservative statements on what the outcome will be?

McGill: They have a very strong sense of the limits of knowledge. "We think this, we see that, we don't know where the complications are going to arise, we don't know how they are going to affect you." The "art" of medicine becomes very striking. A man in the next bed was a young fellow of thirty-two or thirty-three. His family came in. Apparently his wife had almost no experience with hospitals. They had taken the young children almost religiously for medical checkups. For them there was a very vivid difference between the medical professional in a checkup and the medical professional in intensive care. The first time the wife came, I just knew that the whole "yearly checkup" mentality was there. She was waiting for the doctor to say what was wrong so that they could leave. I could see just how totally dysfunctional the yearly checkup was in terms of medical reality. The man's physician was wonderful. If the wife came in while he was tending her husband, he would always go out with her, and I could hear them talking out in the hall. He was really trying to help her understand the limits of medical knowledge. It was very, very impressive.

Bryant: It was very unusual. I'll say that. I'm impressed with the fact that you were impressed with that doctor. There is a certain humility on both sides—in you and in him. I think that's admirable.

McGill: It's not a verbalized humility. There is a lack of confidence in the way the physician steps. They just don't walk as confidently in intensive care.

Marine: It's the difference between *medical* intensive care and *surgical* intensive care.

Florence Schubert, Professor of Nursing, Luther College (to Marine): I'd be interested in your reflections as the doctor who left Arthur McGill at the airport twenty minutes before he had a heart attack.

Marine: In terms of my observation of him, I didn't notice anything unusual. He had a heavy suitcase.

The Religious Aspects of Medicine

Bryant: Did you feel that you had been left out when he first told us his story?

Marine: Yes, I guess I did.

O'Shaughnessy: If the attack had come earlier, you could have been included!

Marine: And he might have ended up in a hospital in Philadelphia instead of Boston.

Shriver: But you didn't want to be sick in Philadelphia, did you? It was far from home. It was a time for being home.

McGill: My most striking experience developed quite unexpectedly after I got home. It turned out that some of my portion of the hospital bill was quite heavy, so that we were under financial pressure. My wife came in to me and commented on this. I replied offhandedly, "Of course, I'm sick." She said, appropriately enough, "What does that have to do with the bill?" It suddenly struck me that, when you are sick, the *whole* of you is sick, including your contact with the details of reality and your patience to cope with those details.

Shriver: I keep wondering what you learned about the theme of your paper from this experience of suffering. What did you learn about how to be human in the midst of suffering?

McGill: Not to confer the responsibility for healing on to a machine or to doctors! I have to take that responsibility. I have to participate in the event, and I can't delegate my responsibility to anyone or anything else. The temptation is to do that, to relieve myself and everybody else from worrying about me by agreeing that "the drug will take care of everything." *If it is not personal and interpersonal, it is not human.*

Bryant: It's a fight against being helpless.

Marine: So you find yourself taking some personal responsibility for your own heart attack. By the same token, I want to apologize if there was anything we did to contribute to it.

McGill: Oh no, it was twenty years of hard work, the culmination of a lot of stuff.

Patrick Prest Jr., Counselor-Chaplain and Professor, Medical College of Virginia, Virginia Commonwealth University: I can't help noticing that there was a notable closeness in the feelings of people in this group when McGill shared this experience with us. It was as if we had been introduced to a common space.

Marine: It brought home to me some of the things in your paper from our previous meeting, Arthur. There you spoke of the religious dimensions of death, the manipulations of the powers of death by the physician-priest, and the like. Does all that seem to mean more to you now in light of your actual brush with death?

McGill: As I said, my sense of death was not altered. But I did feel more strongly the temptation to depersonalize death, to externalize it. It was as though I was saying to myself, "I'm not dying, that thing over there is killing me."

Cyril Moore, Professor of Biochemistry, School of Medicine, Morehouse College: What struck me was the timing—in such close proximity to your meeting with us. It reinforces the fear you have that you will become ill suddenly when you are by yourself. Illness tends to isolate you, to put you away from other people. This happened when you were with people but were really all by yourself.

Shriver: I have had that very thought while jogging in Riverside Park. Usually I leave my wallet home, and I wonder to myself: "If I were to collapse in Riverside Park, how long would it take for people to find out who I am?" Occasionally I jog with my wife, and that is a considerable comfort, because she has some idea of who I am!

O'Shaughnessy: It's the insecurity associated almost uniquely with heart disease. It seems to strike unpredictably. At least if you have cancer you know you have it, and you have some time to prepare to die.

Prest: I'm amazed, really, that you didn't share this experience with the group earlier.

McGill: I was going to share it with Bill Marine, but I thought I should get to the meeting first. The most unnerving thing this time was going by the spot at the airport where the heart attack struck me.

Bryant: So you can appreciate the problems of a traditional society which believes that the spirits cause these things, that the spirits abide in a tree or a rock where traumatic events happen! But it still interests me that you had to go *home*. We desperately want serious things to happen to us while we are with our families, not somewhere else.

O'Shaughnessy: It's not an uncommon story, even with doctors who know better. It's "indigestion" until they get home, or it's "indigestion" until they mention it to someone who says, "You'd better get home or get over to the hospital."

Moore: Can a doctor without faith *face* death?

O'Shaughnessy: Oh, surely. But I'm not sure how they handle it. Religion is at the heart of this, at least for me. Life *is* insecure. I do everything I can for my patients, but I have to acknowledge that I don't really have control over their lives, either. My lack of control over them extends to myself and to things generally.

Bryant: It's important that you add "at least for me." In all this I think we see a sensitization that occurs in professionals *as persons*, at a level deeper than their professionalism, at the level where all of us are "ordinary human beings." Not long ago I went through the death of my mother, and I understand death in a personal rather than an academic way as a result of that experience. But that raises a question of professional education. What if our ability to be a "competent" physician is enhanced by our personal experience and what it means to us? If such experience is important, how do you deal with it, prepare for it, interpret it in the context of *education* for the profession? I feel sure that you can't do it very well by lecturing students. Students have to absorb such understanding indirectly, from the attitudes and casual remarks of their mentors—like one of mine who asked me to "leave my technical equipment hanging on the door."

McGill: There's a version of that problem among students of theology. Medical students may have a problem getting close to their own and their patients' emotions about dying, but theology students are also likely to feel only remotely related to everything connected with dying. Very few of our students in religion and theology have ever been close to someone who was dying. It's the result of your medical success in delaying death to old age, and of our society that separates the residences of the generations.

Marine: In your paper you spoke of your feeling that the physician traditionally sees death as the great enemy. It sounds to me as if your physicians in that intensive care unit were not dealing with death from that perspective.

McGill: My physician would consider death the end of everything, but the physician of that patient beside me, in talking to his wife, was quite different. He insisted that death was really beyond any medical control. It was as if he were acknowledging that "the powers of life and death" belonged to some other power, not to us. I've never heard a physician say that out loud to a patient.

Shriver: One might say that no subject is more regularly a part of "professional" services than someone's death, but that before death all the professionals, like all human beings, literally come to grief. Doctors, lawyers, clergy, even businesspeople, all have something to do when a person dies, but they can do nothing about death itself. The priest says the "last word" over our bodies at our funeral services, but priests know that such words will be said over their bodies as well. Like medicine, religion is only indirectly relevant to death; but death is a notable incident in our negotiation with the "uncanny," the uncontrollable, in our lives.

At the conclusion of the study group, participants were asked to summarize their personal interest in the subject matter. Between the end of the group meetings and writing this statement, McGill had a renal transplant in early 1978. He would never fully recover from that procedure.

As a juvenile diabetic, I have been engaged with medical care for many years. However, my concern for the relation of religion and medicine only began when I came to see that religion is not a matter of being related to a peculiar kind of object, like God. It designates a quality in the attitudes and behavior of people toward all kinds of objects. It seems to be constituted by people's reaction to whatever they think has power over their lives.

Because I adopted this view I realized that religion is not so much an area over against medicine as something that pervades the doing and receiving of medicine. In less developed societies the person who brings healing is seen as channeling a religious powerfulness. This is also true today in the United States. As I found repeatedly in talking to patients and physicians, "going to the doctor" involves a quest by people for defenses against this powerfulness of sickness.

My recent renal transplant has reinforced this perspective. I know that I look upon my taking of a necessary pill not only as producing certain measurable effects, but as carrying with it a powerfulness rich in creative possibilities for my life and as keeping destructive powers away from me.

13

Human Suffering and the Passion of Christ

Published two years after McGill's death in a collection titled The Meaning of Human Suffering, *this essay was originally presented at "The First International, Ecumenical Congress on the Meaning of Human Suffering," at the University of Notre Dame in April 1979. The Congress was sponsored by "Stauros" (the Greek word for cross), an organization formed by the Passionist Religious Order "to promote research and study on the 'Gospel of Christ's Passion.'" McGill was one of ten invited presenters. McGill wrote and delivered this piece while trying to recover from a renal transplant. The analysis of "the meaning of suffering" that McGill had provided in* Suffering: A Test of Theological Method *remains firmly in place here, but new and surely autobiographical accents emerge: first, a relentless assault on white middle class affluence as the most significant barrier in the American experience to accessing the meaning of suffering, and second, a strong emphasis on personal presence as the primary form of love. One cannot help but notice McGill has set aside his earlier critiques of personalism.*

Let me begin with some preliminary remarks which will indicate certain directions that I will not follow.

First, there is something fundamentally misleading in any attempt to examine suffering in isolation. Suffering never occurs in and by itself, nor can we ever examine it properly as if it were an independent and self-contained experience.

Suffering always occurs in a *living context*. The agony is embedded in some project, some hope, some relationship. The physical distress of an injury occurs in connection with some striving on the part of the sufferer. The pain of betrayal belongs to the life of a relationship. Whenever we consider suffering in abstraction from its living context, we not only give it a false isolation, we also miss the way in which a suffering bears on the living situation.

Second, a distinction is sometimes made in discussions of suffering between what is called physical pain on the one hand, and mental or psychological agony on the other. "Physical pain" designates that which comes from the body, while "mental anguish" arises from decisions, attitudes, and experiences in the mind. These latter might include guilt, loneliness, separation, terror, etc.

I find this distinction not very helpful. It means to separate out the bodily suffering which befalls us from beyond the realm of our self-control and self-determination from that suffering to which our freedom contributes. I find, however, that this distinction disappears in real life. My mind will experience a bodily pain and draw it into its own frame of reference, finding it a reason for terror or despair, using it to avoid responsibility or win pity from others. There is never a moment when I endure physical pain by itself. Similarly, psychological afflictions generate and relate to various bodily illnesses. Suffering is a fabric that involves both the mind and the body, and efforts to isolate the one from the other constantly fail.

Third, I would also like to dissociate myself from relying very much on analytic reason to discover and verify some meaning connected with suffering. Today people expect that some intellectual expert will give them some teaching or some truth which will enable them to find meaning in suffering.

I consider this to be an illusion. It is only by passing in and through the actual experience of suffering that we have access to any meaning that it may entail. After doing this we may share our discoveries with one another. But abstract reason can give us only abstract meanings, and these unfortunately are too general to connect with the specificity of our suffering. Perhaps that is why the language of a novel or a poem can expose the meaning or meaninglessness of suffering much better than an intellectual discussion. However, such a discussion can challenge thinking which too easily ignores the difficulties of suffering.

Human Suffering and the Passion of Christ

Fourth and finally, I will not pursue the question of how to free our lives in this world from all suffering. For instance, let us suppose that God might so interfere in situations that all our suffering would be immediately removed. At the first pain of hunger, for example, a meal would miraculously appear on the table. Upon cutting ourselves with a knife accidentally, we would be instantly healed. Upon being defrauded of our savings by some criminal, new money immediately appears in our possession.

We can appreciate the problems which would arise in this "ideal" world. First, much of human creativity and striving are directed to the overcoming of some bit of suffering. Hunger has provoked us to develop hunting skills and agricultural techniques. Against disease we have fostered medicine. The moral patterns we adopt warn us against the sufferings which we may produce in the lives of others. In any deep human relationship we discover how essential it is that the other rebuke and correct us at certain points. A real relationship always involves the suffering experience of being judged. What is a love that does not judge? It does not love us. It simply humors us.

Behind these circumstantial problems of a world devoid of suffering there stands a much more fundamental issue. When we wish for a life that never frustrates our desires, that never complicates our health, that never claims our moral restraint or encumbers us with social difficulties, we are asking for a world that lets us have our own way, that lets us be entirely centered within ourselves. It is against such narcissism that suffering may have a very significant effect.

Further still, when people dream of a world without suffering, they often forget that their suffering arises, not only from circumstances in their environment, but also from their own nature. The capacity to suffer is a measure of *human sensitivity*. Therefore we may realize our dream of a world without affliction, not by the rearrangement of circumstances, but by the removal of sensitivity from human nature. It is along these lines that we may long to possess a solidness that is immune to affliction, that we become heartless and steel-clad. Yet the very sensitivity that is lacerated in our suffering is the very quality that marks us as human.

In my remarks, therefore, I will not be concerned to free this world from all suffering. I will rather be concerned with the occasions of intense suffering, which, far from provoking people to striving and creativity, overwhelm and shatter them. I think here of the grim sufferings that afflict helpless children, though also of the famine and oppression and disease that crush adults.

In considering our suffering in relation to the suffering of the Christ, I will be particularly concerned with that dreadful degree of suffering which seems to stay with us through the centuries and which so lacerates the sensitivity of our humanity that it brings forth our destruction.

The "Problem of Suffering" Today

The first thing which I wish to do is to get some bearing on the rather extraordinary status which "the problem of suffering" has acquired in our day. One can see this clearly if one reads the writings of earlier times. For instance, in the works of earlier theologians, like Athanasius or Augustine or Thomas or Luther or Ignatius, there is simply no mention of the "problem of suffering." Suffering seems to have been accepted as an immovable component of our present human life. No one developed it into a profound religious question.

That, however, is exactly what we do today. In contemporary Western literature no source of atheism is presented so insistently or so dramatically as the existence of suffering. Why is that?

We can begin our inquiry on this matter by observing how deeply we have been affected in our attitude toward suffering by two recent developments.

The first is the way in which technology has given us a control over our environment that was unknown to our predecessors. Much of that technological control we direct to the removal of the sources of suffering. Irrigation eliminates the dangers of drought. Advanced weapons defend us against our enemies. Drugs work against disease.

This pattern of activity, however, creates in us a pervasive expectation: since technology has been able to remove so many kinds of suffering from our lives, can we not look to it to dispel all forms of serious suffering? We find ourselves directing that expectation, not only toward the disasters with which nature afflicts us, but also toward the psychological and interhuman sources of our suffering. If we are afflicted by economic adversity, if we are in conflict with our neighbor, can we not remove these problems by developing a better social order or by taking a drug to forestall our hostility?

That is the first development which has affected us. In many cases, however, we must endure a suffering whose source technology is not able

Human Suffering and the Passion of Christ

to remove. In this eventuality we have recourse to a second help: the development of anesthetics and narcotics. By their effect on us we can dull the sensitivity in us which bears affliction.

We can readily see the bearing of these two developments upon our attitude toward suffering. While earlier ages looked upon suffering as one of the immutable givens in life, we no longer share that view. We look for the physician or the engineer or the political leader or the social conditioner to eliminate these conditions which impose our suffering. And insofar as that cannot be done, we will take an anesthetic or a narcotic to deaden our agony.

This expectation, this demand that suffering be removed, we not only direct to the agonies which we ourselves must endure directly. We direct this with equal insistence toward others, toward people who may suffer in our presence. We require that suffering also be removed from us. Therefore you will find no deformed beggars on the streets of our towns. The sick are sequestered in hospitals, and we can encounter their suffering only by "visiting" them. Moreover, such care is taken in providing these hospital buildings with an attractive landscaping that when we drive by them no hint is given to us of the dreadful agonies that are being endured within those walls.

The demand to flee from suffering also has many subtle effects in the lives of middle class Americans. For instance, in relating to one another they seem to feel prevented from obtruding their real afflictions upon the attention of each other. The lawn is kept mowed, the clothes are kept pressed, the smiles are kept boisterous, even while some difficult ordeal is being endured. On the street where I am living, one family has had their daughter run away. Another family is coping with the ravage of severe cancer in the husband's mother. Another family is being prosecuted by the Internal Revenue Service.

In every case, however, the afflicted families in these ways seem to go out of their way not to impose their pains upon their neighbors. It is as if there were a taboo against the social sharing of suffering, as if suffering should be kept a private matter, as if it were better to pretend to others that one is free from suffering than to relate others to one's agony.

The demand that suffering be removed is having a devastating effect on one situation in particular. What do we do when we face a suffering that no invention or drug is able to relieve? What does the physician do when his or her patient has passed beyond the reach of helpful treatment?

The Uncertain Center

In these situations we can understand how the demand that suffering be avoided pushes the physician and us all to withdraw, to abandon the suffering patient on the grounds that "we cannot do good anymore." As if the only order of good were the removal of suffering.

The work of technology and anesthetics has been somewhat successful. Some of the suffering that has haunted human life has been removed or at least minimized. Yet with regard to the success of this project we can only say "somewhat." People are still afflicted by terrible and widespread suffering; psychological forms of suffering are as intense as ever; and technological developments themselves are yielding their own fruits of difficulty.

Nevertheless, people continue to expect the elimination of suffering with naive and single-minded commitment. Consider, for example, the pattern of education which is given to the children of the middle class. No child is deliberately directed to try out an experience of suffering; to learn the peculiar difficulties which his or her personality experiences along this road; to discover not only how to cope but how to maintain one's human ways under this duress; to develop the strengths of courage and patience in the face of suffering. No one is subjected to this kind of education. Our education is a one-sided development and reinforcement of all those techniques and skills and ambitions by which we hope to avoid suffering and live in happiness. Can you imagine a middle class school providing an opportunity for children to "learn about failure"? Children are taught only to fear and flee from failure, and to condemn themselves for it. They are prevented from learning how to endure failure with a quiet mind.

Behind this kind of education, behind all the social constraints which work to keep us away from suffering, there runs a belief of utmost significance for Christian theology. This is the conviction that suffering is somehow utterly incompatible with being genuinely human. It is widely believed that no human growth and no human developments are possible in suffering. This is exactly the principle which shapes our education. Not only is it assumed that affliction enervates our humanity, it is also assumed that those who suffer have nothing of value to offer us. You know how tubes and masks and narcotics are allowed to obstruct the communication which a hospital patient may wish to make with others. The dominant belief seems to be that no significant humanity remains to be honored and listened to where suffering has taken over.

In other words, to many suffering has become the most dreaded and the most overwhelming form of evil. While earlier ages were preoccupied with the moral evil that issues from the misdirection of human freedom, our time looks upon moral evil as secondary to the evil of suffering. In fact, the most heinous moral evils in the view of many are those which produce human suffering. Also, middle class people tend to "explain" a flagrant moral evil which they find in some individual or some group as the consequence of some suffering or deprivation which has scarred that individual or group.

The reverse side of this perspective must also be observed. Since suffering effectively destroys our humanity, those who exercise their humanity to help the sufferers can only do so from a vantage point apart from suffering. Only because they stand outside of suffering are they able to work humanely and creatively, and thereby deliver others from suffering.

In the prevailing view, then, there are two domains, as it were. There is the domain of successful humanity, characterized by people who are healthy, confident, outgoing, and capable of serving others. We must also observe that these qualities are almost always made possible by the possession of enormous affluence. On the other hand, there is the contrasting domain of suffering, where the humanity in us is so thoroughly twisted and shattered that nothing very human is expected of us, and that we can only recover our creatively human possibilities by being taken out of this dreadful domain to the other.

Thus, in the prevailing attitude there is working a thoroughgoing dualism, with humanity in secure well-being on one side and dehumanized wrecks ravaged by suffering on the other. We can see a vivid example of this dualism in our hospitals. The staff who work there helping others do so in such a way that traces of their fragility and suffering are carefully hidden. The mask of "expertness" identifies each worker with a successful effectiveness that allows no room for his or her victimized agonies. There is an incredible pretense involved in this stance, but it is believed to be essential, so that physicians hardly ever present themselves as sharing in the same misery as their patients. Instead, they stand immune behind the facade of expertise.

The sick, on the other hand, are thought to have lost their creative humanity and to have become only "patients," passively being possessed first by their illness and then by the medical treatment which seeks to deliver them. It seems perfectly reasonable, therefore, that since the suffering sick have lost the power of their humanity, no compunction is felt against denying them speech by putting tubes in their mouths, or denying them reason by keeping them comatose, or denying them the resources of courage by dulling them with drugs. What matters is the removal of their suffering. Until that is achieved, there is no point in so restraining medical treatment as to allow their humanity to function, because their suffering is thought to debilitate and destroy their humanity.

In speaking of the marked dualism—or mutual exclusion—which is believed to exist between being human and suffering, we must be careful not to overlook one peculiar feature of this dualism. For if suffering is able to shatter our humanity, that means that suffering has excessive power over humanity. Apparently a person's humanity is thought to have no resources within itself against the savagery of suffering. It is as if the sufferer's ability to maintain humanity, to exercise discriminations, to be responsive to moral demands was thought to be simply eliminated. It is as if suffering was thought to involve such a heavy and unredeemable evil that all factors within the sufferers which might qualify or transform its overwhelming destruction were automatically dismissed. Suffering has the decisive power, and any human gripped by it is in the position of total victimization.

To identify this extreme destructive powerfulness which is attached to suffering, we may say that in this view suffering is being seen as "demonic," not in the mythic sense of being caused by demonic spirits, but in the descriptive sense of having a destructiveness that can so transcend all human resources that in its presence we are utterly helpless and can see no positive meaning except by escaping from it. The only significant redemption, therefore, is the escape from suffering which technology provides. Why? Because in the prevailing middle class view the really decisive form of evil is not our moral perversity or our self-engendered corruption of our human character or our act of personal sinning, but the imposition upon us of destructive suffering.

We can see the enormous impact which this prevailing cultural attitude has had on contemporary Western Christianity. We can see this impact operating in two opposite directions.

On the one hand, it has been adopted by Christians as illuminating the meaning of their Christianity. For instance, today many Christians identify the love of neighbor almost exclusively with the removal of suffering. Emphasis is given to Jesus' commands that we feed the hungry and clothe the naked and free the oppressed, and to his making our being approved or condemned at the final judgment depend on how well we have fulfilled these particular commands (Matt 25). After all, Jesus calls us into the work of redemption, and what else can an authentic redemption be but the deliverance from suffering?

At the same time, since suffering is thoroughly antihuman, the Christians who seek to help others can do so effectively only from a vantage point apart from suffering. Their affluence (called by Christians "the blessings of God") or their faith is thought to put them in a position which should be immune from suffering and from which, therefore, they can hope to deliver the afflicted. Thus the pattern of love which prevails among the Christians of Western middle class represents an adoption of the view that sees full humanity only in the escape from suffering.

We can see how different this whole attitude is from the viewpoint expressed, say, in the New Testament. For there, in addition to the feeding of the hungry and the freeing of the captive, that is, in addition to directing us to work for the removal of suffering, the New Testament writings seem to give equal emphasis to the work of simply *accompanying* the sufferers in their suffering. For instance, in the letter to the Hebrews, Christians were enjoined to "remember those in prison as if you were there with them, and remember those who are being maltreated, for like them you are still in the world" (Heb 13:3). In this passage no stress is given to the elimination of suffering. The emphasis is rather "remember" the sufferers, in the sense of being with them mentally, because no one is immune from that suffering. The concern here is not on avoiding suffering, but on suffering with, that is, on "compassion," which originally meant to "suffer with." For the prevailing view today, of course, suffering with is seen as a very second-best activity. For what can be gained if one joins another in being crushed by the terribly destructive power of suffering? "Compassion" is, therefore, usually taken to mean that the person who stands outside of suffering is somehow able to reach across the dualistic gap emotionally, though not in actual life, and thus to empathize with the afflicted.

Adoption of the prevailing view, however, is only one impact which it has made on Christianity. It has also been decisive in providing a platform for the attack on Christianity. By stressing the perfection of life hereafter, has not Christianity had the effect of diluting people's struggle against present suffering? Has it not functioned like a drug to instill a kind of passive inactivity before this evil? Far from being in the vanguard to provoke people to strive against the sources of their suffering, it has tried to distract them, to lull them, in short, to serve the interests of those who profit from systems which afflict them. And if Christians today emphasize the removal

The Uncertain Center

of suffering, this is not because of Christianity itself, but because of the very different spirit of humanism and technology, whose abomination of suffering has been only recently adopted by Christianity. In earlier times Christians had no difficulty in believing that their God properly imposed the afflictions of hell upon the non-Christians, and that their duty was also to impose afflictions upon such available non-Christians as the Jews. The seeming hypocrisy of Christianity at claiming to be a religion of redemption while generally doing nothing against the dreadful evil of suffering outrages many today.

Equally vigorous has been the attack which has recently developed against the God that Christians claim to worship. It is a matter of comparison. After two centuries of making remarkable achievement against suffering, humanity by comparison makes the God who established and sustains this world seem morally grotesque. Why could not this God have originally created more provisions against suffering? Why could God not have originally provided an effectively anesthetic plant? Today there is no source of atheism so broadly powerful as the enormity and scope of human suffering.

We find this everywhere today, inside as well as outside of the churches. Let me give one example from the novel *Catch-22* by Joseph Heller. In one scene Yossarian, the main character, is protesting against the prevalence of suffering in the world.

> "And don't tell me God works in mysterious ways," Yossarian continued... "There's nothing so mysterious about it, He's not working at all. He's playing, or else He's forgotten all about us. That's the kind of God you people talk about—a country bumpkin, a clumsy, bungling, brainless, conceited, uncouth hayseed. Good God, how much reverence can you have for a Supreme Being who finds it necessary to include such phenomena as phlegm and tooth decay in His system of creation? What in the world was running through that warped, evil, scatalogical mind of His when He robbed old people of the power to control their bowel movements? Why in the world did He ever create pain?... When you consider the opportunity and power He had to really do a job, and then look at the stupid, ugly little mess He made of it instead, His sheer incompetence is almost staggering. It's obvious He never met a payroll. Why, no self-respecting businessman would hire a bungler like Him as even a shipping clerk."

What Yossarian is doing is assessing God's activity by the prevailing ethic of removing suffering, and by comparing it with human achievements along that line. By that criterion God is grossly evil. Yossarian's castigation of God ends with the fury of moral superiority.

> Yossarian snorted resentfully, "You know, we mustn't let Him . . . get away scot free for all the sorrow He's caused us. Someday I'm going to make Him pay. I know when. On Judgment Day. Yes, that's the day I'll be close enough to reach out and grab that little yokel by His neck" (184–85)

For many today like Yossarian the Christian enterprise of believing in a good God who rules over this world makes absolutely no sense. Suffering is evil, is radically and profoundly evil. Therefore, as Yossarian says, the God who is responsible for this world which inflicts terrible suffering ought to be morally condemned and finally punished.

In these many ways we see how deeply the belief in the dreadfulness of suffering and the ethical striving to remove suffering works in every region of our culture. Therefore, from this point of view, if we ask about the meaning of suffering in relation to Jesus, we expect to learn how Jesus will take away suffering. Nevertheless, that expectation has no support in the New Testament. There Jesus was not seen as removing suffering, either from himself or from his followers. He did not promise a way devoid of suffering. He did not teach a set of values that were supposed to produce the avoidance of suffering. On the contrary, Jesus is reported to have predicted that the world would persecute his followers just as it had persecuted him (John 15:18–20), and that those worthy of him would be taking up their crosses (Matt 10:38).

Therefore, in our approach to the issues before us, we will have to recognize that the belief in the intolerable evil of suffering and the single-minded quest to avoid suffering are peculiarly our own, with roots in our time. It was not the orientation of the New Testament nor of most of the Christian tradition. We belong to the age of technology and anesthetics, and that marks us as having a peculiar intolerance to suffering and an enlarged sense of its evil.

The Passion of Jesus

Let me now turn to the passion of Jesus as variously reported in the four Gospels. The perspective which we find here differs so markedly from the

The Uncertain Center

view that now prevails in the Western middle class that it raises fundamental questions against that view.

The first thing which I will do is to call attention to the three surprises which meet us in the Gospel accounts. These surprises will pinpoint what unusual attitudes toward suffering were called forth by Jesus' crucifixion.

The initial surprise is the one which I have just mentioned, that no hint is given in the Gospel narratives that we may, or should, or must get rid of suffering. We know how some of Jesus' teachings emphatically point in that direction. The power of his miracles to relieve the afflicted reinforces his call that his followers do the same. Feeding the hungry, liberating the oppressed, and succoring the weak, therefore, become ways of continuing the redemptive work of Jesus and extending the kingship of God. Yet in the Gospel accounts of Jesus' passion, that theme disappears. In fact, he is presented as going out of his way to prevent the removal of suffering from himself. Furthermore, the entire New Testament is unanimous in connecting his submission to suffering with his way of relating to God.

In other words, here God was not seen to work in such a way that Jesus was "saved" from his agony. Something else was going on in the passion, something else by comparison with which the removal of suffering would have been not only secondary but a countervailing development.

People have always found this to be a very difficult feature of the Gospel accounts. How could it have been possible for Jesus to be the redeemer and yet in that very role submitted so completely to suffering?

By contrast, the tendency in the early church was to resolve this seeming contradiction by minimizing Jesus' suffering. Hilary of Poitiers (300–367 AD) may be taken as an example of this early tendency. Hilary was a strong supporter of the council of Nicaea, so that for him Jesus the redeemer meant that Jesus was a human nature assumed by the divine son of God. For Hilary this meant that Jesus had "a unique body as befitted his origin." "He was free from the . . . imperfections of the human body." Therefore, Hilary concludes, he could not have felt pain and could not have suffered as we do.

Hilary is very insistent on this point, in order to oppose the Arians. They had argued that because Jesus feared and felt pain and was infirm, we are prevented from treating him as impassible and therefore must not assign to him the likeness of God. Hilary took the opposite position. Since, in his view Jesus was the Son of God, since he became man without departing from the mystery of his divine nature, he must have had a human condition

Human Suffering and the Passion of Christ

that befitted his divinity and therefore that was subject to no pain or sorrow or fear. How, asked Hilary, could he have been thirsty who redeemed by giving forth from himself rivers of living water (John 7:38)?

The common tendency for many today is to give up the notion that Jesus himself is a redeemer. Some find themselves having to reject all connections between the Jesus of the first century and their own lives. Others believe that Jesus exemplifies and arouses humanity to the work of love, but deliverance only comes about through that human work, not directly through Jesus. In any case the pattern today is to resolve the seeming contradiction between Jesus as redeemer and Jesus as sufferer by minimizing his redeeming role.

Then what of the gospel reports of his suffering? Hilary explained these by distinguishing between the infliction of cutting, piercing, and other actions upon Jesus (he called this *passio,* the being affected by another's actions) and the inner experience of suffering (he called this *dolor*), which he argued, that Jesus could never have felt.

> When he was struck with blows or inflicted with wounds or lashed with whips or lifted upon the cross, he felt the force of suffering (*passio*), but without its pain (*dolor*). When a dart cuts through water or pierces a flame or slashes the air, it inflicts all the "sufferings" which belong to its nature—it cuts, pierces and slashes. Yet the "suffering" which it inflicts does not have effect on the things that it strikes, for it is not in the nature of water to be cut or of flame to be pierced or of air to be slashed ... So our Lord Jesus Christ "suffered" (i.e. received) blows, hanging, crucifixion and death. But the suffering which assailed the Lord's body, though it was "suffered" (i.e. received), still did not convey the nature of our suffering ... for his body did not have a nature susceptible of pain (*The Trinity,* 417).

Most Christians today find this minimization of Jesus' experience of suffering impossible. Not only do the Gospel accounts present Jesus as experiencing both pain and great distress—"horror and dismay" came over him in Gethsemane (Mark 14:33) to the point that his sweat was like drops of blood (Luke 22:44) and on the cross he suffered thirst (John 19:28)—but also that distress was reported as occurring at several levels. His most profound agony was the cry of dereliction, "My God! My God! Why have you forsaken me?" However, although today we have little sympathy for the tendency of many in the early church to dissociate Jesus from the agony and destruction of suffering, yet it is striking how restrained the Gospel traditions were on this matter. Their own references to Jesus' own experience of suffering are few and far between. Their emphasis is on what was done to Jesus—he was flogged, mocked, abandoned, and crucified—but his own response to these assaults is mentioned with reserve and only occasionally. If his full submission to suffering is the first thing that surprises us, for the four Gospels the agony of that submission was not the primary focus of concern.

Now we must consider the second surprise that awaits us in the Gospel accounts. Jesus did not seek to remove himself from suffering. He did not come down from the cross or conduct any kind of defense or seek help from the local committee for the liberation of prisoners. Yet in all this submission to suffering the Gospels report on his part no viewpoint which construes his suffering as somehow good and significant. In other words, Jesus' passion was not presented as a vehicle by which suffering in itself and as such could become a positive good.

Efforts to construe it in this way have preoccupied many Christians since the time of the passion. Perhaps the two most recurrent themes have been the claims, first, that suffering is good because it functions as the punishment for sins ("Any transgression or disobedience has met with due retribution," Heb 2:2), and second that suffering is good because by it the Christian is disciplined, tested, purged, and purified (2 Cor 6:9; Heb 12:6–11; 1 Pet 1:6–7; Rev 3:18–19). But these are later reflections. The Gospel narratives do not report that any positive meaning is given to the suffering of humanity by the crucifixion.

In other words, in these accounts suffering is viewed as essentially evil. That is, in the mythic perspective of the New Testament, it is the effect of evil personal beings called demons, who victimize and impose torment. Like human sin, demons and their work may be "removed," or "conquered," or "driven out" by Jesus, but he never puts them in an interpretive context which converts their evil to good.

Suffering is a demonic evil, and that is as true for the crucifixion as for the instances of blindness and madness that Jesus healed. The fact that humans impose suffering does not change its character. This behavior only makes such people partners and servants of the demonic. As we are redeemed from sin, not by the thought that it builds character or has some other good effect, but by its outright removal, so we are redeemed from suffering, not by finding reasons to justify it, but by its elimination. Evil is evil. It stands opposed to God's purpose and will and nature. It is not the servant of God.

From this point of view, then, there is no satisfactory explanation for affliction, no vantage point that we can take in order to see its place in a meaningful scheme, no perspective by which we can transform its destructive and evil character. Redemption is by the removal of evil, not by its reinterpretation. The fact that the Gospel accounts of Jesus' crucifixion do not emphasize deliverance from suffering as the most important event does not mean that suffering can somehow be justified and ceases to be thoroughly evil.

The religious bearing of this can now be seen clearly. So long as there is suffering, a demonic powerfulness is at large and therefore the rule (or kingship) of God is not complete. This is not yet my Father's world. On the contrary, in the way suffering imposes torments it seeks to repudiate God. The fact that affluent people can feel such unqualified gratitude to God for the blessedness of this world only means that their piety distracts them from hearing the cries of suffering that arise everywhere. The Lord's Prayer makes the perspective of the Gospels unambiguously clear: we pray that we may be delivered "from the evil one," that is, from being victimized by the demonic, for the demonic is very much still at large; and that "Thy kingship may come and Thy will may be done," because as yet this is not fully the case.

The third and final surprise for us arises from the fact that the Gospel accounts of the passion show so little place for hope. That is how we ourselves usually endure suffering. We hope that it may be removed or that it may produce something valuable.

Hope figures in the New Testament and sometimes with great force. Yet, as reported in the Gospel narratives, it plays no part in Jesus' suffering at the crucifixion. Jesus there gave no hint of looking to the future and thinking, "My suffering will prompt people to give up such dreadful practices," or "This agony is only for a moment, for I will be raised in three days." There are indications of the very different context in which Jesus placed his suffering, but that context was not one of hope.

The Challenge of the Gospel Perspective

We now come to the heart of our problem: what do the Gospel accounts portray as happening in Jesus' passion?

The Uncertain Center

Emphasis seems to be given by the Gospels to two activities on the part of Jesus. The first kind of activity is indicated by the saying in Luke's Gospel which Jesus gave from the cross: "Father into your hands I commit my spirit." This may be taken in what may be called a weak sense or a strong sense. The weak way is to see Jesus as holding onto an agenda of his own hopes and values, and as committing himself into God's hands in the confidence that now that he is dying, God will fulfill Jesus' agenda. Too often people have looked forward to resurrection in this sense: they imagine that in the resurrection God will do their will and fulfill for them their agenda of expectations.

The difficulty of such a reading is obvious: Jesus did not say that he was committing his values or hopes into his Father's hands. It was his spirit, that is, his central self that he committed, the self from which he could not distance himself. This weak reading becomes more unlikely if we remember that this saying by Jesus echoes the words of Psalm 31, and that there the weak meaning of the words is excluded.

> In you, O Lord, do I put my trust . . . you are my rock and my fortress. Therefore, lead me and guide me for your name's sake . . . Into your hands I commit my spirit (Ps 31:1–5).

The strong reading of Jesus' statement gives to the word "commit" a much more unusual meaning. In this case his act of commitment was not in his mind a means for the realization of some other purpose, of some plan or hope. In itself it was the final and decisive act. He gave himself into his Father's hands, with a trust in his Father that reached beyond his own knowledge, beyond his own expectations, beyond his own grasp of his Father's purpose.

The reason for this is twofold. On the part of Jesus, extreme suffering so debilitated him that he could no longer proceed on the basis of himself. Suffering may so violate a human self that it cannot maintain its own psychic energy. It is driven into helplessness. If Jesus was genuinely subject to affliction at the crucifixion, that helplessness was his condition also.

The second and much more important reason pertains to the status of God. It is not just that God is the decisive context which obtains for Jesus during his crucifixion, as in all the moments of his life. God is the context in relation to which Jesus did not need and did not use any reliance on himself. He passed over all his own strengths and virtues and knowledge and hopes, and gave himself into the care of his Father. When the New Testament writers see Jesus' taking on suffering and death in terms of his

Human Suffering and the Passion of Christ

obedience to his Father (Mark 14:36; Phil 2:8), we must not reduce that obedience to the mere conforming of his outer behavior to God's requirements. His obedience involved the inner conformity of his self to his Father's status as his Father, that is, as the one who established him and nourishes him and cares for him. Therefore, in his extremity, as in his daily life, he trusted his Father to the point of committing his whole self to the Father. The inner content of obedience is trust (Heb 11:8).

We can now see the bearing which this strong reading of Jesus' words has on the question of suffering. Jesus may be seen as actualizing the way in which we may become authentically and fully human. To be a person means committing ourselves into God's care, means not trying to assert our own control over ourselves or our situation or our neighbors. It means living without maintaining a wall around ourselves. But the accounts of Jesus' crucifixion make perfectly clear what it means to live without a wall: it means letting oneself be *vulnerable,* be open even to destructive activities.

This is what takes precedence over the removal of suffering. In other words, the gospel perspective radically challenges the view which prevails among the Western middle class today. What primarily destroys our personhood is not suffering, but rather our way of holding ourselves behind a wall. If you love, if you commit yourself in trusting, if you open yourself in receiving or expend yourself in giving, then the walls which you hold around yourself must go. But in a world where the rule of God is not yet complete and where a demonic powerfulness still moves at large, this abandonment of walls means the acceptance of suffering. What emerges from the accounts of Jesus' crucifixion, then, is that sin and not suffering is the much more critical evil. Or to put this in somewhat different terms, suffering is primarily evil not by causing immediate distress, but by provoking us to build a protective wall around ourselves so as to avoid suffering. This wall may indeed protect us from this enemy, but it also prevents our self-commitment to God or to our neighbors.

But why should things proceed in this way? Why should precedence be given to the removal of sin and not to the removal of suffering? Why should we be called to let go of the walls around us, before we are freed from the forces which torment us? Why must commitment to God involve our becoming vulnerable, not just to God and the good, but also to demonic evil?

At one level we can see this in terms of a comparison between the *power* of God and the *powers* which bring suffering. If it were the case that in order to be God, God had to remove suffering, the reverse of this statement would also be true: suffering had to remove God. Whenever powers would work to produce suffering, God would there be excluded.

In such a belief there is operating just that sharp dualism between the good and suffering that prevails in the middle class today. That dualism implies that God cannot be God, that God has no place wherever suffering is present. Wherever tormenting forces operate they are all-powerful. They wholly dominate. The only way for God to qualify their enormous power is by obliterating them altogether.

What emerges from the accounts of Jesus' passion is a very different notion. God exercised God's power and Jesus was able to keep letting go of all walls around him, thereby stepping into vulnerability, *even while the evil forces worked their dreadful suffering.* Normally in human experience nothing provokes us to hold on to walls around us as much as fear and suffering. Yet even while he was afflicted at many levels, Jesus did not resort to walls. He maintained his openness to God. Even under that physical and psychic torment he continued to exercise what he exhibited as full humanity. He did not "fall" into the belief that his humanity could really operate only in affluence, security, vigor, and happiness.

Therefore, the dread of suffering as being somehow final and ultimate, as that before which humanity is totally "nothinged," becomes misplaced. Suffering has its destructive power, but that power is relativized by God's power to nourish and maintain our humanity even in the midst of suffering.

We can understand the failure of dualism in another way. If the removal of suffering had to be the first and most important thing, then the fundamental human attitude would be the fear of that evil. One often gets the impression that much work today against suffering is primarily motivated by fear. "Love" often becomes simply a name used when fear prompts us to work on behalf of others. In such cases help may be given, but it is not affection for victims which informs this help. It is primarily the dread of suffering.

The kingship of God is not grounded on fear, does not authorize fear, and does not call for a love that is essentially a form of fear. In the passion, therefore, Jesus was not controlled by fear and did not attribute to destructive forces a power comparable to God's. This comes through in that Jesus conformed to the will of his Father and therefore maintained his refusal to defend himself with walls, even at the expense of being vulnerable to terrible suffering. The forces which inflict suffering are really evil, yet even in its most extreme action, evil is not able to exclude or overwhelm the work of God.

There is a second activity alongside of trusting in God which the Gospel accounts indicate in Jesus during his passion. This is the activity expressed by the saying in Luke 23:24, "Father, forgive them, for they know not what they do," or by John's way of seeing Jesus' death as his decisive act of "handing over" his life to humanity (John 19:30). John used the word here of which the noun form is translated "tradition." In spite of the presence of suffering, Jesus also refused to place a protective wall between himself and those humans who crucified him.

The removal of walls between people and the vulnerability that results are a striking theme in many of Jesus' teachings. Love your enemy, turn your other cheek to receive the blows of others, have "com-passion" and accompany those who suffer even into their sufferings. Jesus seems to be warning us that we cannot be with any of our neighbors authentically without suffering. If we wish to avoid suffering, we must keep all of our neighbors at a distance, observing them, relating to them, even helping them, but holding off so as not to share with them in their actual suffering. As Jesus truly joined us in our agonies, he directed us to follow the same course with one another. In the passion where he joined us in our suffering, Jesus exhibited what "com-passion," or suffering with, really means.

Suffering normally forces us to self-preoccupation and self-pity. Then we are tempted to give up trying to reach beyond ourselves and to maintain our responsibilities. The wall of self-absorption takes us over. Jesus' direction to others is that they break through our wall, not just by their doing outer actions which enter our suffering lives in order to take us out of suffering, but by their actually sharing in the same suffering with us. For, in terms of the most important consideration, humanity is not genuine when it gives help from behind a wall that preserves it from suffering. This only makes the sufferer feel hopeless so long as he or she suffers. The helper serves merely to exhibit the conviction that there can be humanity only where suffering is avoided. For this reason passing assistance or strength from those who are well to those who are afflicted is a crucial Christian work, but it is not the primary form of love. In love, getting rid of walls is primary.

This bears directly on the ways in which we impose suffering on one another. Middle class Christians sometimes believe that those who are affluent and healthy and effective are the ones who may deliver others from suffering, may liberate them from victimization. But do those with affluence or health or efficiency prove to be less cruel, less brutal, less pernicious than others? Not at all. Affluent and effective people seem to inflict even more suffering than other groups. For the problem before us it is not enough, even with Christian motives, to stand on that healthy side of the dualism.

The reason is clear: affluent and effective people still enclose themselves behind walls. At their deepest levels they live as isolated selves in isolated societies. When they help the afflicted, they imagine that they are reaching beyond their own kind to "the unfortunate." They do not believe that they can live humanly with and for others while suffering.

Because the training in "com-passion" leads us into living without walls, it knows no limits. One thinks here of the suffering of infants or of the mentally deficient who cannot understand speech. Are they not cut off from the reach of compassion? Does not their suffering lock them within an isolation that compassion cannot cross? Does not Jesus' well-meant diagnosis that the decisive move is to remove walls collapse at this point?

The primacy of God becomes in practice very obscure in such cases. How can we know if our compassion ever reaches the infants or the mentally retarded? We believe that it does; that is, we believe that even on this frontier our humanity is not without meaning.

The work to relieve suffering and to deliver people from it is critically important and receives the full emphasis of Jesus. But it is not primary. First live openly, live to receive and to give, live so that you do not have to identify yourself in terms of what you are and have and do over against others, live by sharing even the agonies of suffering. When the separative walls are removed, when we have learned to suffer with and to let our commitment to others be stronger than our fear of affliction, then we may give our help with love and not out of fear. Then the passion of Jesus shapes and guides our own existence.

The question and answer session that followed McGill's presentation at the Congress was recorded and a portion of it transcribed.

Question: The question was asked about the theme of Christus Victor in the patristic period, and I wonder whether the presentation of the crucifixion doesn't involve a hope that there may be or now is victory over suffering.

Human Suffering and the Passion of Christ

McGill: It seems to me that the Christus Victor theme was in the early church identified with the fullness of God's reign. In other words, it really had a kind of eschatological contact, and one of the most fascinating things about the patristic period is the fullness of life into the eschaton with which Christians lived. I'm much less clear that the Christus Victor theme was thought to sort of be the rule of Christian practice in the sphere where God had not yet removed the powers of evil. There the work of victory was, of course, being advanced, and the work against suffering was emphatically emphasized by Christ and by a few of the early theologians, but at the same time, there was also the conviction that the forms of suffering are so various and so manifold, that suffering works in any human being at so many levels and in a whole society in so many dimensions, that the movement toward a genuine victory over suffering and not just provisional victories at this or that point—that that's really the eschatological fullness. That's when, well in one image, we will have a new flesh, and for that reason, therefore, it was not in the context of eschatological hope that I was speaking this afternoon, but the times between the times in which we are now living.

Question: I want to express my utter gratitude for your presentation. It was a magnificent presentation and very helpful. However, you leave me with some problems because I'm a professor who teaches students to work in the field of therapy—psychotherapy and family counseling—and all that you said was really overwhelmingly beautiful and I am grateful and very moved. However, I'm left with the dilemma of one of the things that we deal with in training our students—the separation of the subjectivity and the objectivity and the necessity of a very real need to empathize, a very real need to hear and have compassion, but the need to control that so that one doesn't begin to intermix one's suffering, the client's suffering with one's own, and I heard you very well and I believe what you said. Could you enable me to find that bridge so that we can enable those who work with those who suffer not to take on that suffering so we do not, as we say, lend our strength and our ego and help our suffering clients out of their suffering by our own strength. Again, I want to thank you for what you've given me—you've given me a great deal, but you've left me with a dilemma. Please help me.

McGill: Well, it seems to me that those who are well ought to be most grateful and giving of their wellness, ought to have no reservations about their being well and, therefore, in relation to those who suffer work in every way to bring those who suffer into the state of becoming well. At the same time, I only suspect, I really don't know, that psychotherapists also suffer—they're also well but they also suffer—and insofar as they suffer or any of us suffer, that also provides an opportunity for us. That also provides a group, a community, a suffering situation in which we can enter, not entering as a person with health or vigor or vitality or effectiveness, but enter as a companion in suffering. And it was not on the roles and methodologies and procedures and effectiveness of the first mode that I was talking about—how the well deal with the sufferers—but rather, it was an effort to open up a door that, at least in my experience is not opened up very much: that even when we are suffering, the work of Christian love, the work of participating in the cross of Christ, the work of moving out of ourselves into the lives of others, being responsive and responsible is as vigorous and as real as on the side of—I must say in the light of your question about eschatology—the side of so-called well-being. What we take as well-being may be from another point of view just another form of sickness, so that the two sides are there and each may work and each should work and in each case the rule of God supports and encourages and elevates our work.

Question: You mentioned our attitudes towards suffering and then Christ's attitude—that of his ultimate commitment to the Father—and that somehow we have to learn from his attitude, not putting more borders around us, but taking the walls away so that we could also become vulnerable. I can't argue with that point. Now the point I'd like to find more about is what kind of relationship there is between contemporary suffering and the suffering of Jesus? Are we to look at Jesus as just a model and example, or is there some kind of participation in his suffering wherever we find suffering people? How does the suffering of Jesus strengthen us and give meaning or give eschatological orientation? You might have touched on those and I may have missed them, so I would appreciate your giving me some explanation.

McGill: Well, in relation to us today, I mean—and this was dealt with a little—one of the bearings of the passion of Jesus is that suffering may not be as immense, as paralyzing, as inhibiting of humanity as we think when we're well; that there are strengths which come into play in the face of suffering that don't come into play otherwise. But, I guess what I'm really also interested in is what I might characterize as the first moment in the act of service, and that is the moment when suddenly the suffering of the other is before us and begins to engage us, and at that moment there is the very critical decision to be made—do I psychically back away and observe

Human Suffering and the Passion of Christ

this other from a distance so as to protect myself, or do I let myself be vulnerable to that suffering? And, for me I guess, one of the meanings of the passion of Jesus is that in and through the sufferings that are right in front of me in the hospital or in the neighborhood, I am involved with and being gathered into him, and the sufferings of the many that are beyond my eye, that I'm indifferent to, that I refuse to see, or, for the sake of effectiveness, don't see. And it's that sense of Christ as gathering in the sufferings, as taking on our sufferings into the horizon of the love of God and transforming their meaning and opening them up to creativity and communication and not just flight—it is in that sense that I would find the call to creativity as well as compassion, to effectiveness as well as sympathy, to be directed to us by the Lord. That's a very immense question you ask and it's immense because it bears primarily upon what I do rather than what I think, and unfortunately, those are not always on all fours with each other.

Question: I wonder if you'd comment on an extrapolation of, I think, a method which you used in your talk, which I thought was excellent, namely to try and understand the meaning of suffering in what our response to it should be. You went back to Christ on the cross, his passion, his death as the exemplar of what human suffering is, and how we should have an attitude towards it. And it seems to me also that Jesus isn't just suffering from some abstract evil. He's not just suffering in general, but all of his suffering is coming from sin on the part of men—he's being rejected; he's wept over Jerusalem; those he has come to show the love of God are not accepting it, and although they may think they are serving religion or God or the Roman state, they are, in fact, paralyzing God, causing God to suffer. And, therefore, at the cross we have not only the message of what is suffering and how we are to react to it, but also the relationship of suffering to sin; that is, on the cross we learn that sin is precisely the rejection of God. Jesus is the Will of God and putting him to death is putting the Will of God to death or contravening the Will of God, and that, therefore, the driving of the nails into his feet and the final act of piercing his heart with a spear is an image for us of the origin of human suffering, namely, our sin which is the rejection of God who has become man in Christ. That's quite a development but I feel that flows organically from what you said in your talk and I'd just like to have you comment on that.

McGill: I made very minimal use of the term "sin," because it's a word with a number of different thrusts in it, and it would have been crucial to distinguish sin as imposing suffering, sin as breaking a law, sin as being offensive to God, and sin as one's own rejection of God. So that with this variety of meanings—like any word, this capacity to have a number of different thrusts—it was really a decision of time not to go into the clarifications of my meanings of that word that led me not to use the term. Sin, in this context, is concretely the rejection of one's participation in not only the will of God, but the life of God, and since the life of God is communicative, loving—in the love of God. And in human existence breaking from the arena of God's life and God's love, the emergence of suffering or the meaning of suffering alters profoundly. One of the most obvious ways can be seen right away, for what is more decisive for suffering than myself, and what is more important to sin than myself, so that not self-centeredness, but self-preoccupation or an evaluation of one's self as the first and essential thing becomes one of the elements, both fostered by suffering and used in order to assess suffering, so that I have difficulty looking over there and finding a relation between sin and suffering, because the relation between sin and suffering I know best is right in here and there sin is a disengagement from the life of God and the love of God. This disengagement constitutes the glasses that I wear when I look upon suffering. And it's in that sense that sin and suffering are in our experience so profoundly interrelated.

Question: As I take it, we can suffer good, as well as evil, as when Jesus said, "Suffer the little children to come unto me," and we must suffer not to come in and take over our lives if we put up walls against that—they are sin—and only when we have suffered the good, especially the good of God taking over our lives, are we able to suffer the evil, and in that way have the evil cured by the good.

McGill: One complication in that passage and in certain others in the First Letter of John in the New Testament is that it seems as if the love of God breaks into my life through the love of the neighbor. God's love may be first in value but not chronologically first. That's the one qualification I'd make—that it's our responsibility to each other which and through which and coinciding with which God is the primary worker, but though God's work is primary and most valuable in the glory and the final horizon for everything, yet our work is in our specific way we live, in the specific way we suffer, the work we do for each other, and the particular person we go and visit. That's also, I would say, crucial in the very situation you beautifully express. Thank you.

Question: Do you think that the Western middle class resistance to suffering and the refusal to become companions in suffering has something to do with the contemporary ascendency of the euthanasia movement which represents the final obliteration of the suffering from the euthanasianist's point of view?

McGill: Well, the fear of suffering, certainly, I would have to say in the women I know who've had abortions, is often dictated by the realization, or at least the medical advice, that their expected child will be deformed or inadequate or suffering in some way, and that the most merciful thing to do in that context is to end the life of such a fetus. That, for me, is the most vivid example of the practice of wanting not to have suffering, and I'm trying to think of any physician I know who's talked to me about his own practice of euthanasia—I usually like to have it firsthand, rather than on somebody else's part. Lots of physicians talk about it, but never as if they'd done it. You know, my imagination would guess that one of the impulses that moves people to impose euthanasia upon others would be the desire that the other not suffer. And, again, it's profoundly a matter of education, not schooling, but of the education and the sense of strengths we have and weaknesses which we have, and in an extraordinary way the middle class strikes me as having a sense of extraordinary weakness before suffering. And, of course, those of you who work in hospitals know that that's not at all the case when people—even middle class people—are actually involved in suffering; they can develop courage and they can develop fortitude and they can develop patience, as well as developing self-pity and other things.

Question: You've spoken a lot about breaking down walls, tearing down walls and being vulnerable, and I guess I need more of a description of that.

McGill: The question is for me to be more specific about the experience of vulnerability, how it feels and what one does in that situation. Well, I think what one does is not merely to suffer; in fact, that's one of the most emphatic themes in my remarks this afternoon—that when we suffer there's still much to be done and still much which we may do. So being vulnerable means that while you're doing something and while you're being open, the impact on you of suffering, the invasion into your life of another suffering, or of distress of psychic or motivational kinds, an experience of any kind of debility would be accessible to that which injures. I can only speak in terms of a medical situation with which I worked for three years, and I must say that the experience of vulnerability there was downright exhaustion. It was crucial for me and for the physicians involved in this—subjected to this exhaustion—not to let the exhaustion so surprise us and defeat us, that it get in the way of our doing what we had to do. So it was necessary there to—if you will—be open to exhaustion; the only way of not becoming exhausted is not to do what you had to do. But to be open to exhaustion, but not to let "Good Heavens, I'm being subjected to suffering! How outrageous! Where is my help? Where is my escape?"—because in that case I would make such moves and, I suppose, the doctors with me would have made such moves, in the effort to escape from our own suffering, that we would have involved really compromising or violating our work with those who suffered and whose suffering we were addressing. Now, you know the forms of vulnerability are really incredible. You're exhausted one day; you're over-pleased the next day; you're confused the next day; you get a stomachache. I mean I'm now convinced after my operation that it's only the healthy that can survive the hospital. If you could only know ahead of time what's going to be vulnerable in you, you could take all the precautions. But you never know and it's that element of surprise and dismay which I'm addressing. I'd like to encourage the work of resourcefulness, the sense of "yes, I can do it, not because I've got energy, but because I'm here, and even though I don't have much energy, I'm here, and there are not many here," or "I'm here and I've been put here, and there are others here who would have their humanity confirmed by my love." So, I really don't have, I'm afraid, a very clear sort of step-by-step procedure for how you cope with vulnerability, but I'm very concerned that there has to be the letting go of walls if we love, and if we love at all—we may not—but if we love at all, we let go of walls so as to reach. We also let go of the walls which protect. In other words, we become vulnerable, and I guess you know more than I do that love always suffers.

Afterword

I no longer remember when I first read Art McGill's *Suffering: A Test of Theological Method*, but I remember why I read it. I read the book because Paul Ramsey told me I had to read McGill. Paul gave me many gifts but telling me to read McGill was surely among the most significant. It was so because to read McGill is to discover a way to do theology without fear. God knows from where he came but McGill, as the chapters in this welcome and important book demonstrate, had the ability to make theology do work so that we might better negotiate the imponderable reality we call "our life."

The power of McGill's reflections surely derives from his refusal to be satisfied with theological simplifications. Perhaps another way to characterize the compelling character of his work is to call attention to the relentless honesty that shapes everything he has to say. That honesty I think was born of his refusal to seek refuge in sentimentality. There is a beautiful hardness to his prose, as well as the content, that is frightening. We do not want to know what we know but live by denial of what we know. McGill will not let us live in denial. He never, therefore, refrains from reminding us that when all is said and done we are all going to be dead.

It is a challenge to know how best to characterize his work as a theologian. If I thought there was an area of theology that could be identified as theology of culture I might think he belongs there. But I have my doubts about attempts to do a theology of culture because it is not clear to me that we know what we are talking about when we designate aspects of our life as "culture." What I do know, however, is McGill was a master of showing us how theological claims can illumine our lives when they are taken, so to speak, "straight-up."

What do I mean by "straight-up"? By "straight-up" I mean to call attention to his presumption that Christians should live what they say they believe. He refuses, therefore, to explain what we believe as Christians in terms of what is assumed are the conditions of truth determined by modern humanism. There is a direct relation between his discussions of rationality in the chapter "The Ambiguous Position of Christian Theology" and his observation in "The Crisis of Faith" that our daily lives are completely at odds with Jesus. McGill seems to have seen clearly that the epistemological presumptions that shape accounts of what someone should be prepared to believe reflect middle class anxieties formed by the desire that somehow they can get out of life alive.

Thus his suggestion that the crisis of faith we confront is not that what we believe as Christians is "unbelievable," but that we are determined to know how to live possessed by our possessions. Thus his reminder that Jesus was one that lived dispossessed. Because Jesus lived dispossessed he was able to face as well as defeat the powers that have rebelled against their Creator. One might say, therefore, McGill understands redemption as learning how to receive without regret.

McGill's observation that we are a people who are terrified of being in need is one that might be made by someone who is not a theologian. But McGill's understanding of Jesus as the one who makes possible our living free of possessions illumines and intensifies that insight. That he turned to medicine as one of the places that makes unavoidable the acknowledgment of our fear of being out of control is an indication of the kind of insight with which he wrote. He was a person of extraordinary wisdom but his wisdom was but the result of his theological reflections.

I think it very important not to overlook the courage he displayed not only as he contemplated the possibility of an early death but also the courage it took to do theology in the manner in which he worked. He was well aware, as the chapter in this book on the rise of religious studies indicates, that theology would increasingly have problems being considered a university subject. His argument in favor of theology being in the curriculum of the modern university is as compelling today as it was then, but equally important is the very quality of the work he produced. He quite rightly maintained that theology asked questions that those associated with the modern university are trained to ignore.

McGill came of age as a theologian when theology was assumed to bear the burden of proof. The presumption, a presumption widely associated with Rudolf Bultmann, was that theology would need to be demythologized if it would be relevant to the lives of modern people. McGill, I believe,

Afterword

saw how dangerous such a view could be just to the extent the convictions that make Christians Christian would be lost. He saw as an alternative that the question is never, "Does the Gospel measure up to the standards of the world?" but "How must we think and live if we are to provide an alternative to a world that refuses to acknowledge that the very fact that we are is a gift we must learn to receive without regret?"

I should like to think that the way I have tried to think not only about the relation of theology and medicine, but more generally about how theology must be done in a manner to expose our endemic self-deceptive strategies I learned from McGill. Just as important, as someone who has written more than McGill I nonetheless should hope that I also learned from him when to say no more than needs to be said. There is a silence that surrounds all that he has to say and that silence I take to be prayer.

Once dead we are often forgotten. McGill was not that well known when he lived. He was not the kind of person or thinker who needed validation by commanding the attention of others. He was profoundly his own person. But hopefully this book will kindle renewed interest in his work because I think few working in theology today have his gift for making theology one of the disciplines we so desperately need to avoid the narcissism endemic to lives that would be free of suffering.

—Stanley Hauerwas

Bibliography

Anouilh, Jean. *The Lark*. Translated by Christopher Fry. Oxford: Oxford University Press, 1956.
Barth, Karl. *Dogmatics in Outline*. Translated by G. T. Thomson. New York: Harper & Row, 1959.
Buber, Martin. *I and Thou*. New York: Scribners, 1958.
Camus, Albert. *The Plague*. Translated by Stuart Gilbert. New York: Alfred A. Knopf, 1948.
Cicero. *Orations: Pro Archia, Post Reditum in Sentu, Post Reditum Ad Quirit*. Translated by N. H. Watts. Loeb Classical Library 158. Cambridge, MA: Harvard University Press, 1923.
Descartes, René. *Discourse on Method*. Translated by Laurence J. Lafleur. Upper Saddle River, NJ: Prentice Hall, 1956.
———. *Meditations on First Philosophy*. Translated by Laurence J. Lafleur. Upper Saddle River, NJ: Prentice Hall, 1960.
Fearing, Kenneth. *Collected Poems*. New York: Random House, 1940.
Gissing, George. *The Private Papers of Henry Rycroft*. London: Constable & Co., 1908.
Hauerwas, Stanley. *Suffering Presence: Theological Reflections on Medicine, the Mentally Handicapped, and the Church*. Notre Dame, IN: University of Notre Dame Press, 1986.
Heller, Joseph. *Catch 22*. New York: Dell, 1978.
Hilary of Poiters. *The Trinity*. 360. Translated by Stephen McKenna. Fathers of the Church 25. Washington DC: Catholic University of America Press, 1954.
Kierkegaard, Soren. *Concluding Unscientific Postscript to* Philosophical Fragments, vol. 1. 1846. Kierkegaard's Writings 12.1. Translated and edited by Howard V. Hong and Edna H. Hong. Princeton, NJ: Princeton University Press, 1992.
———. *Practice in Christianity*. 1850. Kierkegaard's Writings 20. Translated and edited by Howard V. Hong and Edna H. Hong. Princeton: Princeton University Press, 1991.
Lasswell, Harold. *Power and Society: A Framework for Political Enquiry*. New Haven, CT: Yale University Press, 1950.
Longfellow, Henry Wadsworth. *The Complete Poetical Works of Henry Wadsworth Longfellow*. New York: Houghton, Mifflin & Co., 1902.
Marcel, Gabriel. *The Philosophy of Existence*. Translated by Manya Harari. New York: Philosophical Library, 1949.
McGill, Arthur. *Death and Life: An American Theology*. Eugene, OR: Wipf and Stock, 2003.
———. *Suffering: A Test of Theological Method*. Eugene, OR: Wipf and Stock, 2007.

Bibliography

Milbank, John. *Theology and Social Theory: Beyond Secular Reason*. 2nd ed. Oxford: Wiley-Blackwell, 2006.
Nash, Arnold. *The University and the Modern World: An Essay in the Philosophy of University Education*. New York: Macmillan, 1943.
Robinson, John A. T. *Honest to God*. Louisville, KY: Westminster Press, 1963
Stevens, Wallace. *The Necessary Angel: Essays on Reality and the Imagination*. New York: Vintage Books, 1951.
———. *Opus Posthumous: Poems, Plays, Prose*. New York: Alfred A. Knopf, 1957.
Wolfe, Thomas. *You Can't Go Home Again*. London: Penguin, 1968.

Index of Names

Alexander the Great, 88
Altizer, Thomas, 59, 67–68
Anouilh, Jean, 23
Athanasius, 158
Augustine of Hippo, 158

Barth, Karl, 26
Beethoven, Ludwig van, 126
Buber, Martin, 34–37, 41, 60, 104

Camus, Albert, 24, 126
Capone, Al, 15
Cicero, 48-50
Cox, Harvey, 66–68
Crosby, Bing, 3

Darwin, Charles, 95
Descartes, René, 98–99

Edwards, Jonathan, 103
Einstein, Albert, 29

Faubus, Orval, 18
Fearing, Kenneth, 38
Feuerbach, Ludwig, 66
Frank, Anne, 29
Freud, Sigmund, 142

Galileo, 95
Gissing, George, 49
Godfrey, Arthur, 21, 24

Hamilton, William, 59, 67–68
Hegel, G.W.F., 99–100
Heidegger, Martin, 60
Heller, Joseph, 164
Hilary of Poitiers, 166–67
Hitler, Adolf, 15

Ignatius of Loyola, 158

John of Salisbury, 50

Kant, Immanuel, 142
Koestler, Arthur, 67

Lasswell, Harold, 75, 77, 80
Long, Huey, 16–17
Longfellow, Henry Wadsworth, 63–64
Luther, Martin, 158

Mann, Thomas, 126
Marcel, Gabriel, 45
Marx, Karl, 41, 66, 125, 142
Mauriac, François, 22–23
More, Thomas, 50

Napoleon, 65
Nash, Arnold, 51
Nietzsche, Friedrich, 142
Newton, Isaac, 29
Niebuhr, Reinhold, 104

Index of Names

Paine, Thomas, 66
Plato, 49

Raye, Johnny, 3
Robinson, John A.T., 36, 71, 73

Salk, Jonas, 21
Schweitzer, Albert, 88
Stevens, Wallace, 37, 62–63

Tertullian, 103
Tillich, Paul, 104

van Buren, Paul, 59–60, 67–68

Wolfe, Thomas, 124

Scripture Index

OLD TESTAMENT

2 Kings
17:35 — 26

Psalms
31:1–5 — 170

Joel
2:28–30 — 87

NEW TESTAMENT

Matthew
5:39–42 — 53
6:25 — 27
10:38 — 165
25:35ff. — 53

Mark
14:33 — 167
14:36 — 171

Luke
22:25 — 117
22:44 — 167

John
7:38 — 167
15:13 — 53
15:18–20 — 165
19:28 — 167
19:30 — 173

Romans
7:14 — 130
7:17 — 130
13:8 — 34
14:4 — 43, 53
14:8 — 135

1 Corinthians
4:7 — 135

2 Corinthians
6:9 — 168

Galatians
5:13 — 52

Scripture Index

Philippians
2:8	171

Hebrews
2:2	168
11:8	171
12:6–11	168
13:3	163

James
2:15–17	52

1 Peter
1:6–7	168

1 John
3:17	52
4:7	52
4:8	34
4:12	52

Revelation
3:18–19	168

www.ingramcontent.com/pod-product-compliance
Lightning Source LLC
Chambersburg PA
CBHW031359230426
43670CB00006B/596